FREE FOR ALL

Medill School of Journalism
VISIONS *of the* AMERICAN PRESS

———◇———

GENERAL EDITOR
David Abrahamson

Selected titles in this series

HERBERT J. GANS
Deciding What's News: A Study of CBS Evening News,
NBC Nightly News, Newsweek, and Time

MAURINE H. BEASLEY
First Ladies and the Press: The Unfinished Partnership of the Media Age

PATRICIA BRADLEY
Women and the Press: The Struggle for Equality

DAVID A. COPELAND
The Idea of a Free Press: The Enlightenment and Its Unruly Legacy

MICHAEL SWEENEY
The Military and the Press: An Uneasy Truce

PATRICK S. WASHBURN
The African American Newspaper: Voice of Freedom

KARLA GOWER
Public Relations and the Press: The Troubled Embrace

TOM GOLDSTEIN
Journalism and Truth: Strange Bedfellows

NORMAN SIMS
True Stories: A Century of Literary Journalism

MARK NEUZIL
The Environment and the Press: From Adventure Writing to Advocacy

FREE FOR ALL

THE INTERNET'S TRANSFORMATION OF JOURNALISM

Elliot King

Foreword by Jeff Jarvis

MEDILL SCHOOL OF JOURNALISM

Northwestern University Press

Evanston, Illinois

Northwestern University Press
www.nupress.northwestern.edu

Printed in the United States of America

10 9 8 7 6 5 4 3 2

Library of Congress Cataloging-in-Publication Data

King, Elliot, 1953–

    Free for all : the Internet's transformation of journalism / Elliot King ;
foreword by Jeff Jarvis/

        p. cm. — (Visions of the American press)

    Includes bibliographical references and index.

    ISBN 978-0-8101-2328-1 (pbk. : alk. paper)

    1. Online journalism. I. Title. II. Series:Visions of the American press.

PN4784.062K56 2010

070.4—dc22

2009043815

⊗ The paper used in this publication meets the minimum requirements of the
American National Standard for Information Sciences—Permanence of Paper
for Printed Library Materials, ANSI Z39.48-1992.

CONTENTS

◈

FOREWORD

◈

Jeff Jarvis

A 2009 survey of a small sample of mostly old-media journalists in the *Atlantic* found that two-thirds of them thought the Internet was harmful to journalism. The opposite is true. The Internet may have been harmful to the desire of journalists and publishers to avoid disruption of their comfortable hegemony over media, the public debate, and advertising. But, as Elliot King so thoughtfully demonstrates in this volume, the rise of the Internet has brought no end of opportunity to journalism.

Thanks to the Web, we can now tell stories in any and all appropriate media. When I graduated from Medill's journalism school in the 1970s, my cohorts and I had to pick a medium for the rest of our careers (I was a newspaper major). Today, at the City University of New York Graduate School of Journalism, where I teach, every student learns to work in all media, and we no longer require them to specialize in any.

The Web enables us to share our news in new ways and reach new audiences around the globe. Thus, a third of the *Guardian*'s audience online comes from the U.S. and another third from the rest of the world outside the U.K. The *Guardian* has opened up all its content in an API (application programming interface) that enables developers to include its journalism in their own sites and services—in the paper's words, to weave *Guardian* reporting into the fabric of the Web. And the *Guardian* API is one way to meet the challenge of a college student who said in the *New York Times* in 2008 that "if the news is that important, it will find me." News organizations can no longer behave as if they were magnets, drawing audiences to them; they must instead think distribution and go to where the readers are. Indeed, they must make it easy for readers to become distributors, embedding content—like YouTube videos or Google maps—as links in their own space.

Of course, our readers have also become our writers, and that enables us to make journalism two-way and collaborative. News organizations are beginning to use their power to mobilize the public to "crowdsource" reporting, getting help digging into documents or gathering data points no single reporter ever could have done alone. Reporters are using blogs to get more information from the public both before and after writing articles. Thus news becomes less a product and more a process. The article itself as the fundamental unit of journalism is up for reconsideration as blogs and feeds are better at giving updates; wikis are best at collecting a snapshot of current knowledge; links to source material provide depth; discussion can bring perspective; and video, audio, photos, and applications may illustrate or explain better than text.

As journalism changes, so does its relationship with its public. In the blog world, I have learned the value of transparency as an ethic, one that I believe supplants our old myth of objectivity. I have learned that corrections—and the openness and humility they require—do not diminish but instead enhance credibility. And I have learned the power of the link. This simple invention, the link, has changed the architecture and economy of news in ways I have yet to fully grasp. The link affords news organizations an efficiency they desperately need in their suddenly competitive media landscape: now they can do what they do best and link to the rest. The link forces specialization as a news organization is no longer able to—nor can afford to—be all things to all people. This also means that news coverage can become ever more targeted to interests, communities, industries, and locales, each of which can become better served.

The link economy—in contrast to the content economy under which media has operated since Gutenberg—dictates that one no longer profits most by controlling content and selling it multiple times. Online, there need be only one copy of content, and it is the links to it that give it attention, and thus value. Content without links has no value. Content gains value and, in some definitions, authority as it gains links. These new economics have caused confusion and conflict, for example, where organizations such as the Associated Press have accused bloggers and aggregators of theft for publishing snippets with links to articles. The net natives in this situation could not understand the accusation because they thought they were giving content creators value and attention with their links. This is just one of the new economic rules that confound old media.

The challenge for newspapers facing a future dominated by the Web has been that it was not enough to transplant content, organizations, and business models from old media to new. In the past, journalists working in newsrooms produced journalism, and the public paid at least some of journalism's freight. And so it should be in the future, right? No. Now every assumption is a jump ball. The fundamental rules of the economy are changing as we shift from the industrial age to the knowledge age, as the presses and broadcast towers that gave news companies monopolistic power now become cost burdens. Today, everyone has a press.

So now to the refrain: How do we pay for it? Where are the new business models to support journalism? Well, we won't know until we have tried some and succeeded and failed and learned. I believe that journalism will no longer be the domain of single companies in markets producing single products but instead will come from ecosystems of many players contributing for many motives under many models. When the last city newspaper dies, imagine news coming from many sources: from former professional journalists who now start blogs and businesses alongside other bloggers; from foundation- and public-supported entities such as National Public Radio, ProPublica, and Spot.us, which will contribute a small but vital slice of investigative reporting; from volunteers who want to podcast their school board meetings; from a new ethic of transparency that forces government to make its data and actions searchable, turning any citizen into a watchdog.

Will there be news organizations? The historical lessons so ably rendered by Professor King in this volume certainly suggest there will be. I think so, too, and the job of those organizations will be to organize the news: to aggregate it, to curate the best of it, and to educate its creators. These are new roles for the journalists of the future, roles we must teach in journalism schools now. Members of these ecosystems will also depend on someone—it could be a remade newspaper or it could be Google—to support them with technology, promotion, and, most importantly, revenue. The news organization of the future should not see Google as an enemy but instead as a model. That new news company will act as a platform to support a larger network of news—yes, larger. Thanks to the Web, I believe that journalism will not only survive but prosper and grow far beyond its present limitations.

But then, I'm an optimist.

PREFACE

◈

As a child I was so not a gadget person that when my parents gave me a choice between an electric typewriter or a stereo for my high school graduation present, I chose the electric typewriter, not being smart enough to realize that if I had chosen the stereo, my parents would have had to buy me a typewriter anyway. And I continued in that way for a long time. As an undergraduate student I did take a course in programming in FORTRAN but only because I didn't want to take any science courses (and since I thought I was a pretty fast learner, I didn't want to start with BASIC). When I was at the Columbia University Graduate School of Journalism, I was completely oriented toward print journalism. I took none of the nascent video production courses offered and was completely uninterested when several of my classmates found jobs with a new broadcast news effort called Cable Network News.

My relationship to technology changed accidently in the early 1980s. After a short and unhappy stint as a political press secretary, I wanted a real job in journalism. As luck would have it, we were in the middle of a recession and the only job I could find was on a start-up magazine covering personal computers. Within eight months, the magazine was out of business, but by virtue of my eight months of in-depth experience I was considered a veteran technology writer.

In 1984, I was offered a free e-mail account on The Source as a member of the Computer Press Association. I did absolutely nothing with it for four or five years until a magazine editor of-

fered to pay me $25 extra if I filed a story via e-mail. It took a day
but I figured out how to use e-mail. When a student of mine at
the University of California, San Diego, mentioned that she could
send me e-mail from her UCSD address to my CompuServe
account (CompuServe had purchased The Source by then), I
thought it was the most amazing thing in the world.

In the 1990s, while still a graduate student at UCSD, I began to
edit a magazine that covered the use of new technology in science,
a position I held for almost ten years. The scientific research community was one of the first to adopt the Internet, and I adopted
it right along with them. In 1992, I organized a small conference
using e-mail and listservs. Two years later, I was downloading ab-
stracts of grants concerned with scientific computing from the
National Science Foundation and my students at Loyola College
in Maryland were using Gopher at the University of Minnesota
to download on-site English language reports about the war in
Bosnia, comparing them to reports in the U.S. media. I remember
telling somebody that I was so hot that I was cool or so cool that
I was hot. I wasn't sure which.

In the mid-1990s, I set up the first Web sites for a business-
to-business publisher with whom I worked and wrote a book with
Randy Reddick about how journalists could use the Internet in
reporting. I learned a lot from Randy during that period. We had
met and communicated almost entirely online. I also was the guest
editor for three editions of the *Electronic Journal of Communication,*
a pioneering online peer-reviewed journal. The topic: the impact
of the Internet on journalism.

At that point, I was faced with a decision. Should I jump on
the dot.com bandwagon or should I stay in the academic world?
I chose to stay in the academic world. For years afterward, my
mother-in-law, whom I love dearly, would ask me, since I was such

an earlier adapter to the Internet, how come I wasn't rich? Of course, I am the guy who chose an electric typewriter over a stereo coming out of high school.

My academic interests have always been in the history of journalism, and for a long time I joked that I was a journalism historian whose period of study ranged ten years into the future. This book represents the fusion of my interest in history and my interest in the use of technology. It is a history of the emergence of online journalism placed within the context of the emergence of computer-based communications networks and the Internet. It doesn't try to answer every question raised by impact of the Internet on journalism, but it does try to answer some of the important ones. The premise of the book is that the emergence of online journalism cannot be understood if the emergence of the online world itself is not understood.

As with all books, I have had help along the way. I have a profound sense of gratitude to my colleague Neil Alperstein, who volunteered to read the entire manuscript and encouraged me along the road. Neil Alperstein has been my close intellectual companion in my journey through the academic world, and we each take turns playing Sancho Panza to the other's Don Quixote. To me, it is a special relationship.

Loyola College in Maryland awarded me a summer research grant and a sabbatical that helped move the project along, and I cannot thank enough Linda Tanton, Pat Turkos, Ginnie Smack-Harper, and all the librarians at Loyola who joked and chatted with me as I emptied the shelves of books, many of which had never seen the light of day. Three of my students, Cara Wiegand, Raven Smith, and Meg Conley, took cracks at helping me move this project forward, which I appreciated. And I enjoyed talking with my friend Ari Lapidus, who has given me important insight into the world of blogging and has played an instrumental role in making a blogger out of me.

I would like to thank David Abrahamson, the editor of this series, profusely. David was an earlier pioneer in the online world himself. Over the years he has been one of the great academic entrepreneurs of our generation. He has been the driving force behind so many important projects, and I am forever grateful that he has included me along the way.

And then there is my family. I am very proud to have three children, Aliza, Marcie, and Jordan, who actually express an interest in my work and with whom I can talk about it, sometimes at great length. As for my wife, Anita, I am so lucky that no matter how old I get, she always says she believes in my potential. I hope this book is a small down payment on the promise she says she sees in me.

This book itself is a reflection of the new tools available to researchers. I mined all sorts of databases from my home. And if a book I needed was not at the Loyola library but held by a participating institution in the Maryland Interlibrary Consortium, I could order it online and sometimes it would show up the same day. I have no idea how that worked, but it was great. My favorite story, however, is about a recently published book that I found on a database. While the entire book seemed to be available as a PDF, the download button was grayed out and I could not access it. When I called the librarian, she told me that Loyola's subscription did not cover downloading that book. Since it wasn't part of the interlibrary consortium holdings, it would take about two weeks to get it via regular interlibrary loan. I didn't want to wait so I went to Amazon.com and found that even though the book had been published just two months earlier, I could buy a used copy. Three days and eight dollars later I had it. Ten years ago, I would have never known that book existed, much less been able to track it down and access it so quickly.

More information is available in more ways than ever before and so much of it is available for free or for very little cost. Along the same lines, the free-for-all to provide news that is free for all to access is having a profound impact on the way we see the world and that phenomenon needs to be understood. This book is a contribution to that conversation.

FREE FOR ALL

ONE

NECESSARY BUT NOT SUFFICIENT

Nicholas Carr probably never met Neil Postman. In 2003, Carr wrote an influential article in the *Harvard Business Review,* which he later turned into a book, called *IT Doesn't Matter.* In the article, he contended that the use of information technology in business was following the same evolutionary arc as other infrastructure technologies like railroads and electric power. Carr argued that as those technologies were being built into the infrastructure of commerce, for a brief period of time, opportunities opened for progressive and forward-thinking companies to gain a competitive advantage. The first companies to "plug" into the electric grid or to use rail transportation, for example, could potentially gain an advantage over those that were slower to adapt.

But as these technologies become commonplace and their costs drop, they no longer offer companies competitive advantages. They become commodities and no longer matter from a strategic perspective. Along the same lines, in Carr's view, the first companies to network their computers may have enjoyed a competitive advantage over those that hadn't. But once all companies had networks installed, the networks in and of themselves no longer provided an edge.[1]

In 1985, Neil Postman wrote an influential book called *Amusing Ourselves to Death,* in which he argued that communication technology itself—the media—inexorably and definitively shapes and constrains the information that is exchanged between people. Certain information could not exist without the media to give expression to it.[2] In essence, Postman claimed that rational, linear thought was inextricably intertwined with print technology. Sentences were linear constructions, with beginnings, middles, and ends, as was logical, rational thought. Print effectively archived knowledge, changing the definition of who was smart from people with experience to people who could read and remember. Finally, "the printed page revealed the world, line by line, page by page, to be a serious, coherent place, capable of management by reason, and of improvement by logical and relevant criticism."[3]

Television, Postman argued, was an altogether different matter. Nonlinear and based on the image rather than the word, the highest value electronic media held was not in educating the audience but amusing it. No matter how serious the issue, the first and dominant value of television production was to keep the audience amused. As opposed to a serious, coherent world capable of improvement, television, because of the demands of the technology itself, presents the world as fragmented, without context, without value, and essentially not serious.[4] As television technology became ubiquitous, far from becoming invisible, it extended its domination over the ways we see the world. Postman's argument was bold and far reaching: print technology enabled rational thought and democratic self governance. Television technology did not.

Though both Carr and Postman were seemingly trying to understand the same issue—how new ways to disseminate information have an impact on society—their arguments are independent of each other. Carr was talking about the use of information technology, basically computers, in a business setting. He was reflecting primarily on the growth of the personal computer, accessible databases in which information could be stored and reused by many applications, computer networks, and all the high technology that has shaped the way we live over the past twenty-five years. Postman was writing before the use of personal computing became widespread. He was reflecting on television not within the context of the development of information technology but within the context of the development of communication. Societies experienced profound shifts when they moved from oral cultures to written cultures. The world was fundamentally changed again with the introduction of the printing press and mass communication. Broadcasting represented another revolution in communication, and one that was not for the better in Postman's estimation. At the bottom line, Carr was assessing the impact of the new computer infrastructure, particularly on commerce; Postman was assessing the impact of television, particularly on social life.

In many ways, online journalism reflects the nexus of each of the developmental paths Carr and Postman described. The desire to know the news seems to be an intrinsic part of human nature.[5] As far back as the Greeks and before, people communicated the events of the day both orally and through other media ranging from letters to obelisks.[6] Over time, however, three great technology platforms for the dissemination of news have emerged. The first to come was printing, which made the mass distribution of news possible. The second was broadcasting, which made news more readily available to large audiences more quickly and in a dramatically different format. The third great platform for the distribution of news is emerging now with the Internet and the different technologies for the production and consumption of information and content that the Internet supports.

Of course, the emergence of online journalism is no longer news. It has been the subject of study for at least the past fifteen years.[7] Studies have explored early efforts of news organizations to move online.[8] The way that news organizations have tried to employ the new possibilities offered by computer-based communication such as interactivity and the potential to build community has been assessed.[9] There have been a raft of academic studies examining the credibility of online news; the relationship of online news to agenda setting and the diffusion of information; the legal issues involved in online news; and, initially, simply tracking the spread of online news efforts.[10] And there have been serious attempts to place the emergence of online news within an appropriate theoretical context.[11]

One of the more interesting aspects of online journalism is that computer-based communications served not only as a platform for disseminating the news but provided a host of new tools for reporting the news. Starting with *The Online Journalist,* several books explored how the Internet can assist reporters.[12] This book takes a different approach. The premise here is that understanding the emergence of online journalism requires an understanding of the online world in general. Along the lines of Postman, it argues that the kind of journalism that is practiced online is deeply shaped by both the technology and the culture associated with the development of the Internet. Therefore, it tells two parallel tales—the development of the computer-based communication networks culminating with the beginnings of collaborative computer-based social media and what has been called Web 2.0, and the efforts of news media and others to take advantage of those technologies for the dissemination of the news.

These two tales are told in this way. Chapter Two very broadly examines the relationship of the technological development of journalism starting with the emergence of newspapers in the 1500s through the ascendency of cable television in the early 1990s. It suggests that the characteristics of specific technologies themselves play pivotal roles in who produces and consumes news; the kind of content that is considered news and how it is presented; and the social, political, and legal framework that shapes the news. Chapter Three traces the development of computer technology from its beginning as a military technology and the first attempts to provide news and information via computer networks. While computers were not conceived of as communication devices, almost from their inception, visionary thinkers like Vannevar Bush saw the opportunity to use computing technology to capture the world's knowledge and to make it more readily available to everybody. This chapter reflects on the first attempts of news media to exploit the potential of computer networks to disseminate the news through the successful launch of the videotex network Minitel in France and the unsuccessful experiment with videotex in the United States. It also relates efforts to provide news through commercial online services like CompuServe and Prodigy.

Chapter Four sketches the creation of the Internet and its first uses as a mechanism to distribute information. While vibrant communities like Usenet news groups and LISTSERV email groups emerged, the traditional news companies were not yet deeply involved with the Internet. They had been scarred by their experience with videotex and cautious about the possibility of commercial online services. For much of this time, the Internet itself was not yet open for commercial use. Nevertheless, the culture that developed around the Internet at this point would influence the development of online journalism in the future. In addition, in this period the Internet became a common tool for reporters, exercising an influence on reporting.

Chapter Five traces the emergence of the World Wide Web both as a technology and as a platform for news. The rush for news organizations to get on the Web did not happen in a vacuum. The Web beckoned everybody from the largest companies in the world to teenagers who created personal Web pages. While the Web clearly presented a great opportunity as a news medium, for established companies it also presented many threats and posed many barriers to entry of specific concern to news organizations. In fact, during the 1990s it looked as though unencumbered start-up companies would have a significant advantage over established companies that had long operated under radically different cost structures. Despite the threat to their established economic and newsgathering models, however, news media had no choice but to invest in building Web sites. The online world was attracting new participants at an exponential rate. If the established organizations did not offer the news online, other organizations would.

The World Wide Web, however, was just the first compelling broad-based platform for news on the Internet. In the late 1990s, another technology emerged that had an important influence on practice of journalism online. In Chapter Six, the rise and impact of blogging is traced. Blogging deeply embodies many cultural elements and ideological perspectives drawn directly from the open source computing community, including the idea that a community of producers will develop a better product than a top-down organization. It also reflects a deep-seated notion in the open source computing community that, at a fundamental level, information should be free, at least free to be changed and altered by anyone whose information might be of better quality. As important, the technologies that enabled blogging were developed as open source products and were free for anyone to use.

Blogging represents one of the first applications in what has been called Web 2.0. Web 2.0 technologies shift the emphasis of the Web from easing access to static information to easing the ability to share user-generated content and collaborate in creating content. Once again, these technologies offer both opportunities for, and threats to, journalism.

The final chapter explores some of the emerging network technologies being deployed on behalf of journalism. It also reflects on the questions first explored for print and broadcast technologies in Chapter Two: What has been the impact of online journalism on who produces and consumes news? What content is considered news? And what is the social, political, and economic context for the production of news?

In trying to determine how the journalistic value of objectivity emerged over time, Michael Schudson argued that understanding the technological changes could not provide a sufficient answer.[13] If so, in a way, Nicholas Carr was correct. When the underlying technologies that allowed for the production of the modern newspaper were in place in the 1890s, all newspapers began to look the same. The *New York Times* did not ultimately gain a competitive advantage over the *New York Herald Tribune* because the *Times* could print a banner headline or seven columns instead of six. And when all the technologies that enabled the modern television news broadcast were in place by the late 1980s, CBS could not claim a competitive advantage over NBC, for example, because it could transmit its broadcast via satellite or because it used videotape.

But, in a way, Neil Postman is correct. The form of the newspaper itself does provide a framework for what is reported, how it is reported, by whom it is read, and the expectations of the readers. The presentation of news on television is different than the presentation of news in the newspapers, because the technology of television is different than the technology of newspapers. Those differences are important.

The technologies associated with online journalism are still in the process of being developed. Therefore news media that appropriately incorporate them can, for a time, enjoy a competitive advantage over established news organizations as well as new initiatives that do not discover the right formula. But once these emerging technologies become established, the technology itself will shape the reporting and presentation of the news online. So, while understanding the technological developments that provide the foundation for computer-based communication networks may not tell the whole story, understanding those changes tell an important part of the story and is absolutely necessary for understanding the transformation of the journalism being driven by the Internet.

TWO

THE TECHNOLOGICAL
ENABLEMENT OF NEWS MEDIA

In November 1951, CBS launched a new television program called *See It Now,* produced by Edward R. Murrow and his partner and colleague Fred Friendly. Murrow was already famous for his radio broadcasts from London during World War II, and in many ways, *See It Now* was intended to compete with, or perhaps replace, the *March of Time* newsreels that appeared in movie theaters prior to the main feature films. *The March of Time* differed from other newsreel operations in that it did not focus on headline news, celebrity events, or sports, the most common newsreel content. Instead, *The March of Time* tried to bring to light the deeper issues underlying the news of the day. The producers of *The March of Time* saw themselves more as documentary filmmakers than newsreel producers.[1]

See It Now would carry on that tradition in the new medium of television, building on Murrow and Friendly's experience with *I Can Hear It Now,* a series of audio recordings Murrow and Friendly produced that combined historical events and speeches with narration by Murrow. *I Can Hear It Now* was such a commercial success that CBS adapted it as a radio series called *Hear It*

Now, combining sound from events with narration from Murrow and other experts.[2]

Murrow and Friendly were cautious in their first telecast. At a cost of three thousand dollars, they rented a video line from San Francisco for the broadcast. Using a split screen, they showed first the Brooklyn Bridge and then the Golden Gate Bridge in San Francisco standing side by side.[3] Murrow narrated the scene. Despite the mundane images—it was a broadcast of two bridges, after all—Murrow's amazement was palpable. He marveled that through the wonders of television, the image could instantly switch from San Francisco to Brooklyn and back again. It was the first live coast-to-coast transmission. The debut of *See It Now* demonstrated to Murrow the potential of television as a news medium. "There are new and great possibilities in TV," he said at the time of the broadcast.[4]

See It Now did not mark the debut of television as a news medium. In 1946, CBS had begun airing the *CBS Evening News with Douglas Edwards* on Saturday nights in New York City. It also aired news broadcasts on Thursday and Friday nights. And in August 1948, four television networks with a total of eighteen television stations broadcast gavel-to-gavel coverage of the Republican and Democratic National Conventions to nine cities along the East Coast connected by a coaxial cable.[5] The broadcast from the Republican National Convention contained the first live press conference, when Thomas Dewey, the governor of New York who ultimately claimed the Republican nomination, took questions from reporters.[6]

The networks decided to cover the conventions not because they believed that television was an important news medium but because it was less expensive to cover the conventions than to fill the air time with entertainment programming. In fact, at that point, many of the most prominent radio journalists of the era, including Edward R. Murrow, stayed as far away from television as possible. Much of the material that NBC broadcast was actually produced by reporters from *Life* magazine, a major advertiser. Nevertheless, the convention represented the first live broadcast of a major news event.

Following the convention, both CBS and NBC launched nightly news broadcasts—*Douglas Edwards and the News* on CBS and the *Camel News Caravan* on NBC with John Cameron Swayze.[7] Both of those broadcasts relied heavily on film developed for newsreels and outside sources. In contrast, for *See It Now,* Murrow and Friendly put together their own film crews and began filming on location and insisting that interviews with their sources not be rehearsed beforehand.[8] In short, *See It Now* marked a milestone in the process of adapting traditional techniques of journalism to the needs and potential of television. Over the next two decades, broadcast journalism emerged as the dominant news medium. By the 1970s, more than 60 percent of Americans reported that they received most of the news about what was going on in the world from broadcast news and more than half reported that television news broadcasts were their most believable source of news.[9] In 1970, the researcher Adnan Almaney bluntly declared broadcast news was the primary source of news for most Americans.[10]

The emergence of television not only changed the way people received the news, it marked the next step in freeing journalism from the constraints of print technology, the medium that had dominated the news since its modern inception. In addition to changing the way news was delivered to audiences, television changed every aspect of journalism. As television became increasingly important, different kinds of stories were reported by new types of journalists in different ways using different techniques and different standards. New audiences were developed and the business model of journalism changed. The emergence of broadcast news raised serious questions concerning who is a journalist, what is news, what is journalism, and the social and political roles of journalism.

The development of television news was not the first time these kinds of questions were raised. Indeed, journalism as it is currently understood was enabled by and rooted in the development of a series of technological innovations starting with the improvement of roads in the sixteenth century, and, most important, the invention of the printing press and movable type. The relationship between the emergence of new technologies, particularly communication technologies, and the practice, product, and delivery of journalism is complex. The diffusion of all technological innovation is intimately intertwined in a jumble of social, political, legal, and economic factors that are difficult to unravel and isolate.[11] The same large and small technological and social forces that have an impact on journalism have an impact on many other aspects of social life, making it difficult to claim that the emergence of new communication technology causes changes in journalism. Nevertheless, every major new innovation in communications technology has had a profound impact on every aspect of journalism including who produces journalism, the audience for journalism, the content of the products of journalism, the business model for journalism, the speed and frequency with which news reaches audiences, and the political and social impact of journalism, as well as the legal environment within which journalism operates. The emergence, significance, and impact of online journalism can be best understood within the broad context of the influence of technological innovation on the practice of journalism over time.

TECHNOLOGY AND THE INVENTION OF NEWSPAPERS

Newspapers, defined as reports containing noteworthy public events and information distributed at regular time intervals, began to appear throughout Western Europe in the seventeenth century. The consistent dissemination of news was made possible by two technological innovations—the development of a more efficient postal and carrier system in Europe, followed by the development of less-expensive printing technology.[12] These changes were accompanied by the collapse of legal restrictions on printing in several countries in Europe.

The need for a more efficient postal system was driven largely by economic development and the growth of international trade. As commerce increased, merchants needed to correspond with each other about prices in markets throughout Europe. The efficiency of that correspondence bore greatly on economic success. By the late fifteenth century, both Spain and France had postal services utilizing couriers and by the sixteenth century, the Hapsburg Empire and the Holy See also had efficient systems.[13] Bankers' agents and merchants, among others, began to write reports about their local conditions, which they sent to their colleagues, representatives, and partners throughout Europe. By the late 1500s, given the improvements in the general postal and carrier services, merchants and diplomats expected weekly reports from their far-flung correspondents. Merchants in particular would share the public aspects of those reports, and in Venice in the late sixteenth century professional newswriters began to copy the public news for wider distribution. The term "gazette" is purported to derive from the word *gazetta,* the smallest Venetian coin, which could be used to purchase a handwritten newsletter.[14]

Similar handwritten newsletters soon appeared in Rome, Holland, and elsewhere. And while it is not entirely certain exactly who wrote the handwritten newsletters of Venice, it is clear that they were widely circulated. As evidence, a collection of Venetian newsletters survives in a library in Leipzig, Germany, as well as in London.[15] While the handwritten Venetian newsletters may or may not qualify as the first newspapers in Europe, they are noteworthy for several reasons. Most important, they were made possible by improvements in communication networks, in this case the transportation system. The regular and timely delivery of newsletters was directly tied to the development of more reliable and extensive roads. In countries in which development of the transportation systems lagged, the appearance of regularly published newsletters lagged as well.[16] For example, handwritten newsletters did not appear in England or France until after the emergence of printing.[17]

Second, although written by various authors, newsletters assumed a regular format—a format that would survive their transition to printing in the decades that followed. Newsletters consisted of summaries of the letters received by the compiler of the newsletter and included trade news, business intelligence, military information, and other events of public interest described one after another, often with little or no commentary.[18] The format is linked to the available production technology, which in this case consisted of copying by hand both the letters that provided the content of the newsletters and the newsletters themselves.

Around the same time or shortly after handwritten newsletters began appearing throughout Europe, printed news books made possible by the invention of movable type and the modern printing press gained currency. As early as 1484, governments began to print proclamations. And in 1513, a pamphlet filled with government propaganda concerning the battle of Flodden Field, where King James IV of Scotland and an army of 30,000 were defeated by English forces under the Earl of Surrey at Northumberland, England, was published.[19]

The market for news broadened with the English intervention in the war between the Netherlands, France, and Spain in 1580. In 1590, the year that marked the assassination of Henry III of France, thirty-eight news books, almost one per week, covering news from France, were printed and circulated in England. With the need to attract a new audience to each publication, news books, as opposed to newsletters, tended to report on crime, sensational events, pageants and ceremonies, and reports of the supernatural in addition to war news.[20] The innovations represented by periodic manuscript newsletters and printed news books began to converge in the late 1500s and early 1600s. The first European news periodical, the *Mercurius Gallobelgicus,* was published in Cologne, France, in 1594. Issued twice a year and printed in Latin, it contained mostly war news.[21] On December 2, 1620, an English coranto was published in Amsterdam with news from Italy, Germany, and elsewhere. It appeared regularly through September of the following year, making it the first regularly printed news publication in English, although it was produced in Amsterdam.[22] Once again war, this time what came to be called the Thirty Years' War, drove the appetite for news. Corantos quickly grew in size, ranging from eight to twenty-four pages. The growing market for news publications attracted the attention of printers, and by 1622 five printers were producing news corantos.[23]

Printers, however, were not the only community that began to produce newsletters, news books, and newspapers, nor were they the only participants in the growing community developing around news media and other printed material. In addition to printers, booksellers emerged as key players, commonly serving as news publishers. The bookseller Thomas Archer, who claims to be the first to publish a printed English language newsletter in England (as opposed to Amsterdam) in 1621, first entered the historical record in 1603 with an account of a battle between a Dutch warship and the Portuguese, an account which he offered for sale.[24] And while printers or booksellers might also serve as the editors of the news in addition to printing and publishing it, merchants, clerics, poets, and even craftspeople from more humble trades, such as tailors, tried their hand at compiling and distributing the news, both printed versions and manuscript newsletters. For example, the tailor John Dillingham compiled *The Moderate Intelligencer* in the 1640s.[25] And a new trade emerged as well—the trade of copyist or scrivener, people whose primary responsibility was to compile the news and write newsletters.

The emerging news media in England found an enthusiastic, if relatively small market. Readers became accustomed to receiving news weekly. And if that news was not provided by their customary source, they would seek out other publications to satisfy their desires. Of course, with literacy levels low, readership was still quite limited. Most publications published less than four hundred copies per issue. Most readers were drawn from the ranks of the gentry, lords, courtiers, and professions.[26]

Interestingly, a similar development pattern for emerging news media was evident throughout Europe. In Germany, for example, weekly newspapers began to make their appearance in the early 1600s, and by the middle of the century, around thirty cities had German language newspapers.[27] These publications had common structures. Most had correspondents in major European cities such as Antwerp, Prague, and Rome who would send letters through the postal system on a fairly regular basis. The correspondents'

identity was often unknown to the readers. The correspc
reports, which covered a wide range of topics, were often p ..ced
in order with little or no editing. Newspapers carried reports of
trade, church activities such as pilgrimages and processions, news
from the royal courts, and natural catastrophes. The reports were
often simply factual statements that an event occurred.

For an extended period of time, both printed and manuscript
newsletters existed side by side. It was not uncommon for the
news reports to be drawn from the handwritten newspapers with
which the printed newspapers competed. In the early part of the
seventeenth century, handwritten newspapers had several advantages over printed newspapers. They could be customized to the
interests of a specific reader. And they were subject to less governmental regulation. On the other hand, handwritten newspapers in
Germany cost five times as much as printed newspapers, which
were geared to generate as large an audience as possible.[28] As the
demand and the market grew, news publications began to have
an impact on political life by making the activities of politicians
more visible to their constituencies. By the 1620s, news publications were an integral part of political process which politicians
could not ignore. Moreover, the image of politics presented in the
news was often very different than the political rhetoric favored
by the ruling classes. While the dominant political ideology was
loyalty and deference to the monarch, who had a divine mandate
to rule, politics as it was presented in the news painted a picture
of conflict and struggle.[29]

Since the circulation of news had an impact on public opinion
and public attitudes, it is not surprising that European governments systematically passed onerous laws to restrict the circulation
of news and other materials, particularly printed news, since manuscript newsletters were more difficult to control. For example, in

the Netherlands, the first law controlling printing was enacted in 1550 and aimed at controlling and punishing heresy. For the next seventy-five years, the rulers of the Netherlands passed a series of laws and regulations constraining what could be published. Although heresy ceased to be the animating motive for the laws, tight regulations remained in place.[30] Similar efforts were made throughout Europe. In England, the Star Chamber passed a decree in 1586 strictly limiting the number of printers in England and what they could print. And in 1621, just a year after the appearance of the first English language corantos from Amsterdam, King James I banned the importing of corantos to England, although the ban was not enforced.[31]

While censorship laws and the control of access to printing presses had a significant impact, stifling the growth of the news media, in 1641 the regulatory regime broke down in revolutionary England. The new freedom, coupled with a sharp reduction in the cost of printing, led to an explosion in the accessibility of news pamphlets, sermons, weekly news books, and other printed news material. Suddenly, for as little as a penny, new forms of printed news were available to a much broader segment of the population, often sold by armies of street vendors. And although postal rates added to the cost, people outside the main population centers also had access to these new news media.[32]

The power of the printed word became obvious. In December 1641, the English Parliament published its Grand Remonstrance, the list of grievances it held against Charles I, not only in script but as a printed pamphlet. Charles I responded with a published pamphlet of his own.[33] From there, the English Civil War was fought by the press as well as on the battleground.

The first blow, however, which would eventually lead to the

launch of fully recognizable newspapers in England, had been struck the month before with the publication of *The Heads of Severall Proceedings in this Present Parliament,* a weekly newspaper apparently edited by Samuel Peake. The publication was filled with news about the proceedings of Parliament. The next month, a competitor called *The Diurnal* appeared, and a third newspaper entered the field shortly thereafter. The appearance of these newspapers signaled that the king had lost his ability to control the press—and, indeed, eight years later another newspaper, also edited by Samuel Peake, would laconically report on the beheading of Charles I. The newspapers that began to be published during the English Civil War carried a full diet of domestic news and used many of the same storytelling techniques that would characterize newspapers for several hundred years.[34]

Although the content was primarily political in nature and closely associated with either the Royalist or the Parliamentary party, the newsletters and news pamphlets were created to make money for their proprietors as well. From the beginning, the publications carried advertising to generate revenue in addition to the revenue raised through subscriptions. For example, in May 1660, *Mercurius Publicus,* a republican news periodical, also carried a series of ads promoting the use of toothpaste. By this time, journalism had metamorphosed into a legitimate business.[35]

The ebb and flow of English politics continued to exert a heavy influence on the environment in which the news media developed. As Oliver Cromwell consolidated his power, he reasserted control over news media. But after his death in 1660, a brief relaxation of the censorship rules allowed for the publication of the first daily news book, *A Perfect Diurnal,* which reported on the daily activities of Parliament. Although *A Perfect Diurnal* was short-lived, lasting only twenty-one issues, and the government of England soon reverted to allowing only a single, censored official news publication, the appetite for news among a class of people willing to pay for it had been irreversibly whetted.[36]

During the Restoration, the publishing and dissemination of news was strictly controlled, but the thirst for news was satisfied by the expansion of the number of coffeehouses. In 1666, there were eighty-eight coffeehouses in London; by 1700, there were more than five hundred. People from all social classes would gather to learn and discuss the news.[37] The Licensing Act had reimposed most of the press restrictions originally promulgated in 1637. Throughout the years of the Civil War, the act had lapsed and then been renewed several times. But as Parliament increasingly asserted its authority in opposition to the monarchy, the desire to renew the act waned, and in 1695 the House of Commons formally declined to renew it. At the same time, it revoked the monopoly of the Stationers Company on publishing and copyrights.[38]

In the wake of the demise of the Licensing Act, prepublication censorship collapsed, setting in motion a new era marked by an increased freedom of the press to operate as it wished.[39] In 1702, the *Daily Courant,* London's first daily newspaper, was founded, followed by the *Morning Post,* the *Times,* and others. By the 1730s, there were six daily newspapers.[40] The year 1730 marked the launch of the *Daily Advertiser,* considered by some to be the first modern newspaper. When the newspaper first appeared, it announced that it would include advertisements, stock prices, and other business news such as bankruptcy announcements and shipping news. As a daily publication, it was as efficient a medium as word of mouth for disseminating commercial news to the merchant class.[41]

THE IMPACT OF THE HIGH SPEED PRESS
AND THE TELEGRAPH

The general form in which newspapers emerged in England and elsewhere in Europe remained remarkably consistent for more than one hundred years. Generally speaking, the editorial mix consisted of political and business news, crime and punishment including executions, tales of the grotesque and unusual, as well as advertising.[42] Newspapers were most often associated with a specific geographic location. Newspapers published in larger urban areas generally had larger circulations. But circulations were constrained by three factors—the ability to print a sufficient quantity of copies daily, the cost of printing, and the number of literate people with the means and motivation to buy newspapers.

Wider newspaper distribution depended on continued improvements in the postal service. In the United States, shortly after the ratification of the U.S. Constitution, Congress guaranteed reduced rates for sending printed matter through the mail in the Postal Acts of 1792 and 1794. Publications accounted for nearly half the mail volume in early America. So while newspapers were identified with specific cities or geographic regions, they had the potential to circulate to wider areas. Giving preferential treatment to publications in the postal system was an effort to build a national identity and knit the new country together.[43] And in the same way that news publication had been identified with the different protagonists in the English Civil War, in the United States newspapers continued to be identified with different political parties. For example, in Isaiah Thomas's *History of Printing in America,* published in 1810, of the 350 newspapers listed, all but 50 were identified as being affiliated either with the Federalist or

Republican Parties.[44] Both political parties, however, supported the use of the postal service to distribute newspapers. The Federalists believed that broad dissemination of the news would strengthen the central government, and Republicans felt that widespread distribution of news would help bring to light the abuses of the central government.[45]

In the 1830s and 1840s, two major technological developments had a significant impact on newspapers. The first was the invention of the steam-driven high speed cylinder press. The press improvements were accompanied by innovations in the production of newsprint. Together, these new technologies meant publishers could print more newspapers each day and sell them at a lower price. By reducing the cost of newspapers and increasing their availability, newspaper publishers could significantly expand their markets. High speed printing and cheaper newsprint enabled the birth of the penny press.

Since the time of Gutenberg, printing press technology had advanced very slowly. As late as the early 1800s, newspaper publishers were still dependent on presses that were cranked by hand. Then, in 1813 in Philadelphia, George Clymer reengineered the printing press, relying on levers instead of a screw technology. While an improvement and widely adopted, it would be soon eclipsed by a revolutionary new technology—the steam-driven press.[46]

Friedrich Koenig of Saxony was the first person to couple steam power to the printing press effectively. First introduced in London in 1811, paper was fed into a cylinder and a movable bed carried the type back and forth to make each impression. A few years later, he introduced a two-cylinder press that could print on both sides of a sheet. This press was adopted by the *Times* of London, which quickly boasted that it could print 1,100 papers an hour.[47] In 1825, the New York *Daily Advertiser,* the first American newspaper to use the Koenig steam press, claimed that it could publish 2,500 newspapers an hour.[48]

But that was only the beginning. In 1830, David Napier, also of London, introduced a series of improvements for the Koenig steam press, raising its production capacity significantly. The Napier model was adopted by Richard Hoe, who created a double cylinder press with the ability to print 4,000 newspapers an hour.[49]

The dramatic improvement in printing technology was matched by equally important improvements in the production of paper and the beginning of mass manufacturing of ink. Through the 1700s, paper had been manufactured in single sheets using rags as raw materials. The first prototype of the Fourdrinier papermaking machine was built in 1798 and first went into operation in 1804. In this process, wood pulp is placed on a continuous screen made of wires. Through a series of steps, the water is squeezed from the pulp, creating continuous rolls of paper. The Fourdrinier process allowed for high-speed production of paper needed for the mass production of newspapers. Using the new machine, a mill could produce the same amount of paper as with the older process at less than one-third the cost. Fourdrinier machines began to be manufactured in the United States in 1830, and the introduction of chlorine as a bleaching agent in 1831 meant that a much wider array of fibers could be used as the raw material for paper, including dirty and colored rags as well as hay and straw.[50]

The response to the opportunity presented by the high speed printing press and the high-speed production of paper was dramatic. After a number of failed attempts, in 1833, Benjamin Day launched the *New York Sun,* which sold for a penny, instead of the six cents that newspapers generally cost at the time. In 1835, James Gordon Bennett, who is sometimes seen as the "father" of modern American journalism, took the wraps off the *New York*

Herald, which also sold for a penny. With the low per-copy cost, Day and Bennett increased the circulation of their newspapers exponentially compared to their competitors. Instead of selling perhaps 4,000 newspapers a day, they sold 30,000 or even 40,000 a day.[51]

The increased circulation meant that the penny press had a more secure economic foundation than the competing six-penny newspapers. Bennett was quick to declare his independence from the political parties that typically sponsored and financially supported newspapers. Moreover, in his effort to appeal to a wider community of readers, he broadened the editorial coverage in the *Herald.* Finally, to more fully reach his potential audience, Bennett adopted a method of distribution that had been pioneered in London. He sold his newspapers to retailers who bought them with cash and could then resell them by subscription to readers on a short-term basis, often a week or so. Or, the retailers could resell the newspapers to newsboys who sold them on the street. Proprietors of penny newspapers recruited an army of newsboys to hawk their product. The *Philadelphia Public Ledger,* Philadelphia's penny newspaper, used the "London" plan, its publisher noted, because that was the only method of distribution that would allow for the newspaper to be sold at such a low price.[52] There are many reasons that the penny press was successful in the 1830s. America was industrializing and there was a growing skilled urban working class that had an interest in public life. Literacy was on the rise. The notion of democracy was broadening with the franchise to vote reaching more and more people. The penny press was not created by the high speed press and high-speed papermaking alone. But without the technological improvements in printing and papermaking, newspapers could not be mass produced and sold for a penny. As it happened, shortly after the successful launch of the

Sun and the *Herald,* penny newspapers could be found in Boston, Philadelphia, and Baltimore. The penny newspaper was the logical application of new technology within specific social conditions.

The second significant new technology with an impact on journalism was the invention of the telegraph in 1844. The telegraph meant that news could travel from place to place faster than ever before imagined. To demonstrate its power, in 1842, Samuel F. B. Morse secured $30,000 in funding from Congress to build a telegraph line along the tracks of the Baltimore & Ohio railroad between Baltimore and Washington. To quiet skeptics about the potential of the new technology, in the spring of 1844, with the line almost complete, he proposed to transmit the names of the people nominated for office at the Whig National Convention, which was to meet in Baltimore on May 1. After the nominations were announced, the names were rushed to a transmitting station fifteen miles outside of Baltimore and then transmitted to Washington. While the nomination of Henry Clay to head the ticket had been widely expected, the announcement that the unknown Theodore Frelinghuysen had secured the vice presidential slot made the demonstration of the telegraph's prowess to deliver the news quickly all the more dramatic. A train with the same nominees' names arrived in Washington more than an hour later. Less than a month after that, the telegraph was officially inaugurated when Morse sent the message, "What hath God wrought," from the chambers of the Supreme Court in Washington to his assistant Alfred Vail in Baltimore.[53] With the formalities for posterity out of the way, the next line Morse transmitted to Vail was, "Have you any news?" The Democratic Party was holding its nominating convention in Philadelphia. Over the next several days, crowds would gather in a room in the north wing of the Capitol to get updates from Morse about the convention. And on May 29, Morse was the first to announce that James Knox Polk and Silas Wright would be the Democratic standard-bearers.[54]

At that point, there was little doubt that the telegraph had the potential to play a major role in transmitting the news. In August 1844, the birth of the second son of Queen Victoria of England was announced by telegraph from Windsor. Within forty minutes, the *Times* of London was in the streets with the news.[55] The impact of the telegraph on the production and practice of journalism was profound. Although news media had relied on far-flung correspondent networks since the days of manuscript newsletters and were dependent on the transportation infrastructure to ensure that the news was delivered in a timely fashion, telegraph technology led to a complete restructuring of the competitive landscape and newspaper proprietors invested heavily in the creation of the telegraph's infrastructure. William M. Swain, the proprietor of the *Philadelphia Public Ledger,* was the largest investor in the Magnetic Telegraph Company, which was established to string telegraph wire from Washington, D.C., to New York. Horace Greeley, James Gordon Bennett, James Watson Webb, and Moses Yale Beach, all newspaper owners, provided a significant part of the capital needed to run telegraph lines from New York to Boston.[56] But even with the preferential pricing the press enjoyed, the cost to any one newspaper to transmit news by telegraph on a regular basis could be staggering.[57]

The response was for newspapers to band together to defray the cost and share the burden. A telegraph line was completed between Albany, New York, and Buffalo, New York, in late January 1846, and the first cooperative news association was established by four newspapers in western New York within the next several weeks.[58] While the New York City papers were slower to band together formally to share the telegraph transmission costs, there is evidence of their cooperation as early as 1846, when identical dispatches with news of the Mexican-American War began to appear daily in the *Herald* and the *Tribune*. In 1848, Henry Raymond, working for the *New York Courier and Enquirer* and later the founder of the *New York Times,* contracted with a Boston telegraph operator to provide foreign news via telegraph for six New York City newspapers. And in January 1849, the same six New York City newspapers, including the *Tribune,* the *Herald,* and the *Sun,* created the Harbor News Association, the forerunner of what was to become the Associated Press. Although the Harbor News Association was first established to share the news gathered from ships arriving at the New York harbor, by 1851 the association was also sharing news received via telegraph as well.[59]

The invention of the telegraph raised the stakes for newspapers to deliver news quickly. The changes played themselves out in several ways. With the growth of international telegraph lines and the completion of a transatlantic cable in 1858, the public's appetite for foreign news increased sharply. At the same time, during war, information that was once safe for the government to reveal could be instantly received by the enemy. Although geographically unchanged, the informational distance between enemy capitals collapsed. At the same time, dispatches from the front lines gave the public a much clearer idea of how a specific campaign was progressing. For example, William Howard Russell, reporting from the battlegrounds of the Crimean War in 1854, helped arouse public indignation about the British government's conduct of the military effort. Russell regularly sent back stories about ill-equipped troops being dispatched to the wrong place with the lack of proper medical equipment.[60]

Moreover, the argument has been made that the incorporation of telegraph technology into news reporting and dissemination may have been a factor in a change in the nature and presentation of the news. The constraints and costs involved in transmitting information via the telegraph may have led to the rise of the notion that news reports should be "objective," reporting just the facts without political bias, and to the use of the inverted pyramid form for news articles in which articles start by answering the questions who, what, where, and when. Because news associations sharing telegraph services included newspapers of differing and even opposing political stripes, the news transmitted via the wire had to be stripped of language that might color it in one direction or another.[61] Studies indicate that the discernible bias in news stories transmitted by telegraph declined over time.[62] An early example of the pyramid style for news articles can be found in the telegraphic dispatches of Edwin Stanton, who served as secretary of war during the Civil War. The argument goes that since telegraph transmission was so costly, all the important information had to be efficiently jammed into the initial paragraphs with little or no verbal adornments.[63]

As printing technology improved and transportation and distribution networks were upgraded, newspapers grew in size and in their scope of coverage. As newspapers increased the number of pages printed, news itself became a larger part of the overall editorial mix, which also included editorial opinion and other material. The improvements in manufacturing and distribution for newspapers took place within an overall improvement of American manufacturing and distribution. Those improvements led to a revolution in retailing, which, in turn, buttressed advertising support for newspapers.

In the 1880s, newspapers were once again in a position to increase their circulations exponentially. And once again, key technological improvement enabled the growth in the size of newspapers. Almost since the time of Gutenberg, printers had required about one minute to set a line of type. With the expansion of newspaper circulations in the 1830s and 1840s, efforts were made to increase the productivity of typesetters. The breakthrough came in 1886, when Ottmar Mergenthaler sold a machine that could set entire lines of type at once to the *New York Tribune.* Working with a machine that resembled a typewriter, using Mergenthaler's linotype machine, printers could set five lines of type a minute, a fivefold increase in productivity.[64]

As newspapers became bigger businesses, chains in which a single company operated newspapers in many different cities emerged. Starting with a single newspaper in San Francisco, William Randolph Hearst built a newspaper chain that reached coast to coast. Lord Northcliffe did the same in England. E. W. Scripps operated newspapers in forty cities in the United States. And several other newspaper chains were launched in the late 1800s and early 1900s. These chains shared editorial material and realized other economies of scale, enabled by the general improvements in transportation and manufacturing. Scripps newspapers, for example, shared telegraphic services and an illustrated news syndicate service.[65]

Finally, technological enhancements enabled the increased utilization of illustrations and photography in newspapers and magazines. Beginning in the 1830s, publishers began to experiment with illustrations. What is generally considered the first illustrated newspaper, the *London Illustrated Gazette,* appeared in London in 1842. Matthew Brady's photographs taken during the American Civil War represent a significant contribution to the record of that conflict, but the technology of photography developed slowly. What is called documentary photography—photography that seemed to capture what could be seen as an objective view of a live event—did not really emerge until the 1920s in Europe. And while photographs became an important component of newspapers, of great significance were the improvements in photography that led to the creation of major magazines such as *Life* and *Look* in the 1930s. With the introduction of color photography and color printing for magazines, the 1930s through the 1950s became known as the golden age of photojournalism.[66]

RADIO AND THE INVENTION OF BROADCAST NEWS

Newspapers and other print publications remained the dominant news medium throughout the nineteenth and into the early part of the twentieth century. Protected to a degree by the First Amendment of the U.S. Constitution, newspapers and magazines reflected a huge array of political, religious, and social viewpoints. But in the 1920s, new technology created a new medium for news—broadcast radio.

In the same way that the birth of newspapers is shrouded in the uneven evolution of news pamphlets and newsletters in the fifteenth and sixteenth centuries, the birth of commercial radio in America is also a question of debate. There were reports of radio broadcasts as early as 1907. But the origins of commercial radio broadcasting are generally marked on November 2, 1920, when KDKA, a newly established radio station in Pittsburgh, Pennsylvania, owned by Westinghouse Electric and Manufacturing Company, began broadcasting the election results of the U.S. presidential campaign waged between Warren Harding and James M. Cox. This date is used as the starting point because KDKA was the first station to be licensed by the United States government for general broadcasting. Moreover, Westinghouse set up the station as part of its effort to turn radio into a consumer product in households across America.[67] The goal of the broadcast was to stimulate the sale of radio receivers built by Westinghouse.

KDKA made its debut a little more than twenty years after radio, or wireless telegraphy as it was originally described, received its first widespread publicity in the United States. In what was the next step in a series of inventions stretching back to the early nineteenth century, Guglielmo Marconi had demonstrated his wireless telegraphy to British audiences in 1896. In 1898, he used wireless telegraphy to send news updates about the Kingstown Regatta to the *Dublin Daily Express.* Those reports were read by James Gordon Bennett, Jr., the owner of the *New York Herald* and an international yachtsman. Bennett hired Marconi to use his wireless telegraphy to send updates to the *Herald* about the America's Cup yacht race in 1899. In October 1899, the *Herald* promoted the use of wireless technology to report on the America's Cup as a major breakthrough in journalism and asserted that it would be widely used to report on more significant events in the future.[68]

The path from Marconi's demonstration of wireless telegraph to commercial acceptance was technologically arduous. Marconi himself had initially focused on using wireless technology to send Morse code. Competitors in the field were more intrigued by the potential of wireless technology to transmit sound and voice. Armed with a research grant from the U.S. Department of Agriculture to explore the uses of radio, Reginald Fessenden, who had once worked for Thomas Edison but by that time was a professor of electrical engineering at what is now the University of Pittsburgh, successfully broadcast the voice of a woman singing as well as a speech on Christmas Eve 1906.[69] But radio technology still required several major refinements before it could be more than a novelty.

The development of radio was driven by two major forces. First, the American Telephone and Telegraph Company became interested in radio technology as it explored the challenges associated with establishing coast-to-coast telephone service.[70] Second, the United States Navy took a serious interest in the technology. During World War I, the navy took control of all U.S. radio transmission aboard ships and on shore. After the war, the navy played a significant role in the creation of the Radio Corporation of America (RCA).[71] Indeed, it was the collaboration of the U.S. Navy and AT&T that led to the first wireless transmission of voice across the Atlantic Ocean in 1915.[72]

Unlike newspapers, which developed through the efforts of locally based entrepreneurs, to a significant degree radio technology was developed and promoted by large companies. After the launch of KDKA, General Electric and RCA both laid plans to establish competitive networks. But Westinghouse, General Electric, and RCA were all focused on selling radio receivers. Little thought was given to developing programming or content.

Moreover, while newspapers emerged in an era in which there were strict controls on what could be published, their basic form developed only after those restrictions were loosened. Radio broadcasting in America, however, was regulated by the federal government almost from its inception. In 1912, Congress mandated the Commerce Department to regulate radio and require radio operators to obtain licenses. At the time, radio was used only for ship-to-shore communication. Seven years after the launch of KDKA, there were 733 broadcasting stations in operation and the broadcast spectrum appeared to be saturated. In part to prevent signal jamming and wavelength jumping, Congress passed the Radio Act of 1927, which was designed, according to the authors of the act, to serve the public interest, convenience, and necessity. Part of the rationale for the federal government having the authority to regulate radio broadcasting was that radio used the public airways. The act was also intended to prevent any one company from monopolizing radio by initiating a series of high-powered radio stations, monopolizing the manufacture or sale of radio receivers, or through exclusive agreements with cable operators or telegraph companies. The result, however, was to cut the number of radio stations operating in the U.S. by almost 20 percent.[73] Congress extended its control of radio and all telecommunications with the passage of the Communications Act of 1934, which created the Federal Communications Commission (FCC) and required radio license holders to operate their stations in the public interest.

As more radio stations began broadcasting, the need for consistent, high-quality programming grew. In the same period that wireless technology was being developed, new technology focusing on sound recording was being developed as well—the phonograph. Like wireless technology, the efforts to record sound were first directed toward different goals from the ones that would ultimately attract a mass market. In the 1880s, when Thomas Edison refined his approach to recording sound to the point at which it was of practical use, he thought the best application would be to capture dictation in business settings. He was wrong. In the period from 1895 to 1910, the phonograph was reinvented as a consumer entertainment product, with recorded music an essential component of the content. By 1910, recorded sound was a mass medium, the first new mass medium since the emergence of print.[74]

In 1926, RCA, GE, and Westinghouse incorporated the National Broadcasting Company, which was soon operating two networks. In 1927, the rival Columbia Broadcasting System was established. And in 1934, the Mutual Broadcasting System was launched. In 1945, three out of four radio stations in America

were affiliated with a radio network.[75] Having already established
its ability to attract an audience, live and recorded music was an
attractive, relatively low-cost option for radio content. From the
earliest days of radio, standard phonograph music was the chief
source for radio programming.[76]

News and public affairs were also seen as attractive content
for radio broadcasts. The 1924 Democratic and Republican presidential nominating conventions were broadcast via radio. An estimated three million people listened, or potentially could have listened, to the nomination of Calvin Coolidge on the Republican
ticket.[77] The press at the time recognized the impact that radio
could have on politics and political reporting. Radio networks
made it more difficult for a candidate to express one point of view
in one part of the country and a different point of view elsewhere.
On the other hand, political oratory on the radio often seemed
flat and stale. Nonetheless, politicians understood that radio could
have a profound impact on the elections and democracy.[78] In 1928,
the presidential candidates Al Smith, the Democratic candidate,
and Herbert Hoover, the Republican candidate, spent more than
$1 million on radio broadcasts.[79]

Although newspaper companies were among the early investors in radio and early content included special events such as
election returns and the 1925 Scopes trial concerning evolution,
in the first several years news was not an important source for
broadcasts. An American Newspaper Publishers Association report
in 1927 observed that 48 newspapers owned radio stations, 69
sponsored programs, and 97 provided on-air news broadcasts.[80]
However, in general, in the early days, there were no daily news
broadcasts and radio stations did not support their own news gathering operations. Some stations, however, did have lecturers and
commentators to discuss current events on the air. Perhaps the

most prominent was H.V. Kaltenborn, an assistant editor at the *Brooklyn Eagle* who began airing weekly news commentaries on WEAF in October 1923.[81]

The relationship between newspapers and radio broadcasters began to change in the late 1920s with the organization of radio networks and the onset of the Great Depression. While radio advertising climbed, advertising in newspapers shrank. As a result, newspaper publishers came to see radio as a competitor. In 1933, the Associated Press voted against providing its news bulletins to radio chains and to charge an additional fee to newspaper clients who used the bulletins on radio stations they owned. The competing International News Service also refused to supply dispatches to radio stations. In response, CBS organized its own news gathering operation, establishing news bureaus in major cities and subscribing to news services for foreign news. Many newspapers answered by eliminating CBS program listings from their pages.[82]

In December 1933, representatives of the radio networks, the newspaper publishers association, and the wire services struck a deal. According to the ten-point agreement, radio stations would receive limited daily bulletins and broadcast not more than five minutes of news from each of the bulletins. In return, CBS agreed to disband its news gathering operation and NBC agreed not to enter the arena. Broadcast commentators could reflect on the news but not provide spot news reports. The agreement was announced in January 1934, and the Press-Radio News Bureau, which was responsible for implementing its terms, was established in March of that year.[83]

But the move to block the entry of radio into news gathering and presentation did not work. Independent stations, notably WOR in New York, did not adhere to the agreement, giving them a competitive advantage over the network stations. Moreover, smaller wire services continued to supply news to the radio market. By 1935, the deal had collapsed. Newspapers began to buy radio licenses more aggressively, and with war clouds gathering over Europe, in 1938 CBS and NBC established their own news gathering operations to supplement the wire services.

Nonetheless, the radio networks did not see themselves in the same light as newspapers when it came to covering the news. Although newspapers played an active role in shaping public opinion, William Paley, the owner of the CBS radio network, declared that radio had to be militantly nonpartisan in politics and even in the realm of social ideas. Radio was different, Paley said, because while anybody could establish a newspaper, a broadcaster's exclusive right to use a specific radio frequency was protected by a government license.[84]

Throughout the 1920s and 1930s, radio won widespread consumer acceptance. Within ten years of the launch of KDKA, radios were found in more than 45 percent of all U.S. households and ten years after that, in 1940, more than 80 percent of all U.S. households had radios.[85] Radio continually demonstrated its power as a medium for news and information. Perhaps the most vivid demonstration of radio's immediacy was President Franklin Delano Roosevelt's fireside chats. To be sure, Roosevelt routinely communicated with the American public through newspapers. He convened 337 press conferences in his first term of office and 374 in his second.[86] But it was the thirty-one radio addresses he delivered, which came to be called "fireside chats," that helped Roosevelt create an intimate, almost personal bond with the American people. It was through the fireside chats that Roosevelt worked to restore Americans' confidence in themselves and their country.[87] Equally as powerful were the broadcasts of Edward R.

Murrow and others during the lead up to and throughout World War II.[88]

Radio, however, represented a completely different model for journalism than newspapers in several significant ways. Radio did not depend on its listeners' literacy, as newspapers did. Instead, radio required that listeners purchase radio receivers to hear broadcasts. The first radio broadcasts were intended to stimulate the purchase of radio receivers. Beyond the acquisition of a receiver, in the economic model established in the United States, radio content was available for free to the listener. It was completely supported by advertising. In the early 1920s, several different economic models were proposed for radio, including having the government impose a tax on radio to support programming—a model adopted in the United Kingdom and elsewhere—or to charge a subscription for programming. The advertising-supported commercial model, however, triumphed.[89] Newspapers, on the other hand, relied on a mix of subscriptions, single-copy sales, and advertising for their revenue. As a result the potential listening audience for radio was always greater than the potential audience for newspapers, although the specific audience for each radio station was limited by the reach of the broadcasting signal.

Furthermore, the economics of advertising on radio sharply contrasted with the economics of advertising in newspapers. In radio, advertising consumed time, which is a finite commodity. In newspapers, advertising required space, which could be increased as the volume of advertising increased. Being a time-based advertising medium constrains the amount of time that can be devoted to other elements in the content mix. The potential limitations for news reporting and commentary for a medium entirely dependent on advertising for revenue quickly became clear. In 1935, the CBS

Radio network had a show called "The Town Crier," in which the respected writer and critic Alexander Woollcott commented on current events. In one commentary, he focused on the dangers posed by Adolf Hitler's anti-Semitism and extreme nationalism. The National Biscuit Company (Nabisco), the parent company of the show's sponsor, received a stream of letters taking issue with Woollcott's commentary. Officials at Nabisco asked Woollcott to use better judgment in the future. He refused and the show was cancelled.[90]

Perhaps not surprisingly, the content mix for radio, particularly during its start-up phase, was quite different than the content mix for newspapers. Unlike newspapers, where business news and politics were among the primary drivers of the launch of newspapers, news was only a small part of the content mix on radio. The network that was to become CBS, for example, broadcast a five-minute daily newscast and fifteen minutes' worth of commentary in the late 1920s. While newspaper companies worked hard to limit the entry of radio into journalism, particularly the broadcasting of breaking news, radio relied heavily on music, both prerecorded and live, as a well as entertainment programming.

Another significant contrast between radio as a medium for journalism and newspapers is that radio was regulated by national governments. While public newspapers first appeared when censorship laws were in force, newspapers flourished as those rules crumbled. The First Amendment of the U.S. Constitution represented an effort to create an almost completely unfettered news medium. As radio technology became more prevalent, the direct application of the First Amendment to this new medium seemed impractical.[91] Since radio could reach directly into every home, radio could be required to operate for the public convenience and necessity, and licenses could be withheld if the Federal Communications Commission found that a station was broadcasting objectionable content.[92]

The net result was that radio never emerged as a serious rival to newspapers as a news medium in that time period. Newscasts on radio were short and largely consisted of reading short bulletins and headlines. On the other hand, radio demonstrated the potential of broadcasting to command attention and create celebrities. Vaudeville comedians such as Jack Benny, Fred Allen, and the Marx Brothers, as well as writers of popular songs, such as Irving Berlin, became famous nationally because of their exposure via radio, as did Walter Winchell, Edward R. Murrow, William Shirer, H.V. Kaltenborn. and others.[93] But if radio did not fundamentally change journalism, television would.

THE DOMINANT NEW MEDIUM—TELEVISION

Generally, a new medium is first explained and understood publicly in relationship to an existing medium. For example, when recorded sound was introduced to the public, it was explained in terms of writing, reading, and particularly speaking.[94] If analogies to old media are generally used to explain the functionality of new media technology, the transition to television from radio represents an extreme case. Not only was the name "television" intended to convey some degree of consistency with, and connection to, the telephone and the telegraph; it was understood, to a large degree, as radio with pictures. Moreover, the same companies that pioneered the formation of radio networks moved aggressively into television, with NBC, CBS, and ABC, which was a spin-off of a second NBC network, leading the charge. Most of the entertainment content broadcast on radio and the entertainment stars associated with radio shows eventually made the transition to television. Like radio, television reserved a limited amount of time for news broadcasting in its overall mix. And, like radio, in the United States, television was regulated by the FCC (television in the United Kingdom also inherited the model used there by radio). Finally, television initially adopted the same economic model as radio. Once somebody purchased a television set, programming was free, supported entirely by advertising.

But while the conditions of radio curtailed its emergence as a news medium, from the early 1950s when it started to become widespread in American households, television as a news medium steadily grew in stature. By the early 1970s, television was seen as the dominant news medium, and with the growth of cable television and Cable Network News not long thereafter, television news had established the 24-hour news cycle. The news was always available.

The power and reach of news broadcasting on television grew incrementally. About the same time that Edward R. Murrow marveled at television's ability to shift instantaneously between images of the Brooklyn Bridge and the Golden Gate Bridge, television's potential power to focus the public's attention on news and propel people into prominence was vividly demonstrated in 1950 and 1951 when Congressional hearings examining organized crime chaired by Estes Kefauver, an obscure U.S. senator from Tennessee, were televised. The publicity Kefauver generated through the hearings and the impressive way in which he could communicate to people through television led him to run for the Democratic nomination for the presidency in 1952 and to garner the nomination for the vice presidency that year despite the opposition of the incumbent president, Harry S. Truman, and other leaders of the Democratic party.[95]

Television's coverage of the Civil Rights movement in the South brought shocking images of nonviolent demonstrators being assaulted by angry crowds and the police into living rooms from coast to coast, generating sympathy and support for the cause. In 1963, television provided nonstop coverage of the events surrounding the assassination and funeral of President John F. Kennedy. Television viewers could witness the event as it unfolded, and 93 percent of U.S. households with televisions watched as the funeral procession made its way to Arlington National Cemetery. Television journalism was seen as playing a central role in the nation's mourning process, and the coverage the television provided was seen as a sign of its maturation as a news medium.[96] "The highest power of television," wrote Reuven Frank, later president of NBC News, "is not in the transmission of information but in the transmission of experience."[97]

CBS and ABC also expanded their evening news broadcasts to thirty minutes in 1963, and although the networks and local stations had a large array of news formats, the nightly news broadcasts were each network's flagship operation. By the late 1960s, CBS's nightly news anchor Walter Cronkite was considered the most trusted man in America. His influence was so great that when he closed one of his nightly broadcasts with the observation that the war in Vietnam had become a stalemate, President Lyndon Johnson remarked that if Cronkite had turned against the war, the war had lost the support of middle America. In fact, television coverage of the war in Vietnam played a role in shaping public opinion as opposition to the war mounted in the late 1960s and early 1970s, and Vietnam became known as the first war broadcast into America's living rooms.

Broadcast news operated in a very different environment than newspapers. First, despite the status and prestige of the network's news division and the investments local stations made into news gathering, news was a relatively small part of the content mix on television. Entertainment constituted the bulk of programming, including most of the prime-time viewing hours between 8 P.M. and 11 P.M. Network news was not seen as the same kind of profit center as the other broadcasting divisions. In fact, television was seen primarily as an entertainment medium with television news the tail on the dog, a tail that could generate status for a network but not much else.[98]

Moreover, broadcast news operated in a more restrictive regulatory environment. Because television news was a more powerful and prominent source of news than radio, governmental regulation was more visible. Through a series of administrative decisions following the passage of the Radio Act of 1927, the FCC required that when issues of public interest were broadcast on radio, and later on television, proponents from all sides of the issue must be included in the report. In cases where personal attacks were launched against individuals, the individuals had the right to respond. This requirement to include all sides of a debate and to give individuals the right to respond to personal attacks became known as the Fairness Doctrine. In the case of *Red Lion Broadcasting v. Federal Communications Commission* in 1969, the U.S. Supreme Court ruled that the Fairness Doctrine did not violate broadcasters' right to free speech. In vivid contrast, in 1974, in *The Miami Herald v. Tornillo,* the Supreme Court ruled that newspapers could not be required to publish the replies of people who had been attacked in their pages.

The Fairness Doctrine was not the only restriction on broadcast news. In an acknowledgment of the potential impact of broadcasting on politics, the FCC instituted what became known as the Equal Time Rule, which mandated that broadcasters treat all candidates for political office equally both in coverage and in advertising time sold to their campaigns. Moreover, broadcasters were expected to make a reasonable amount of airtime available to candidates running for public office.[99]

Broadcasters who did not adhere to FCC regulations could have their broadcasting licenses challenged. The potential for the federal government to challenge a broadcaster's licenses and effectively force them off the air was not an idle threat. In the late 1960s and early 1970s, President Richard Nixon launched a campaign of intimidation against broadcasters, arguing that their coverage was biased and unfair. At the time, nobody believed that the federal government was prevented from placing restrictions on television content, including broadcast news.[100]

During the late 1960s and early 1970s, network news emerged as the dominant news medium. Not only the anchors but other broadcast journalists such as Dan Rather and Barbara Walters became celebrities. CBS's news magazine, *60 Minutes,* premiered in 1968. It was the top-rated show on television for five years and among the top ten shows for twenty-three years.[101] By 1963, television had become the source of most news for most Americans, and by 1974, 18 percent more people reported television as their primary source of news than newspapers, the second most popular medium for news, according to a study by the Roper Organization.[102]

THE NEXT WAVE OF TELEVISION NEWS

As with newspapers in the 1880s, new technology in the 1960s and 1970s reshaped broadcast news. Advances included the increased use of videotape, the spread of community antenna television

(CATV), which became known as cable television, and the invention of satellite broadcasting. The enormous growth in television in the late 1940s and early 1950s generated a huge demand for a method of recording television shows. When television was first launched, shows could only be captured using blurry kinescope technology. As a result, like theater, television broadcasts disappeared once they had been aired.

In 1951, Desi Arnaz, who produced *I Love Lucy,* a television show with his wife Lucille Ball, suggested that CBS record the show on 35-millimeter film. The network said no, reasoning that nobody would want to see an episode more than once. But Arnaz persisted and agreed to pay for the filming if he could retain the rights.[103]

Film was expensive. But in the same year, engineers at Bing Crosby Enterprises demonstrated a videotape recorder, based on the same principles as audio recording, which was able to capture and play back black-and-white images. Two years later, engineers at RCA developed a videotape recorder that recorded images in color. However, because of the speed at which the tape had to pass through the recorder heads, it was not possible to produce a stable picture.

The breakthrough came in 1956 from a small electronics firm in California called Ampex. Using a different approach, Ampex developed a practical technique for video recording. By 1958, the networks were recording shows on videotape, and by 1960, videotape technology was integrated into the television production process.[104]

The development of videotape had a significant impact on broadcast news. With videotape, networks could tape their nightly news programs and rebroadcast them three hours later on the West Coast, creating truly national news broadcasts. Videotape was a much more efficient production medium than film, which required laborious processing. The use of videotape enabled television news reporters to capture images in the field and prepare them for broadcast quickly. To report on the trial of the alleged murderer of Emmett Till in 1955, an event that would emerge as a major milestone in the Civil Rights movement, CBS, ABC, and NBC used private jets to shuttle film back to New York City for processing and broadcast. The broadcasts were restricted to what was filmed and limited by the time needed to process the film. But by 1963, NBC could air eleven special reports and three hours of coverage about Martin Luther King's march on Washington. Since videotape was so much more efficient than film, more events could be recorded and aired more quickly. The reports included taped interviews with celebrities participating in the march, which would have been too expensive to do using film.[105]

The march on Washington also demonstrated the impact of another significant new technology that would have a profound impact on broadcast news. In July 1962, Telstar, a communications satellite, had been lifted into orbit. Using Telstar's capacities, the march was broadcast live to six European countries, while other countries received a videotaped version of the broadcast that could be shown later.[106] Satellite broadcasting had first been envisioned by the science fiction writer and futurist Arthur C. Clarke in 1945. He suggested that three satellites orbiting 22,300 miles above the equator and positioned 120 degrees away from each other could provide almost blanket communication coverage of the earth. By positioning them at the proper distance from the earth, the satellites would be in geosynchronous orbit and appear motionless, providing a feasible target for signals, which they would then amplify and retransmit earthward.[107]

Technological competition between the United States and what was then the Soviet Union led to the launching of Sputnik by the Russians in 1957 and the first U.S. satellite, Explorer I, on January 1, 1958. With satellites now feasible, AT&T, RCA, and others began developing communications technology for orbit. AT&T built the medium-orbit satellite, Telstar, which was launched in 1962, and Hughes Aircraft Company, under contract to the National Aeronautics and Space Administration, built a satellite to orbit 20,000 miles above the equator, called Syncom. By 1964, two Telstar and two Syncom satellites were in orbit.[108]

The recognition of the potential for the application of satellite technology to broadcast news was swift. In 1964, the Syncom 3 satellite was used to televise the Olympics in Tokyo. The following year, Early Bird, the first commercial satellite in geostationary orbit, established a live television link between the United States and Europe. In addition to telephone signals, Early Bird could broadcast one television signal.[109]

The next significant new technological innovation that would have a profound impact on broadcast news was the spread of community antenna television (CATV) or cable television. Cable television was first developed in the early days of television broadcasting to address a vexing problem. Television reception depended on the strength of the broadcast signals the television set received. People living in remote and mountainous areas where there was no economic base to support local television stations simply did not receive strong signals, if they could receive any signals at all. The solution to the reception problem was to erect large central antennas in rural areas and then connect individual households to those antennas via coaxial cable. The first CATV systems were developed in rural areas in Pennsylvania and Oregon in 1949. Subscribers would typically pay a small fee to receive programming. The growth of cable television was slow. In 1952, there were only around seventy systems serving 14,000 viewers, and in 1960, there were still only around 650,000 cable subscribers. At the time, 52 million households had television sets.[110]

The breakthrough came in 1973. On June 18, 1973, the heavy-weight boxing championship match between Jimmy Ellis and Ernie Shavers was broadcast live from Madison Square Garden in New York to the Disneyland Hotel, where the National Cable Television Association was holding its annual convention. The transmission via the Anik 2 satellite was arranged by a fledgling start-up company called Home Box Office, and it represented the marriage of cable technology and satellite broadcasting. No longer just a local retransmission system, combining cable and satellite technology restructured the television industry by pro-viding a cost-effective national distribution system for television programming, bypassing the terrestrial microwave network used by traditional broadcasters.[111]

The new transmission infrastructure of cable and satellite sparked a flurry of entrepreneurial activity. Systems operators such as TCI and Teleprompter began consolidating existing cable sys-tems and building new ones, promising to install the cable needed in target regions in exchange for the exclusive cable franchise in the area. By 1975, TCI, the second largest cable operator, con-trolled 149 cable systems in 32 states and served more than 650,000 subscribers itself.[112]

The new infrastructure touched off the race to create innovative new television programming. In 1975, HBO began transmitting feature films, with subscribers paying a monthly fee. A competitor, Showtime, was established shortly thereafter. By 1979, there were ten premium programming channels offered to cable subscribers either individually or in a bundle for a monthly fee.[113]

In Atlanta, an entrepreneur named Ted Turner was also

intrigued by the possibilities of cable. Turner owned an outdoor advertising company and several radio stations when, against the advice of his closest business associates, he purchased an under-powered, money-losing UHF television station, Channel 17, in 1968. He struggled with the operation for the next couple of years, but in 1972, the cable operator Teleprompter, which had 200,000 subscribers in Alabama, approached Turner about making his signals available to them. The deal required investing in the earthbound microwave transmission technology but the advan-tages were clear. Teleprompter could offer its viewers additional programming while Turner significantly increased his advertising base. Within a year, Turner was trumpeting Channel 17 as the top independent UHF station in the country.[114]

But that was only the start. With the launch of HBO in 1975, Turner quickly realized that his station, which was then called WTCG for Turner Communications Group and would eventu-ally carry the call letters WTBS, for Turner Broadcasting System, could transmit its programming to cable operators nationally. And in 1978, about a year after Turner began transmitting nationally via satellite, he had another idea. He announced that he intended to start a 24-hour news network. The concept of Cable News Network was premised on the cost-efficiencies associated with being able to transmit programming via satellite. The network would be headquartered in Atlanta and have offices in New York, Washington, D.C., and elsewhere. It would also have exchange agreements with local stations.[115]

On June 1, 1980, Cable News Network began operations. With three hundred employees and bureaus in nine cities, including London and Rome, it reached viewers in thirty states. While Dan-iel Schorr, a veteran of CBS News, and Bernard Shaw, who had

worked at ABC, were in CNN's lineup, most of its on-air personnel were relatively obscure broadcasters who had gained their experience at local television stations.[116] Within a year, CNN had 7.3
million subscribers and was on the verge of turning a profit.[117]

Although CNN did not create the idea of a 24-hour news
service—all-news channels could be found on radio, for example—its success revolutionized broadcast news. All-news radio
was little more than 20 minutes of headlines repeated over and
over again. The success of CNN augured in the idea of a 24-hour
news cycle, in which news could break any minute of the day and
be reported promptly. The reporting of important national and
international news was untethered from the evening time slot.

With its 24-hour presence, Cable News Network soon came to
be monitored continually by the power elite in Washington, D.C.,
including reporters for other media outlets. Offices in the Penta-
gon, the State Department, and the White House reportedly had
CNN turned on at all times.[118] With fast-breaking stories, CNN
viewers often had as much information as top-ranking government officials, or so it seemed.

Perhaps the epitome of the impact CNN could have on the delivery of the news came in 1991 with the attack on Baghdad that
signaled the start of the first Gulf War. At 7 P.M. Eastern standard
time, CNN correspondent John Holliman, who was holed up in
a hotel room in the Iraqi capital, reported in a flat voice that the
war had begun in Baghdad as he observed bombs dropping and
antiaircraft guns blazing in the night sky. For the next fifteen to
twenty minutes, Holliman and his colleagues, Bernard Shaw and
Peter Arnett, took turns looking out the window and reporting
what they saw. It was as though viewers around the world were in
Baghdad as the war began.[119]

NEWSPAPERS VERSUS TELEVISION NEWS

Almost from the introduction of radio broadcasting, the relationship between broadcast news and newspapers has been uneasy. The competition between newspapers and television news was shaped to a degree by the different regulatory structures in place, difference driven by the different technologies on which they were based. Newspapers were largely free from governmental controls while broadcasters needed governmental licenses to operate and were required to meet certain expectations. If they did not, the government could revoke their licenses and effectively put a company out of business.

The absence of First Amendment protection for broadcasters was felt in several ways. Newspaper companies were early investors in television, and in 1948, 48 percent of newspapers owned television stations. But owning a television station made newspapers vulnerable to governmental pressure. If an official in the federal government was unhappy about the editorial stance or coverage provided by a newspaper, a company's broadcast license could be threatened. Of equal significance, even if newspaper companies wanted to continue to own television stations, the federal government put up legal obstacles. In 1975, the FCC banned cross-ownership of a newspaper and a television station in a single city. Newspaper companies could not operate television stations in markets in which they operated a newspaper. After the rule was passed, ten companies that owned both radio stations and newspapers and eight companies that owned both television stations and newspapers in a single city were ordered to divest.[120]

The different regulations covering print and broadcast media driven by the differences in their technological foundations also had an impact on the content as well. Historically, newspapers had a long history of partisanship activity and coverage. The move toward objectivity in newspapers was a long, slow trend.[121] In broadcast journalism, "objectivity" was mandated by the Fairness Doctrine. All sides of a story, or at least two sides, had to be included in controversial reports.

Beyond the regulatory differences, the technological differences between the media manifested themselves in many other ways. Very early on it became clear that in providing even just a summary of the important news of the day, television was not nearly as effective as newspapers. But television excelled in giving viewers a sense of being there.

Given the technical complexity of creating a news report for television, coupled with television being an advertiser-supported time-bound medium, until the advent of CNN, television stations devoted only a limited amount of time to news in general, and each individual news story was usually short, lasting one to three minutes. In the 1950s and 1960s, the networks devoted resources to creating one-hour and two-hour news documentaries for television; by the 1980s the networks cut back significantly in that area.

Moreover, the different news media required different skill sets from their practitioners. The differences can be best illustrated perhaps in the representation of journalists in two movies from the 1970s and 1980s. In *All the President's Men,* the 1976 account of the efforts of Carl Bernstein and Bob Woodward, reporters with the *Washington Post,* to track down what became known as the Watergate scandal, reporters are shown interviewing unwilling sources, scouring documents, and putting tough questions to people in power. In *Broadcast News,* a 1987 fictionalized version of life inside the Washington bureau of a major television network, there is as much emphasis on the way the news anchors look and the way they read their news scripts as there is on actual reporting.

Finally, with the ability to attract a national audience and the resources to attract national advertisers, network news was seen as exerting an enormous influence politically and socially in America.[122] Moreover, as broadcast news continued to grow in scope and influence, newspapers began to encounter stiff economic headwinds. By the mid-1960s, competition among newspapers within a single city had largely been eliminated, the culmination of a trend that had begun in the 1920s, coinciding with the introduction of radio. As part of the same trend, large newspaper chains were actively purchasing locally owned newspapers. The ongoing consolidation among newspapers was due to a wide variety of factors, but competition from television was seen as an important component in the mix.[123]

With broadcast news seen as eclipsing newspapers along many dimensions, some newspapers began to fight back by trying to adapt television news techniques to newspapers. In 1982, the Gannett Company launched *USA Today,* the nation's first national newspaper. Widely reviled when it was first unveiled, *USA Today* consciously adopted many aspects of broadcast news: its stories were short, it made heavy use of graphics, there was a heavy focus on sports and entertainment, and it was printed in color. One observer at the time remarked that reading *USA Today* was like reading the radio.[124] In part, advances in technology made *USA Today* possible. The same satellite technology that enabled cable television to grow enabled Gannett to print *USA Today* at multiple printing plants around the country, and improved printing technology enabled companies to move to color printing for daily newspapers. Other newspapers followed suit: the *New York Times* and the *Wall Street Journal,* among others, built national circulations. And scores of newspapers began to print in color.

For *USA Today,* the experiment worked. Fifteen years after its launch, it had a circulation of more than two million and was generating profits of $40 million a year.[125] But if, by the early 1990s, it appeared that the practice of journalism had settled into two dominant technology platforms, print and broadcast, that would coexist for the long term, that appearance was deceptive. A new and disruptive technology was edging into the mainstream— online communication.

TECHNOLOGY AND THE NEWS

From the beginning, the ability to deliver news reports to larger and then mass audiences on a regular basis was made possible only through technological innovation. Periodical newsletters were not possible without improved roads. Mass newspapers were not possible without high-speed printing, improved papermaking, and mechanical typesetting. Broadcast news was also the result of an ongoing series of inventions, starting with the wireless telegraph.

In most cases, the seminal, turning point innovations were not developed to further journalism. Nevertheless, the specific characteristics of the technologies, to a significant degree, shaped the way news was reported and transmitted, and contributed to the definition of the audience for the news delivered by each medium. Moreover, the regulations governments developed to control the use of communication technology also played a large role in the way those technologies were applied in journalism.

By the late 1980s, two major platforms for news were firmly entrenched—print technologies, predominantly newspapers, and broadcast technologies, predominantly television. Although newspapers and television were competitors and regulated differently, each played a role in reporting and disseminating news.

The development of a third technological platform for news, computer-based communication networks that came to be called computer-mediated and then online communication, followed a similar developmental trajectory. Computer-based communication networks were invented for different reasons, but the underlying computer technology has shaped the reporting and delivery of news through that medium, as have the efforts to regulate online communication. Online news competes with both print and broadcast news; the terms of the competition, to an important degree, have been defined by its technological development.

---◇---

THREE

THE ACCIDENTAL NEWS NETWORKS

In 1936, during the same period that David Sarnoff was aggressively pushing the development and testing of television at RCA, Alan Turing, a brilliant student of mathematics and recent graduate of King's College, was working in the laboratories at Cambridge University. That year he wrote a paper describing an abstract computing machine that consisted of unlimited memory and a scanner that could move through the memory, reading symbols and then producing an output in symbols. The movement of the scanner would be dictated by instructions made of sequences of additional symbols that would be also stored in memory.[1] In a public lecture more than a decade later, Turing suggested the machine would have the capacity to alter its instructions; in effect, the machine would be able to learn from its experience.[2] Turing's vision, known as the universal Turing machine, articulated the fundamental principles of what would become the modern computer.

The desire to automate mathematical calculations had long been an objective of mathematicians and others. In 1822, the English mathematician Charles Babbage, who served as Lucasian

Professor of mathematics at Cambridge University from 1828 to 1839, proposed building a machine to calculate automatically the polynomial equations associated with astronomical and mathematical tables using a numerical approach called the differences method. After twenty years of work and an investment of £23,000, including £6,000 of his own, Babbage's attempt to build what he called a differential engine ended in failure. In the process, Babbage developed several improvements to the original design, including the use of punch cards to specify the calculator's actions. Babbage called the improved approach the analytical engine, and it was intended to serve as a general calculation engine and not be limited to calculating polynomial equations. The mature analytical engine came to be considered the world's first general purpose computer.[3]

Turing's proposal differed from mechanical calculators in several key aspects. The foremost difference was the abstract, binary representation of both the input and output for the machine, as opposed to an analogue representation of the input and output. And, of course, the proposal was for an electronic machine, not a mechanical one.

Many of Turing's central principles were incorporated into a proposal developed in the 1930s by Howard A. Aiken, a graduate student in physics at Harvard University. After presenting his plan to the Harvard faculty in 1937, Aiken approached IBM for funding. With the approval of his engineering team, in 1939 IBM president Thomas J. Watson agreed to fund Aiken's idea. Work continued slowly during the war years, but in 1944 the IBM Automatic Sequence Controlled Calculator, also known as the Harvard Mark I, was shipped to the university. IBM had spent $200,000 to build the machine and donated another $100,000 to Harvard to cover its operating expenses.[4]

The Harvard Mark I was controlled using prepunched paper. It could carry out basic mathematical operations including addition, subtraction, multiplication, and division and had special subroutines to calculate logarithms and trigonometric functions. The results from one operation could be used as input for another operation. Data was stored and counted mechanically using decimal storage wheels and rotary dial switches. Its electromagnetic relays classified the machine as a relay computer. All output was displayed via a typewriter. Fifty-one feet long and eight feet high, the five-ton device contained almost 760,000 separate components. It could add two 10-digit numbers in 0.3 seconds, about thirty times faster than people using paper and pencil. Its first task was to calculate ballistics for the U.S. Navy.[5]

The largest electromechanical calculator ever built, Harvard Mark I is widely acknowledged as the first automated digital calculator and seen as an important step toward the dawn of the computer era. But the Harvard Mark I was not without its competitors. While Aiken was working with IBM, John W. Mauchly and J. Presper Eckert at the Moore School of Engineering at the University of Pennsylvania were working on a machine for the U.S. Army's Ballistic Missile Laboratory that could calculate missile trajectories even more quickly.

From the start of World War II, the Moore School had served as the base for scores of young women with degrees in mathematics, who as members of the U.S. Army's Women's Auxiliary Corps were engaged in ballistics calculations. But given the rapidly changing design of artillery and other changes in warfare, the human computers, as they were called, could not complete the needed computations quickly enough. Calculating a trajectory could take forty hours to complete using a desktop calculator. That time could be slashed to thirty minutes using the most advanced mechanical calculator, the differential analyser developed in the 1930s by Vannevar Bush. But the University of Pennsylvania had only one of those available. And even so, with so many trajectories to calculate, it could take a month to complete a single table.

Mauchly, the son of a meteorologist, and a professor of physics at Ursinus College, a small school in the Philadelphia area, had a long-term interest in devising ways to speed statistical calculations on large data sets. When the U.S. government underwrote a program in engineering, science, and management war training, Mauchly enrolled. He was soon added to the faculty at Penn to replace professors who had been called into military service.

J. Presper Eckert was one of the most promising and innovative graduate students at Penn at the time. He had already developed an electronic device for measuring magnetic fields and for recording this information on film, a device the U.S. Navy had adopted to assess the performance of their airborne minesweeping operations. In 1941, Eckert was running the electronics lab, and he and Mauchly soon found themselves discussing Mauchly's ideas about how to apply electronic techniques to the problems of high-speed computation. Eckert felt that Mauchly's theoretical ideas could be implemented practically. Mauchly also consulted with John Atanasoff, a professor at Iowa State University, to whom historians now generally give credit for actually building the first electronic digital computer in the years from 1939 to 1942. In that period, working with graduate student Clifford Berry, Atanasoff had developed a machine that used base-2 binary numbers instead of base-10 decimal numbers. It also separated memory and computing functions. A full-scale model cost only $850 to build and performed one operation every fifteen seconds. However, its operational capacity was quite limited, and the prototype of the machine remained for its lifetime on the floor of the physics department at Iowa State.[6]

With the invasion of North Africa in 1943, the Allied armies found themselves fighting on a completely new type of terrain. The need to recalculate trajectory tables became acute. The year before, Mauchly had written a memo to the Army Ballistics Research Lab outlining how an electronic computer could calculate trajectories one thousand times faster than the differential analyser. The U.S. Army funded the project to build what was called the Electronic Numerical Integrator and Computer, or ENIAC. The effort was conducted in secret for four years.

By the time the ENIAC was functional, in November 1945, the war was over. The first tasks the ENIAC performed in production involved millions of discrete calculations as a part of top-secret studies leading to the creation of the hydrogen bomb. The following February, it was formally dedicated and unveiled to the public, and it served as the Army's primary computer for nine years.[7]

The ENIAC was the first functional electronic digital computer and could add two 10-digit numbers in 0.0002 seconds—50,000 times faster than a human, 20,000 times faster than a calculator, and 1,500 times faster than the Harvard Mark I.[8] The ENIAC did not have all the features envisioned by Turing. Most notably, it lacked the ability to store instructions or programming or to switch easily among different tasks. Overcoming those shortcomings, however, were clearly on the development agenda. The real unanswered question was what would be the use of a high-speed computer in peace time? Not only were the first generation of computers massive in size and cost, their application was geared to high-end and complex calculations. The visible market for such a machine seemed extremely limited.

However, others working on developing advanced computational tools had a broader and more robust vision of the role computers could eventually play. The clearest expression of this alternative vision came from Vannevar Bush, who, in 1916, had received his doctorate in a joint program between Harvard University and the Massachusetts Institute of Technology. Bush is credited with making a major scientific and engineering contribution to the Allied victory in World War II and played an instrumental role in establishing a system for federal support for basic scientific research. He was one of the scientists who convinced President Franklin Roosevelt to establish the National Defense Research Committee in 1940 to apply basic scientific research to the war effort, and then, after the war, he was one of the architects of what was to become the National Science Foundation.[9] In the 1930s, Bush had invented a differential analyser, one of the most advanced analogue calculators. At the time, Bush, a photography enthusiast, had become interested in the use of microfilm. He proposed building a machine for the Federal Bureau of Investigation that would be able to scan one thousand fingerprints a second. The FBI chose not to fund the project, but Bush continued to experiment with high-speed information processing.[10]

Although he put aside his work in this area during the war, in July 1945, Bush published the article "As We May Think" in the *Atlantic Monthly* magazine. In it, he painted a picture of an information processing machine that could replicate the ways people produce, store, and consult knowledge. He coined the term *memex,* for memory extension, and described the memex as a mechanized private file and library designed to enhance people's memories. The machine would store a user's books, records, and communication. Most importantly, the user could create associations between the different records contained in the memex, which would have virtually unlimited memory. In this way, a lawyer could have immediate access to all the opinions and decisions associated with his career, and a physician, baffled by a patient's symptoms, could review similar case histories as well as the relevant anatomical and physiological data. Results could be saved to become part of a storehouse of information to be consulted in the future. The memex could be the size of a desktop, Bush suggested, and it would be an electrical, rather than an electromechanical device. Ultimately, Bush argued, the memex would help create whole new forms of encyclopedias with associative trails embedded in them, ready for consultation.[11]

While Bush's vision was compelling, even before the ENIAC was operational, Mauchly and Eckert were working on improvements and upgrades. In 1944, the Ballistics Research Laboratory at the Aberdeen Proving Grounds in Maryland agreed to fund what might be called the next generation of computers. In 1945, Dr. John von Neumann, who was on leave from the Institute of Advanced Studies at Princeton University as well as the Manhattan Project to build a nuclear weapon at Los Alamos, New Mexico, wrote a memo outlining the key features of what he called a very high speed automatic digital computing system. The computer came to be called EDVAC for Electronic Discrete Variable Automatic Computer. EDVAC had five key principles, including a central logical processor to control the machine through a series of instructions, the ability to store information in memory and then record it on an outside device, and a focus on performing the four basic arithmetic functions of adding, subtracting, multiplying, and dividing. After a long period of development, in 1949 the EDVAC was delivered to the Ballistics Research Laboratory. It was the first computer with the capacity to store programs internally, and with several improvements in the interim, it was still operational in 1961.[12]

With the end of World War II, however, the most pressing need was to identify civilian applications for computers and organizations and companies that could afford to develop and fund them. In 1946, Eckert and Mauchly left the University of Pennsylvania and started their own company. In the spring of that year, they received a deposit from the U.S. Census Bureau to build a computer. It took two years for the design and the contract to be finalized. Eckert and Mauchly were to receive a maximum of $400,000 and would have to absorb any cost overruns themselves. The development process did not go smoothly, and in 1950, Eckert and Mauchly sold their company to Remington Rand.[13] Remington was an established U.S. company that had manufactured the first commercial typewriter in 1873. Remington Rand was formed in 1927 when Remington Typewriter merged with Rand Kardex Bureau, Inc., a manufacturer of office equipment and furniture. At the time, along with International Business Machines (IBM), Remington had a leading position in the tabulating equipment market. In 1949, the company introduced the Remington 409, its computer that used punch cards to direct its operations.[14]

On March 31, 1951, Remington Rand delivered the first UNIVAC to the Census Bureau. The name was an acronym for Universal Automatic Computer. The final cost was estimated to be close to $1 million. The Census Bureau put it to work crunching numbers from the surveys that it conducted, including economic surveys. The UNIVAC came into the public's eye in 1952 when it was revealed that the UNIVAC had successfully predicted the outcome of the presidential election being waged between Dwight D. Eisenhower and Adlai Stevenson. Interestingly, while news media had fed the UNIVAC incoming data, they initially reported that the computer could not determine the results, as reporters were not confident of their accuracy. Only later did reporters admit that UNIVAC's prediction had been correct.[15]

The UNIVAC was the first commercially manufactured computer, and ultimately Remington Rand, which merged with the Sperry Corp., a defense manufacturer, in 1955 to form Sperry Rand, produced more than forty UNIVAC computers. General Electric was the first commercial customer to purchase a UNIVAC, using it to calculate payroll at its appliance facility in Louisville, Kentucky.[16] But Sperry Rand was not the only competitor in the field. In 1952, Thomas Watson Jr., the president of IBM, announced that his company, which dominated the tabulating market in which Remington Rand competed, would build what he called the "most advanced, most flexible high-speed computer in the world."[17] Developed in part to meet the needs of the U.S. military during the Korean War, IBM introduced the IBM 701 Electronic Data Processing Machine in 1953, marking its transitions from manufacturing punch-card tabulators to manufacturing electronic computers.

Several other companies soon entered the computer market, including the National Cash Register (NCR) Company in 1952, when it purchased Computer Research Corp., a producer of digital computers for aviation applications; Honeywell in 1955, when it formed a joint venture with the Raytheon Corp.; Burroughs Corp., a manufacturer of adding machines, in 1956; and in 1957, Control Data, a company started by former Sperry employees that initially focused on computer subsystems. As could be expected, competition in the marketplace heated up. From the late 1940s through the early 1960s, a series of important technical innovations and improvements were made that broadened the market and the usage of computers.

Perhaps the most important innovation was the invention of the transistor in 1947. Called by some the most important invention of the twentieth century, the transistor became the essential component in the ongoing development of radio and the telephone network as well as computers.[18] The problem that the transistor eventually resolved had its roots in telephone technology. In the early 1900s, Alexander Graham Bell's telephony patents were about to expire. To stave off growing competition, officials at AT&T lured its former president, Theodore Vail, out of retirement. Vail decided to launch a transcontinental phone service. The technological challenge for such a service was how to amplify the signals on telephone lines sufficiently so they could travel from coast to coast. The solution was found in a 1906 invention by Lee De Forest, who had developed a triode consisting of a positive and negative element and a control element in a vacuum tube. After improvements by AT&T engineers, the vacuum tube enabled telephone signals to travel across the country as long as they were periodically amplified.[19]

In addition to its role in telephony, the vacuum tube became the core component of the Harvard Mark I, ENIAC, and UNIVAC computers. For example, the ENIAC had more than 19,000 vacuum tubes. But vacuum tube technology had many drawbacks. Vacuum tubes were bulky, they consumed a lot of energy, and they were unreliable. As a result, the ENIAC filled an entire room, weighed thirty tons, and consumed 200 kilowatts of power. It generated so much heat that it had to be housed in one of the few climate-controlled rooms at the University of Pennsylvania. Working at Bell Laboratories in Murray Hill, New Jersey, a team led by William Shockley, Walter Brattain, and John Bardeen experimented with using solid-state semiconductor material, which had been suggested as an alternative to the vacuum tube as early as the 1930s. Shockley created what is called the junction or sandwich transistor, in which two layers of one material sandwich a layer of another material; then, by changing voltage, current can be directed in one direction or the other. As the newscaster Chet Huntley reported, the solid-state transistor could amplify and switch.[20]

The solid-state transistor was destined to change many industries, including radio, where Sony engineers Masaru Ibuka and Akio Morita created the transistor radio, a battery-powered radio that could fit into a shirt pocket. Shockley left Bell Laboratories to establish his own electronics company. Apparently difficult to work with, several of his top engineers, including Robert Noyce and Gordon Moore, left to set up Fairchild Semiconductor and then Intel Corp. In 1958, Jack Kilby, an engineer at Texas Instruments, which also manufactured transistors, had the insight that all the components of an electronic circuit could be manufactured from semiconductor material, not just the transistors. Using semiconductor material would make them easier and less expensive to manufacture as well as reducing the size. The resulting product became known as the integrated circuit. In 1959, Robert Noyce at Fairchild Semiconductor had a similar insight. He realized that an entire circuit could be made on a single small piece of silicon—which came to be called a chip.[21] From that point, improving the number of transistors that could be packed on a single chip became one of the driving factors that reduced the size and cost of computers while driving up their processing power exponentially.

If the invention of the transistor and the integrated circuit were the key enabling factors driving the development of the computer, they were not the only significant innovations. When development of the computer started to accelerate in the 1940s, information was stored on punch cards and punched paper tape. Magnetic memory was first used in the late 1940s, but data was erased every time it was read. UNIVAC used magnetic tape for storage.[22] In 1956, IBM unveiled the RAMAC, the random access method for accounting and control. It was the first commercial computer hard disk drive, and its approach became the standard for data storage. Within a second, RAMAC's random access arm could retrieve data from any one of ten spinning disks. At a demonstration at the 1958 World's Fair in Brussels, IBM used RAMAC technology to retrieve answers to world history questions in ten languages.[23] As with transistors and integrated circuits, the move to random access magnetic memory meant that as disk drives became more dense and read/write technology became faster, more and more information could be stored on smaller and smaller physical devices less expensively. Vannevar Bush's vision of a desktop machine with which people could create, store, and retrieve vast amounts of information and connect the information in different ways became technologically more feasible.

Throughout the 1950s and early 1960s, however, computers remained extremely costly devices that only governments and very large organizations could afford to own and operate. Given their cost and complexity, computers could only be applied to sophisticated and highly valued tasks. Moreover, since computing time was so valuable, any time a computer lay idle represented a loss for the organization.

The pressure grew to devise ways to better utilize computers. In the mid-1950s, computer engineers began to explore the concept of time-sharing. With time-sharing, individual users could use the same central computer resource simultaneously, and it would appear as if the computer was processing only their jobs. In 1959, Herbert Teager and John McCarthy of the Massachusetts Institute of Technology presented a paper to the Association of Computer

Machinery conference called "Time-sharing Program Testing." McCarthy had been working on the problem since 1957, when he had joined the MIT Computation Center on a Sloan Foundation fellowship from Dartmouth College. The idea gained traction, and when McCarthy presented his ideas about time-sharing to engineers at the engineering consulting and research firm Bolt, Beranek and Newman (BBN), he learned that time-sharing could be implemented on a new kind of computer, the PDP-1, made by a start-up computer company called the Digital Equipment Corporation.[24]

Launched in 1960, the PDP-1 (PDP stands for programmable data processor) represented a radical shift in computer technology. It was designed from the start to incorporate the latest innovations in computer engineering. Soon dubbed a "minicomputer," the PDP-1 was relatively small, measuring eight feet by two feet by six feet, and relatively inexpensive, costing $120,000, which was less than the cost to rent some IBM mainframe computers for three months. The PDP-1 was engineered to give feedback to the user via a graphics terminal. It did not require air conditioning or a special power source. And its operating system was compatible with the concept of time-sharing; it allowed multiple users to access the machine at the same time.[25]

Although only around fifty units of the PDP-1 were ever shipped, it had a dramatic impact on computing. Geared toward scientific research as well as process control and graphics, the PDP-1 brought computer technology within reach of a much broader spectrum of businesses and organizations. With time-sharing, jobs did not have to be queued up and executed sequentially; the computer itself shifted back and forth among the requests sent to it from different users and different programs. Remote users could log onto the computer using acoustical modems and submit jobs.

They no longer had to rely on computer technicians behind glass doors in the computer center. With the PDP-1 and its successor machines, including the IBM System 360, which was introduced in 1964, computer users began to develop their own culture. Computer scientists, engineers, and technicians began to experiment with their own ideas about how the technology should be used. Working on the PDP-1, programmers developed text editors and music programs. In 1962, Steve Russell, a programmer at MIT, led a team that created the first computer game, a shoot-'em-up package called "Spacewar!" that utilized the PDP-1's operating system allowing multiple simultaneous users. In Spacewar!, which reportedly took around 200 hours to program, players maneuvered their space ships, trying to shoot down their opponents while avoiding the gravitational pull of the sun.[26] Computer games would slowly win a large following within the offbeat, almost hip, eclectic community that began to develop among computer users.

By the early 1960s, it began to be understood that computers could have a much wider application than originally imagined. Far from being relegated to the sophisticated calculations associated with advanced scientific research or the massive number-crunching conducted by the largest companies in the world, computers potentially could be used for almost anything from the most significant aspects of business to games. In 1960, J. C. R. Licklider, a psychologist with a specialization in psycho-acoustics who was leading a group exploring what is called human factors research, or the study of the way people interact with machines, published an influential paper called "Man-Computer Symbiosis" in a technical journal. In it, he argued that people and computers could develop a symbiotic relationship to solve complex problems. People would "set the goals, formulate the hypotheses, determine the criteria, and perform the evaluations."

Computers would "do the routinizable work that must be done to prepare the way for insights and decisions in technical and scientific thinking." To achieve that vision, Licklider suggested, improvements were needed in time-sharing, memory, the languages with which people interact with computers, and input and output equipment including speech recognition. Those improvements were achievable within the foreseeable future, argued Licklider, who would go on to play an important role in the creation of the Internet. The result would be the incorporation of computers into real-time thinking processes and the tighter coupling of people and machines.[27] Interest in Vannevar Bush's vision of a storehouse of accessible knowledge was renewed in the early 1960s by Ted Nelson, then a sociology professor at Vassar College, who began to promote the term *hypertext* to describe a system in which all data information was stored once, linked, and never deleted. Users could navigate through the information of the world in a nonlinear fashion.[28]

TIME-SHARING INFORMATION SERVICES

Time-sharing helped to create a new model for computing, particularly in the corporate world. Entrepreneurial companies purchased large-scale computers and resold their computing time to organizations that did not have the resources or expertise to support a computer operation of their own. In 1962, Ross Perot started Electronic Data Systems (EDS) by purchasing the unused computer time on Southwestern Life Insurance's IBM 7070 mainframe computer and then contracting with Collins Radio in Cedar Rapids, Iowa, for data processing services. It was a complex business as EDS employees would physically pick up data from one location and drive it to another for processing. In 1965, EDS purchased its own IBM 1401 mainframe computer. The following year, it won the contract to design a system to process insurance claims and payments for Texas's new Medicare program managed by Texas Blue Cross and Blue Shield. In 1967, with contracts to manage Medicare and Medicaid data from both Texas and Kansas, EDS established a data processing center and debuted a distributed transaction processing center. It also constructed a private voice and data network to transmit the information.[29]

EDS was just one of several companies scrambling into the market to take advantage of time-sharing and other advances in computing. Earlier, in 1957, Automatic Data Processing had purchased an IBM mainframe computer to process payroll data for its clients, pioneering the concept of business data processing outsourcing. In 1963, Sam Wyly and his brother Charles Jr. set up University Computing Company by installing an IBM mainframe computer at Southern Methodist University. In return for hosting the computer, SMU received free time. Using the remaining computing time, Wyly sold data processing services to Sun Oil Company, Texas Instruments, and others.

The idea that companies could put their computer expertise to work for others had many ramifications. One possibility that presented itself was that efficient, centralized computers could manage access to and retrieval of information from vast storehouses of information. In 1960, Roger Summit, a doctoral student at Stanford University, took a summer job at Lockheed Martin Missiles and Space Company, where he was assigned to work on problems of information retrieval under the supervision of E. K. Fisher, the director of information processing. The central issue was how to locate and retrieve stored information in a cost-efficient, timely manner. At the time, according to Summit, the feeling was that it was often easier to redo scientific research than it was to determine if it had been done before.

In the course of his assignment, Summit encountered the work of H. Peter Luhn, a researcher at IBM who had invented two significant schemes for the large-scale management of information—Key Word In Context (KWIC) indexing and Selective Dissemination of Information (SDI). In 1964, at Summit's urging, Lockheed Martin established a laboratory to study the application of these technologies. A project team of six led by Summit set out to create a technology that could facilitate efficient information retrieval. Among the criteria he established were that the system had to be usable by end users without the intervention of computing staff and it had to be interactive and recursive so that searchers could immediately see their results and modify their queries accordingly. Finally, researchers wanted to include an alphabetical list of searchable terms near a desired term and the number of items in the database containing that term.

By 1965, the team developed the prototype of what became the Dialog Information Service. To test the system, Summit submitted an unsolicited proposal to apply Dialog to NASA's Scientific and Technical Aerospace Reports (STAR) database, a database with 200,000 citations and one that was in great demand. NASA had been established by the Space Act of 1958 to spearhead America's drive into space, and part of its mandate was to disseminate information about its activities and findings as widely as possible. From its inception, the agency aggressively indexed books, reports, and research concerning aerospace, and in 1962, NASA's staff, working with a contractor, started entering the bibliographic citations into a computer.[30]

When Summit discovered a contract had already been awarded to a competitor, he proposed a smaller, less expensive parallel project as backup if the competitor failed. For the test, Summit leased a data line from the Lockheed offices in Palo Alto, California, to the NASA Ames Research Center near the San Francisco airport. The test was conducted in January 1967. The turnaround time for a query was cut from fourteen hours when conducted at NASA headquarters to just a few minutes using the Dialog system.

Based on that success, Lockheed won a $180,000 contract from NASA to build what was called the Remote Console Information Retrieval system or NASA RECON. This was followed by contracts to install Dialog at the Atomic Energy Commission and the European Space Research Organization and, in 1969, a contract to provide the U.S. Office of Education with a retrieval service on the Educational Resources Information Center (ERIC) database. In 1972, Lockheed launched a commercial information service under the name Dialog. The initial service provided users access to ERIC, the NTIS database from the National Technical Information Service, and PANDEX, a science citation index. At its launch, Dialog had six customers.

Other vendors were working with government agencies to make information more readily available as well. In 1969, Systems Development Corp. (SDC), a spin-off of the Rand Corporation, completed a project with the National Library of Medicine to provide access to its Medline database. The SDC version of Medline was a backup version and when the National Library of Medicine decided to terminate the contract, Systems Development Corp. decided to launch a commercial service as well, despite conducting market research that seemed to indicate that the market for online access to information would be small or might not exist at all. When Roger Summit got wind of SDC's plans to launch a commercial service, he lobbied for Lockheed to convert Dialog into a commercial service.[31]

Online services were being developed with primarily commercial applications in mind. In 1964, Bunker-Ramo, which later became part of Honeywell, was formed by the merger of three companies with expertise in aerospace, computers, and data communications. Its president, Simon Ramo, who earlier had founded the company that became the defense contractor TRW and who was an instrumental figure in the creation of the intercontinental ballistic missile, assigned Herbert Mitchell the task of determining how the new company could apply its expertise to online retrieval. Mitchell had deep roots in computing, having worked with Howard Aiken on the Harvard Mark II as well as on the UNIVAC. He proposed combining several government databases into what he called the direct electronic library. Bunker-Ramo eventually won a contract from NASA to fund the project, and in 1966 they set up the first online retrieval system with the ability to order source documents remotely—an early version of what became Dialog's NASA RECON system (the name had been set by NASA before the system had been built).[32]

After losing the NASA contract to Lockheed Martin, Bunker-Ramo moved in a different direction. In 1963, the Securities and Exchange Commission issued a report calling for the establishment of an automated system for buying and selling stock for what was known at the time as the over-the-counter (OTC) market, publicly held companies whose stock did not trade on the New York Stock Exchange, the American Stock Exchange, or a regional stock exchange. The specifications for the system, called the National Association of Securities Dealers Automated Quotation System or NASDAQ, were set by 1968, and Bunker-Ramo won a seven-year contract to build and operate it.[33] NASDAQ came online in 1971, and that same year, Bunker-Ramo signed a deal to provide online access to the *Wall Street Journal* and other financial news and information published by Dow Jones, Inc.[34] In 1974, Bunker-Ramo unveiled a news retrieval service that enabled subscribers to tap a database containing all significant business and financial news of the past ninety days.

Clearly, by the late 1960s and early 1970s, researchers were proposing uses for computers beyond the original conception of high-speed number crunching. Computer processing capacity could be shared with many users, even those working on terminals at distant locations, allowing computer processing power to be applied to a much broader range of applications and accessible to a much wider variety of agencies, organizations, and businesses. Data could be generated at one facility and then sent to another for processing and storage. Along the same lines, computers could be efficiently deployed as remote information retrieval devices, enabling users in one place to locate and retrieve information they needed that was stored elsewhere.

The desirability and the need to send data from location to location put a focus on the way that computers could be linked or networked with each other. The National Library of Medicine retrieval system developed by SDC relied on the AT&T Teletype Writer Exchange Network (TWX), an extremely slow network of teletype machines. TWX terminals were installed in five hundred libraries and used primarily to facilitate interlibrary loan requests. While they could be used without additional charge as analogue terminals, getting TWX to communicate with SDC's digital on-line service was challenging.[35]

To build time-sharing systems that could be accessed efficiently by remote terminals required building a data network. With TWX not really suitable for high-speed data transfer, researchers would lease dedicated data lines from AT&T for many of the early tests of online information retrieval. This represented a significant expense and limitation.

The solution emerged as part of the evolution of time-sharing in general. In 1966, a company called Tymshare was started in Palo Alto, California. Using the phone network, clients could call into Tymshare's computer, which could support sixteen terminals at once. The company established a second data center in Los Angeles, and with future expansion planned, the need to more closely integrate their operations was clear. In 1968, Norm Hardy, a former IBM researcher, his wife Ann Hardy, LaRoy Tymes, and others came up with the idea of using minicomputers to log onto mainframe computers.[36]

At the time, AT&T was considered a natural monopoly and controlled all the devices that were attached to the telephone network, including modems. Modems had been created in Bell Laboratories in 1958 and could convert analogue and digital signals, making it possible to transmit computer data via the telephone network. Tymshare engineers developed acoustical couplers to interact with the modems and devised engineering strategies to move more information on each telephone circuit and to ensure the quality of the data transmitted. They also explored ways to centralize the communication operation, minimizing the technology need by the remote terminal, or node. Finally, engineers developed routing tables to manage traffic as new users logged on. The Tymnet network, which had been named by Tymshare engineers at a casual meeting, was unveiled publicly in 1971. As the use of time-sharing burgeoned, companies wanted to connect their own host computers to Tymshare. In response, Tymshare engineers developed methods for attaching different terminals to the network and set up a separate division of the company called

Tymnet. Over time, as Tymnet established local presence in cities across the United States and Europe, a nationwide data network was assembled in which companies could dial into local host computers using remote terminals.[37]

Tymshare did not use the same kind of network technology that would eventually become the basis of the Internet. In 1972, the U.S. Department of Defense's Advanced Research Projects Agency (DARPA), one of the agencies driving the development of the system that would ultimately become the Internet, saw a need for an advanced national data network based on a new technology called packet switching (as opposed to circuit switching, which was what the telephone system used). Packet switching had been developed in the 1960s primarily as a way to ensure that the Defense Department computer networks could continue to function even if a part of the network was attacked and destroyed.[38]

AT&T turned down a request to build a packet switched data network, determining that the technology was not essential to the direction in which it was moving in developing what was called circuit switched networking. So DARPA turned to the engineering firm Bolt, Beranek and Newman (BBN), which was deeply experienced in time-sharing and computer networks, and a primary contractor to DARPA. To provide the service, BBN organized a company called Telenet. By 1975, Telenet was running a publicly accessible packet switched data network as well as manufacturing switches and other equipment needed to link to the network. Other companies, such as Southern Bell, began to use Telenet technology to build their own data networks. The more networks linked with each other, the more valuable they became. The Telenet network was more reliable than leased lines and more flexible than Tymnet. Perhaps most important, with

Telenet computers needed no special technology to connect to the network.[39]

The emergence of data networks came at a critical time in the history of telecommunications in America in general and in the history of AT&T in particular. The United States government lodged regulatory authority over telephone service in the Interstate Commerce Commission with the Mann-Elkins Act of 1910, and by the 1920s the notion that telephone service was a "natural monopoly" and that there was little to gain through competition was widely accepted. In 1934, the FCC was empowered to set telephone rates and regulations.

As a protected industry with nearly insurmountable barriers to entry for others, AT&T became the predominant provider of both local and long-distance telephone service. However, the consensus that AT&T should hold a monopoly on telephone service began to break down in the 1960s and 1970s, driven in part through the new possibilities opened up by microwave and satellite technology. In 1963, John Goeken, who owned a mobile radio business, petitioned the FCC to allow him to establish a direct microwave link between Chicago and St. Louis. By relying exclusively on microwave technology, which had been developed primarily at Bell Labs, Goeken contended that he could deliver more services to his subscribers at perhaps as low as five percent of the prices charged by AT&T. Moreover, his network would be able to transmit data as easily as voice. In response, AT&T petitioned the FCC to deny Goeken's request, arguing that Goeken's service would undermine universal access to the telephone network by skimming off AT&T's most profitable services. Moreover, it would be redundant. Goeken, who called his company Microwave Communications Inc. (MCI), responded that his service would be too small to have an impact on AT&T. Eventually, the FCC approved Goeken's petition and ensured that his company could access AT&T equipment. When William McGowan was named the chief executive of MCI, he saw an opportunity to contest AT&T's monopoly on long-distance telephone service. McGowan launched a multi-prong strategy. He lobbied Congress and the FCC, and eventually he sued in U.S. Federal Court to break up AT&T.[40] It was during MCI's long political and legal battle with AT&T that private data networks entered the arena. With the drive to deregulate telecommunications underway, the issue about how computer networks should be regulated had to be addressed as well.

The FCC first began to consider whether computer networks should be regulated in the 1960s as time-sharing gained ground. In 1966, the FCC initiated a study that led to what become known as the Computer I decision. The study focused on two major questions: Should data processing services be regulated? And should common carriers be allowed to engage in data processing and, if so, under what conditions? In Computer I, the commission ruled there was no need to regulate data processing companies and that common carriers could only enter the industry if they established completely independent subsidiaries. The FCC did not want rate payers subsidizing the entry of telephone companies into the data processing marketplace. Moreover, the telephone companies could not use the computers they bought to operate their networks for nonnetwork activities. In 1956, AT&T was barred by the Justice Department from entering unregulated activities. Since Computer I declared data processing an unregulated business, AT&T was effectively forbidden to compete.[41] Problems with the Computer I decision began to emerge almost immediately. The distinction between data processing companies and communications companies blurred as more uses for computers were found and networks like Tymnet and particularly Telenet were established. In 1976, the FCC started the process that led to the Computer II decision. At the core was the realization that the distinction between data processing and communication was unsustainable. In its place, the FCC distinguished among the services offered. Basic service consisted of a transmission capacity, with no interaction with the user data. The definition of basic service could be applied to voice, data, video, or other types of information. The key was that information was unchanged during transmission.

Enhanced services were defined as "communications, which employ computer processing applications that act on the format, content, code, protocol or similar aspects of the subscriber's transmitted information; provide the subscriber additional, different, or restructured information; or involve subscriber interaction with stored information."[42] In short, enhanced services were layered on top of the basic service and, in some way, fundamentally changed the service. Enhanced services, the FCC ruled, should be unregulated because the market to supply them was competitive. Over time the FCC ruled that e-mail, voice mail, store-and-forward fax, interactive voice response, audiotext information services, news groups, and the World Wide Web should be considered as enhanced services and not regulated. While the FCC claimed it had the constitutional authority to regulate enhanced or value-added services, with Computer II decision it chose not to do so.[43]

Although not widely noted or even remembered, with this ruling the FCC established what would become a national unregulated medium of mass communication which ultimately would have international reach. Unlike newspapers, whose birth triggered censorship regulations that were then, to some degree, cast aside, and unlike radio and television, which were subject to governmental regulation virtually as soon as they began to win commercial acceptance, the layer of the data network that added value for the end user remained unregulated, and companies that provided enhanced services were guaranteed access to the underlying transmission technology. It was as though the FCC required television stations and television networks to maintain their broadcast function but did not allow them to develop their own programming. Instead, broadcasters, whose fees and services were regulated by the federal government, would have to open their facilities to others who would provide the programming and could operate without regulation. What couldn't be anticipated in the mid-1970s was that the costs and barriers to entry for providing enhanced services would soon come tumbling down.

NEW NETWORK NEWS

In the early 1970s, television and newspapers were the primary news media. But with the development of data networks, the increasing technological sophistication of telephone networks, and the desire to put to work underutilized parts of the broadcast spectrum, experiments to explore the potential of delivering the news and other information through these newly available networks were soon under way. Improving the delivery of telex seemed particularly promising. Teletype, also known as telex or the TWX network, had its roots before and during World War II. Developed both in Europe and in the United States by Bell Labs, the technology basically allowed typewriters to be connected to the telephone system and was seen as a replacement technology for the telegraph. Indeed, the roots of the technological development that led to the telex reach back to the early 1900s. After the war, teletype became a significant channel of communication for business, government, and military use. As late as the mid-1980s, more telex minutes were logged than international phone calls.[44]

The use of telex was intertwined with the development of computing as well. In the 1950s and 1960s, the teletext typewriter became a standard input/output device for computers. Moreover, the code used to transmit letters via telex later became the basis for ASCII, the standard representation code of computers. Despite the advantages compared to the telegraph, telex was slow, cumbersome, costly, and limited to organizations that could afford the relatively expensive technology.

Perhaps the earliest effort to harness an existing communications network to provide the delivery of additional news and information by improving the transmission of telex-like messages came from the British post office, which in the 1970s and 1980s controlled both the telephone network and the television networks in the United Kingdom. In the 1960s, engineers from the British Broadcasting Corporation (BBC) and Independent TV (ITV), the second British television network at the time, began to experiment with ways to send digital information via an unused part of the television signal. One concept was to use that signal to supply captioning for deaf people watching television. They found that a normal television picture had unused bandwidth at the top that could be used for transmitting words and numbers.[45]

In October 1972, BBC and ITV announced a new teletext service called Ceefax. The name was a play on the words "see facts." By 1974, the standards were set, and BBC and ITV began transmitting thirty pages of information including news, weather, traffic information, and stock market quotes.[46] A "page" was the name of a unit of information, in the same way a file became the unit of information when the Internet emerged. When it launched, Ceefax had thirty pages total to transmit. At the same time, a similar system was under development by the Independent Broad-casting Authority (IBA), which called its system Oracle, for Op-tional Reception of Announcements by Coded Line Electronics. In 1976, the standards for the two systems were merged, creating an international standard for teletext. A page of teletext consisted of 24 lines with 40 characters per line. Transmission speed quickly climbed from one page per second to four pages per second and the number of pages transmitted reached eight hundred. The new specification also allowed for color backgrounds and navigational buttons.

When first launched, Ceefax was expensive. A teletext set-top box cost £300 and a television equipped with teletext capabili-ties cost more than twice that amount. But as the prices dropped, the service proved very popular. By 1985, more than two mil-lion television sets had access to Ceefax and Oracle. And on the thirtieth anniversary of Ceefax's launch in 2004, with 20 million people a week still using Ceefax, BBC chairman Michael Grade contended that Ceefax was at "the forefront of journalism," lead-ing the way to instantly breaking stories. At the same time, Tessa Jowell, the United Kingdom's minister of culture, described Cee-fax in a press release issued by the BBC on September 22, 2004, marking 30 years of service as the "precursor to the Internet news revolution."

By 1977, delegations from eighty-five companies had visited the Ceefax newsroom on the seventh floor at BBC Television Centre in West London. At the same time that the BBC and IBA were working on Ceefax, the British post office was working on a similar concept that would use the telephone lines to transmit data. Post office engineers called the idea Viewdata and, since the post office also regulated telephone service at the time, Viewdata was seen as an ideal way to increase the use of telephones.

The post office participated in the 1974 effort to set standards for teletext so television sets were compatible with Viewdata information, or videotext as it came to be known. The post office wanted to launch a two-way electronic newspaper, and in 1979, it unveiled Prestel, for "press telephone."[47] By 1983, more than nine hundred companies were contributing material to the 230,000-page Prestel database, with major publishers paying a fee to have their information distributed via Prestel. Like Ceefax and Oracle, the text display consisted of 24 lines with 40 characters each, and users navigated through pages using a keypad to access the information they wanted. The system's major drawback was cost. In the early 1980s, Prestel charged a flat monthly fee of $50 plus per minute usage charges of 30 to 50 cents. In addition, some information providers required a separate charge to access their information.

Ceefax, Oracle, and Prestel signaled a growing awareness that the delivery of news would change as new technologies won consumer acceptance. With newspapers already under pressure from broadcasters, networks like Ceefax and Prestel could deliver the news to viewers even faster.

INTERNATIONAL EFFORTS

The British effort to expand the use of the telephone network and unused portions of the broadcast signal did not go unnoticed around the world. In the late 1970s, the French Postes Telephones Telecommunications (PTT), the state-owned monopoly that controlled the nation's postal and telephone services, wanted to modernize its offerings and find ways to increase the use of its system. Company officials saw an opportunity to use teletext to cut down on the number of telephone books they printed. With the encouragement of the French government, the company proposed to offer consumers a small data terminal consisting of a keyboard and a screen that could be connected to the telephone network via a modem. Using the Minitel terminal, customers would not only be able to access directory assistance, they could also set up a payment system, allowing clients to invoice Minitel transactions to their phone bill. Moreover, third parties were invited to provide content over the network.[48]

Since it cost PTT the equivalent of about $20 to print a telephone book, the company reasoned that the cost of providing a $100 terminal for free to subscribers would be recouped within five years. Testing of the system began in western France in 1980 and was made generally available in 1983, with terminals being broadly distributed to homes and businesses.[49] The system quickly grew in popularity. By 1986, more than 1.4 million terminals were in use, and that year PTT anticipated adding another one million users. All users were able to read newspapers, bank, shop, chat, and play videogames using the system. In 1986, Minitel generated more than $70 million for PTT from additional telephone usage, cost savings, and terminal leasing. Although terminals were free to consumers, businesses paid a monthly rental charge. The most popular feature on Minitel was called le Kiosque, after the corner newsstands found throughout Paris. Le Kiosque was made up of more than two hundred separate services and allowed consumers to read updated news synopses, browse through want ads, and chat. Le Kiosque had a usage charge of about 10 cents per 45 seconds, which was added to the monthly phone bill. Information providers, primarily French newspapers and magazines, kept 60 percent of the charge, and PTT pocketed the rest. By the middle of the

1980s, Minitel was considered the first commercially successful videotext system.[50]

The business model used in the United Kingdom and France could not work in the United States, where there was no state-owned monopoly to explore the possibilities. The only American entity that could assume that effort was AT&T, which was embroiled in the long-running antitrust litigation that led to its breakup in 1984. AT&T was perceived as a potential rival to other information providers and AT&T's potential competitors as well as government officials feared that it would have significant technological advantages if it were allowed to enter the online information business. Indeed, the consent decree that it signed as part of the breakup of its system banned AT&T from electronic publishing using its own transmission facilities for seven years. Instead of the telephone carriers leading the way, as happened in the United Kingdom and France, newspaper companies like Knight Ridder and Times Mirror and cable television companies like Warner Communications pioneered entry into videotext in the United States.

By the early 1980s, newspaper publishers were acutely aware of the threat to their businesses posed by the electronic delivery of information. For example, at the 1982 convention of the American Newspaper Publishers Association, Alan Gillen, a vice president of Knight Ridder, warned that if newspapers did not embrace the delivery of news via video screens, somebody else would.[51] So it is not surprising that perhaps the best known and most costly effort to launch a commercially viable videotext service in the United States was Viewtron, which was funded by Knight Ridder. Knight Ridder had been formed in 1974 through the merger of the Knight newspaper chain and the Ridder newspaper chain.

The merger made sense on many levels as the Knight chain, whose flagship newspaper was the *Miami Herald,* was strong in the East and South of the United States, while Ridder was stronger in the West and the Midwest. At the time of the merger, Knight Ridder was the largest newspaper company in the United States. The combined company had thirty-five newspapers in twenty-five cities from coast to coast and a total circulation averaging 3.8 million daily and 4.2 million on Sunday.[52]

In 1979, a small Knight Ridder team led by James Batten, then the vice president for news at the company and later its chairman and chief executive officer, traveled to the United Kingdom to learn more about Ceefax, Oracle, and Prestel. According to Roger Fidler, who was part of that initial team and served as director of design for Viewtron, Batten and other Knight Ridder executives were already deeply concerned about the impact teletext and videotext might have on printed newspapers. Although it was not clear if the services should be viewed as extensions of newspapers or broadcasting, it was clear that they posed a threat.[53]

In the United Kingdom, the Knight Ridder team explored how to create pages using the Prestel technology. Although the tools themselves were limited, within several days the team was producing what it felt were presentable results. After the team's return to the United States, Knight Ridder entered into a joint venture with AT&T and the Scripps-Howard and McClatchy newspaper chains. The telephone company would develop the tools needed to create videotext pages and terminals for customers. Knight Ridder would supply the content. To pursue the opportunity in videotext, Knight Ridder set up a subsidiary, Viewdata Corporation of America (VCA). Within a year, in Coral Gables, Florida, Viewdata launched the first videotext service in the United States. The company called it Viewtron.

In the first test, 160 families were able to pull up 15,000 "pages" of information using a typewriter-like keyboard connected to a modified color television and a remote control keypad. The information included a continually updated news report, including the *Miami Herald* and the Associated Press wire, a home shopping service, and in-home video banking, among other features. A full commercial service was launched in south Florida in 1983, but despite the optimism, Viewtron got off to a rocky start. The terminal to use the service cost $900. In addition, subscribers had to pay a monthly access charge, additional fees for some premium services, and, in some locations, long-distance telephone charges. When consumers balked at the high price, Knight Ridder first cut the price to $600. It then moved to a scheme to charge $39.95 a month for access with the rental of the terminal in the monthly fee. The terminal itself was also cumbersome to use. In the first year, the company signed up only about half of its projected target of 5,000 subscribers. Nonetheless, in 1984, it expanded the service throughout Florida, and by the following year, it was operating beyond Florida in at least fifteen cities, including Philadelphia, San Jose, Detroit, Charlotte, Baltimore, Boston, Fort Worth, Kansas City, Seattle, and New Orleans. Other newspaper companies, including Affiliated Publications, parent company of the *Boston Globe,* joined Knight Ridder in marketing Viewtron services.[54]

Knight Ridder was not the only major newspaper company that saw videotext as a way to respond to what was perceived as a need for news on demand and other electronic services. Shortly after Viewtron's launch, the *Chicago Sun Times,* the Centel Corporation, and the Honeywell Corporation started a videotext service called Keycom. Next, in the wake of a field test of 350 households in 1982, Times Mirror announced that it would launch what it called its Gateway service to subscribers in southern California in

1983. The plan was to charge consumers between $25 and $35 a month, which would include the cost of the terminal. Times Mirror also signed agreements with thirteen newspaper companies around the country to offer Gateway if the service was rolled out nationally. When it announced the service, Times Mirror officials projected that enrollments would reach 160,000 within the first several years.[55]

Newspaper publishers were not the only information providers interested in videotext services. In 1984, Sears, Roebuck and Company, IBM, and CBS formed a videotext venture known as Trintex. Citicorp, the J. C. Penney Company, and the RCA Corporation and its NBC subsidiary indicated they were in discussions to form a joint venture to provide videotext services.[56] And in 1985, the most feared competitor, AT&T, revealed that it was planning to enter the market directly through a joint venture that included Chemical Bank, Time Inc., and the Bank of America. The idea was that since AT&T would own less than 50 percent of the venture, it could circumvent the ban on entering the electronic publishing arena. The move was seen as a direct response to the proposed $250 million Trintex project.[57]

Despite the roster of blue-chip companies involved, the air seeped out of the videotext balloon before it even fully inflated. In 1986, Knight Ridder pulled the plug on Viewtron. The service attracted 20,000 subscribers but had lost $16 million in 1984. Over its lifetime, Knight Ridder invested more than $50 million in its videotext efforts.[58] Around the same time, Times Mirror also abandoned its videotext effort and the *Chicago Sun Times*'s Keycom service was shuttered as well.

Several reasons were offered for videotext's failure to capture a significant market. Despite Minitel's success in delivering news—

the Paris newspaper *Liberation,* which had a print circulation of around 160,000, netted more than $300,000 through readership and advertising on its Minitel service in 1985—the question was still open as to whether consumers wanted to read their news on the screen. A two-year experiment conducted by eleven newspapers, the Associated Press, and the CompuServe Information Service in 1982 seemed to indicate that people were not prepared to read the news on their television screens. The study revealed that interest in reading news on screen declined markedly over time.[59] Others felt that the technology itself was not sufficiently mature or that the timing of the service was not right.

But most of the criticism focused on the cost of the service and need for specialized equipment. The Knight Ridder service required the use of a specialized terminal that transmitted sophisticated graphics, which the publishers felt were necessary to attract advertisers. Moreover, the system used a proprietary standard for data transmission. Although France's Minitel was also a proprietary system, observers believed that the key to its success was the low-cost terminal provided to consumers. Based on the failure of Viewtron, many observers believed that the delivery of news online would be limited to a niche market. "The market is thin and probably limited to the computer hobbyist. There's no prospect for it being a mass medium in the foreseeable future," Reid Ashe, chairman of Knight Ridder's videotext subsidiary, said in 1986 after Viewtron was switched off.[60] Others were not so sure. They argued that the publishers had misread the market and underestimated the cost of building such systems, and that new technology and a different approach to videotext could bring the next generation of systems success.

Viewtron's failure did not put an end to Knight Ridder's efforts to develop a commercially viable method for delivering the news online in a way that came close to reproducing the experience readers had with newspapers. In the late 1980s and early 1990s, Roger Fidler, who was a member of the original Viewtron design team, headed Knight Ridder's effort to develop a tablet computer that could display a newspaper in color and would cost little more than a standard newspaper subscription. Readers would use a stylus to navigate through the information. Given the apparent failure of videotext, many executives doubted if readers would ever choose to read news daily on a video screen. But a portable device roughly the size of a notebook with improved screen technology and a low enough cost could be attractive to consumers.[61] But in 1995, Knight Ridder pulled the plug on that effort as well.

The low-cost terminal that ultimately proved to be essential to the development of online journalism was already available in the early 1980s. It was called the personal computer. At the time, the personal computer was still expensive and relatively primitive. It could not display sophisticated color graphics like videotext terminals could. But the personal computer had a more general utility: it supported a wide array of applications in the form of relatively inexpensive software. The availability of software stimulated the proliferation of personal computing, which in turn pushed the development of the hardware into overdrive. One of the first ways in which the personal computer was put to use was as a terminal for online information services.

THE UPSTART INFORMATION SERVICES

The development of a microprocessor—bundling the entire array of processing functions on a single chip—was an evolutionary development for computers. Once integrated circuits were developed, one of the prime engines to increase computer processing power was to cram more transistors into smaller and smaller packages. By the late 1960s, many computer engineers felt a microprocessor could be feasible but the technology was not quite there yet.

In 1969, a Japanese company named Busicom contacted a start-up company in the Silicon Valley in California named Intel to design a set of twelve chips to control an array of functions including keyboard, display, and printer control for a calculator Busicom planned to manufacture. Intel (the name was a contraction of Integrated Electronics) had been set up a year earlier by Gordon Moore and Robert Noyce, two veterans of Fairchild Electronics, a pioneering integrated circuit manufacturer. As a new company, Intel did not have the resources to design twelve separate chips. But Intel engineer Ted Hoff believed that by using newly available technology, Intel could design a single chip to perform all the functions Busicom wanted. Busicom agreed to fund the project and, working on a team headed by Federico Faggin, Hoff, and Stan Mazor, another Intel engineer, Hoff designed the first general purpose microprocessor. Measuring one-eighth of an inch by one-sixth of an inch and packed with 2,300 transistors made from metal-oxide semiconductor material, the Intel 4004 had as much processing power as the original ENIAC computer which had filled an entire room. It could perform logical operations, contain operating instructions, and manage data flows, meaning that it could perform all the essential tasks of a computer. Realizing that the chip represented an important technical breakthrough, Intel bought back the design rights to the chip from Busicom for $60,000. The next year the Japanese company went out of business without ever building the calculator for which the Intel 4004 was designed.[62]

Intel developed the next version of its microprocessor, the 8008, for a company called Computer Terminal Corporation. Gary Kildall, then a professor at the Naval Postgraduate School in Monterey, worked with Intel to develop a programming language for the chip. A key turn came when Ed Roberts, who was running a mail-order business in Albuquerque, New Mexico, selling assembly kits for electronics devices, decided to try to build an assembly kit for a home computer. He purchased a large volume of the next generation Intel 8080 chips at a low price and marketed the kit through *Popular Electronics* magazine, which featured a nonworking prototype on its cover in January 1975. The Altair, as it was named, was very primitive. It had no keyboard or video display. Data was entered by toggling switches and the output consisted of flashing lights. Nonetheless, thousands of orders from computer hobbyists around the county flooded in for the kit, which sold for $397.[63]

The Altair had caught the attention of computer buffs around the country. At Harvard University, two undergraduate students wrote to Roberts, telling him that they had developed programs using the BASIC computer language to run on the Altair. Roberts said that he would purchase the programs if he actually saw them working on the Altair. Six weeks later, after reprogramming a computer at Harvard to simulate an Altair, Bill Gates and Paul Allen delivered the programs. During the same period, Gary Kildall developed an operating system that would make it much easier to utilize the Altair in a productive way.

In March 1975, the Homebrew Computer Club was founded in Palo Alto, California. It was a motley assortment of engineers, leftover 1960s free spirits, and others, who gathered together to talk technology. Among its members were Steve Jobs and Steve Wozniak, high school friends who shared an interest in electronics and, according to Wozniak, pranks. Jobs also had a deep desire to form a company, so they began to build a computer using the MOS Technology 6502 microprocessor, which they could buy for $20 as opposed to the $370 that the Intel 8080 cost for a single unit. As the pair built computers in their garage, Wozniak continually looked for ways to improve the design and reduce the number of chips involved. He added a graphics processor, a keyboard, and a video display. Magazines catering to computer hobbyists were hitting the market, and Wozniak compared his designs against those that he read about. Finally ready to start a company, Jobs and Wozniak quit their jobs at Hewlett Packard and, in 1977, debuted their Apple II computer at the West Coast Computer Faire, a gathering of thousands of computer enthusiasts held at Brooks Hall in San Francisco.[64] The Apple II is generally considered to be the first "personal computer." That same year, Radio Shack introduced its TRS-80 Model I computer, which included its own screen. The computer itself was housed in the same casement as the keyboard and cost $599. Expecting to sell 1,000 the first year, Radio Shack sold more than 50,000.[65] A third competitor, Commodore International, also debuted a general-purpose computer geared toward individual users with a built-in monitor and a tape drive that sold for $795. The mantra of Commodore's CEO Jack Tramiel was "computers for the masses, not the classes."

As consumers began to snap up low-cost computers, the question was what would they do with them? In the spring of 1978, Daniel Bricklin, a graduate student in business at Harvard University, conceived the idea of an electronic spreadsheet that could automate many routine calculations. That summer, he decided he would create a product to sell after he received his MBA from Harvard, and in one weekend he developed a prototype on an Apple II, working in Apple BASIC. Bricklin and his friend Bob

Frankston then made a deal with another acquaintance, Dan Fylstra: Bricklin and Frankston would create the program, which Fylstra, who was running a small company called Personal Software, would publish. They called the program VisiCalc, for Visible Calculator. Written to run on the Apple II, it made its debut at the West Coast Computer Faire in 1979. At the same time, Fylstra began an advertising campaign for VisiCalc in the computer hobbyist magazines such as *Byte.*

That summer, VisiCalc came to the attention of Ben Rosen, a semiconductor analyst for Morgan Stanley who later became an important venture capitalist. Rosen lauded VisiCalc as an important first step in developing useful software for the personal computer, emphasizing that users did not have to know anything about computers or programming to benefit from VisiCalc. Rosen reported that using VisiCalc he completed a calculation in fifteen minutes that took him twenty hours to program conventionally. The first commercial versions of VisiCalc were shipped in the fall of 1979, and it quickly won widespread acceptance in the business community.[66]

The success of VisiCalc signaled the birth of a new industry. Entrepreneurs began to flood the market with new software applications for word processing, database management, games, and other tasks. Many start-up companies manufactured personal computer hardware as well. After IBM debuted its personal computer, *Time* magazine named the computer "Machine of the Year" in 1982 in place of its usual practice of naming a person of the year. The cover signaled the profound impact and excitement the proliferation of personal computers was generating.

As the availability of personal productivity applications such as word processing and spreadsheets along with video and computer games grew, more and more consumers wanted to own their own personal computers. The idea of attaching a computer-like device to a television set at home had grown in popularity since Nolan Bushnell debuted Home Pong, an early home videogame player in 1975. That year, 150,000 units of Home Pong flew off the shelves of the department store Sears, Roebuck and Company, which had exclusive distribution rights. Two years later, with the financial backing of Warner Communications, the Atari Video Computer System was released.[67]

By the later part of the 1970s, Jeffrey Wilkins was convinced that personal computers could easily become new fixtures in homes across America.[68] Wilkins had founded Compu-Serv Networks, a computer time-sharing company, in 1969 primarily to make better use of the DEC PDP minicomputer used by his father-in-law's company, Golden United Life Insurance based in Columbus, Ohio. Initially a subsidiary of Golden United, over the years the time-sharing operation had been spun off into a separate company that had gone public in 1975. It changed its name to CompuServe in 1977. The business consisted of adding value to its data network, which used lines leased from AT&T, with its own proprietary technology that allowed it to use regular telephone lines for transmission as opposed to special data lines. Moreover, because it bought the time in bulk from AT&T, it enjoyed sharply reduced rates, allowing it to offer a lower cost service.

At the time, the main problem with the time-sharing business model was that the high-powered computers at the data centers lay idle at night. Most of the capacity was used during regular business hours. The thought came to Wilkins that to better utilize his investment perhaps he could convince the growing legions of computer hobbyists to log onto his computers at night. He set up a team that came up with four applications that hobbyists might want. The first two directly addressed the interests of computer buffs. He could offer them access to the processing power of the DEC minicomputers and more efficient storage for their data. At the time, most personal computers used tape storage if they had storage capabilities at all. The other applications would appeal to a more general audience. CompuServe could provide personal and public communication. Network e-mail had been created by Ray Tomlinson in 1971 while working on a new time-sharing system called TENEX for DEC PDP-10 computers. He improved a local e-mail program called SNDMSG, which only allowed users to send messages to mailboxes of users working on the same computer, by enabling SNDMSG to transmit messages to and from different host computers.[69] CompuServe supported an early e-mail system called Infoplex, developed for corporate customers like American Express.

E-mail provided private communication. For public communication, CompuServe would support computer bulletin boards. The idea of electronic bulletin boards that combined features of e-mail and private computer conferences had been proposed by researchers at the University of California at Berkeley, Carnegie-Mellon, and Stanford University, who were all participating in an experimental network funded by the United States government.[70] Wilkins felt that it would not be difficult to set up a bulletin board service in which participants could post messages, with each message connected in "threads." The final service that CompuServe would offer was the ability to download software.

After testing the idea with Radio Shack TRS-80 computer users in the Columbus area, CompuServe's MicroNet, soon to be renamed the CompuServe Information Service, was launched in 1979. After a start-up fee of $9, subscribers paid $5 per hour for access during evenings, nights, weekends, and holidays. Access during the day cost $12 an hour. By the middle of 1980, Compu-

Serve had 3,000 subscribers paying $5 per hour for access. It was also running a successful promotion with Radio Shack stores in which users could essentially sign up for CompuServe for free. The $29 cost for a starter kit was rebated in the form of free access time.[71] Free access time would later emerge as a key marketing strategy for proprietary information services like CompuServe and America Online, which eventually became the leading service providers in the field.

In 1980, CompuServe added what it called a CB simulator, a real-time chat service. That year, the company was purchased for $23 million by the tax preparation company H&R Block. H&R Block had been established as a bookkeeping service by Henry and Richard Bloch. As a part of their service, they offered free tax preparation advice. When the Internal Revenue Service discontinued providing free tax advice to citizens, the demand for Block's tax preparation services leaped. The brothers began to set up storefront operations to provide tax preparation services to the mass market and eventually franchised the concept. The business model required little capital investment and no inventory. With a great deal of cash on hand, by the late 1970s, Block wanted to diversify its revenue base. CompuServe, whose time-sharing services looked attractive, was its second major acquisition. Block retained Jeffrey Wilkins to run the company.

Wilkins, however, was moving in a different direction. With deeper pockets and a mandate to expand, he began to explore different services to offer. In July 1980, CompuServe signed a deal with the *Columbus (Ohio) Dispatch,* the local newspaper for the company's headquarters, to deliver the newspaper via its service, making the *Dispatch* the first online newspaper. That was the first step in a trial that eventually attracted eleven newspapers and the Associated Press to provide news via CompuServe. For example, in 1981, the *Washington Post* joined the *New York Times* and others in providing news through CompuServe. For the *Post*'s entry, called the *Electronic Washington Post,* it established a separate staff of *Post* editors and sent CompuServe 60 to 70 news, sports, and financial stories from the next morning's paper for viewing that night. It also opened the *Post*'s database to CompuServe subscribers, providing access to editorials and editorial commentary; movie, television, record, and book reviews; a selection from the wires of the Associated Press; entertainment guides; hobby columns; and letters to the editor. The electronic version also had some added features such as guides to Congress and the administration of then President Ronald Reagan, as well as other news and information about the federal government. Donald Graham, the *Post*'s publisher, said at the time that the *Post* was getting involved in the project to learn about the new opportunities available to deliver the news. At the time of the announcement, CompuServe had less than 10,000 subscribers and less than 500 in the Washington, D.C., area.[72]

If CompuServe was the first consumer-oriented online information service, like many technological developments, it would soon not be alone. At the same time that CompuServe was evolving from a time-sharing service to an information service, another entrepreneur, Bill von Meister, who earlier had set up a private data network he established called Infocast, began pursuing the idea of setting up a national online information service for consumers.[73]

Not surprisingly, his idea was to link personal computers to mainframe computers via the telephone network. Online users would have access to e-mail, news, weather, and all sorts of schedules, and unlike cable television, the service would be interactive.

Unlike CompuServe, the focus of the new service would not be on computing but on communication. He decided to call the company Compucom.

All von Meister had was an idea and a mixed record as an entrepreneur. He began to assemble the services he wanted to offer component by component, contracting with one provider for e-mail services, another for computer bulletin board services, and a third to supply the data network. He convinced the *New York Times* and the wire service United Press International to provide news and Dow Jones to supply stock ticker prices on a delayed basis. Compucom was announced in the trade journal *ComputerWorld* in early 1979 and went live under the name The Source in April of that year. Von Meister and his backers anticipated signing up 10,000 users by the end of the year and hoped to break even within six months. It didn't work out that way, and when The Source ran low on cash in 1980, *Readers' Digest,* then the largest magazine in America, bought a controlling interest for $6 million.

As the number of households with personal computers climbed, the number of subscribers to online information services like CompuServe and The Source climbed as well. So did the number of online services, even though the text-based systems were perceived as difficult to use. In 1981, Wesley Kussmaul, an entrepreneur in Cambridge, Massachusetts, typed the nearly 2,000 pages of the *Cadillac Modern Encyclopedia* into ASCII code and made it available online, launching the Delphi online service. By 1983, it included AP News, weather, gateways to other information services such as Dialog, and computer bulletin boards for special interest groups. A year after Delphi was launched, NewsNet, which provided access to more than one hundred independent newsletters, was established. In 1985, General Electric, which ran the largest data network in the world at the time, joined the effort to provide online services to consumers when it launched GEnie, the GE Network for Information Exchange. And in 1988, Sears, IBM, and CBS finally launched what they had originally announced as the Trinitex videotex service. Instead, it was called Prodigy and was a computer-based online service that reflected more than a decade of experiments with videotex.[74]

The company that would turn online information services into a must-have consumer item was launched in 1989, when Steve Case gave a facelift to his Quantum Computer Services, which had started as a bulletin board service for Commodore 64 home computer users, and renamed it. He called his new company America Online, and it grew from having 100,000 users at its inception to 14 million in 1998.[75]

While newspapers demonstrated a willingness to explore the potential for the online delivery of news, there was a certain wariness as well. In 1982, nearly 20,000 people subscribed to CompuServe, but it was clear that accessing news stories was not the most popular feature of the service. The process was cumbersome—users had to dial into the CompuServe computers and then access stories from an index one by one. It was expensive—at more than eight cents a minute, if CompuServe users spent twenty minutes reading news online, which was the average time spent reading a newspaper, they would rack up more than $1.60 in usage charges, far more than what a single issue of a newspaper cost at the time. And there were fundamental doubts as to whether consumers even wanted to read their news on a screen. People could read newspapers wherever they wanted, commuting to work, in bed, or elsewhere. Newspapers were easier to scan than the news delivered online. And at the time, online services could not transmit sophisticated graphics.[76]

Although they cooperated from the beginning with the upstart online services even as they explored the potential of their own videotex services, newspapers also understood that, like AT&T, online services could be potential competitors. For example, newspaper publishers were cool to CompuServe's plans to launch a home shopping service because they worried that the service could disrupt the newspapers' advertising relationships to local retailers.[77]

If the jury was still out about the desirability of transmitting news from mainstream news organizations through online services throughout the 1980s, another feature of those services proved to be extremely popular—their bulletin board services for special interest groups. The first computer bulletin board system had been created in 1978 by Ward Christensen, a physicist by training and a mainframe computer programmer by profession living in Chicago. It operated like an electronic version of a regular bulletin board. People could post and read messages. Later that year, he published an article in *Byte* magazine, which catered to computer hobbyists, describing the bulletin board and how to create one.

By the early 1980s, bulletin boards were a standard feature on both The Source and CompuServe, catering to a range of special interest groups. But bulletin boards represented a larger entrepreneurial opportunity. Since the software needed to set up a computerized bulletin board service was both simple and inexpensive, equipped with a cheap modem, individuals could set up their own computer bulletin board systems, known as a BBS. Anybody could dial into a BBS to read and post messages. Along with the bulletin boards available on CompuServe and The Source, hundreds of hobbyists soon set up their own computer bulletin boards addressing a myriad of different interests ranging from politics to computer gaming to genealogy and family histories. Telephone numbers for new bulletin boards would be posted on established boards.

As with so much of computing, many BBS pioneers were teenagers who kept their computers turned on all day to accept telephone calls. Beyond the initial purchase of a personal computer, a modem, and a telephone line (many programs supporting BBS services were available for free or were very inexpensive), supporting a BBS entailed virtually no cost to the systems operator or "sysop," as BBS operators came to be known. Users would log in and post messages, enhancing the content posted by the sysop. The technology was rudimentary: often using just a single telephone line, callers would have to try repeatedly before they actually connected to the BBS.

By 1985, CompuServe reported that its membership had climbed by 70 percent in the previous year and that it supported more than one hundred bulletin boards catering to special interests. That same year, Mike Cane, author of *The Computer Phone Book,* estimated there were at least 2,500 privately operated bulletin boards. Publishing companies, particularly those catering to the growing personal computer market, began publishing material both on CompuServe bulletin boards and their own. In 1984, Eastman Publishing, a small publishing company in southern California that published a trade magazine called *Computer Merchandising,* launched a daily computer news service edited by Ronnie Gunnerson, via CompuServe. It was one of the first online-only news services. In 1984, another computer publication, *Byte Maga-*

zine, which had been established in 1975, set up what it called the Byte Information Exchange, or BIX. BIX was intended to allow readers to interact with the editors of *Byte,* posting questions and comments and engaging in discussions about the hot technical issues of the times.[78] Columnists such as Jerry Pournelle would often post original material to BIX. Other nascent efforts at providing original journalism online began to appear as well. In 1983, Newsbytes was founded by Wendy Woods, a former correspondent for CNN. Newsbytes provided daily coverage of the computer and telecommunications industries. By the mid-1990s, more than 180 media outlets, including print publications, online services, and database companies, were licensed to publish Newsbytes wire material.

Although largely driven by hobbyists in the beginning, bulletin board technology led to more ambitious projects. In 1985, Stewart Brand, who received international attention with the publication of the *Whole Earth Catalogue,* which had captured the zeitgeist of the counterculture in the 1970s, was one of the driving forces in the establishment of the Whole Earth Electronic Link, known as The WELL. Using a DEC minicomputer in Whole Earth's offices in Sausalito, California, The WELL was conceptualized as a public-access computer communications utility serving the Bay Area. Brand's idea was to replicate the *Whole Earth Catalogue* in a computer conferencing system, to turn every topic into an online discussion not just for the readers of the *Whole Earth Review,* his magazine, but for journalists, technologists, and anybody else who might want to chime in.[79] In the beginning, it supported only six modems, but over time The WELL became an information exchange for tens of thousands of technologists, artists, and writers. It was seen as an inexpensive, relatively easy way for people to come online.

AN UNREGULATED NETWORK?

Whether sponsored by a commercial venture like CompuServe and The Source, a community effort like The WELL, or simply the hobby of a single teenager, BBSs were quickly recognized as representing a new, dynamic, and largely unregulated medium of communication. Should BBSs be considered in the same light as print publications and therefore enjoy the strong protection of the First Amendment against censorship and other government regulations? Or, since the information was transmitted over telephone and data lines, could the information be regulated by the FCC? While in its Computer II decision the FCC had opted not to regulate the value-added services provided on data networks, it had reserved the right to do so. Moreover, was a teenager running a bulletin board filled with hate speech, for example, what the FCC had in mind when it opted not to regulate value-added services?

Almost from the moment that bulletin board services began to enter public awareness, it was clear that some bulletin boards were being used for questionable activities. In 1983, an Australian newspaper, the *Sydney Morning Herald,* reported that over the course of two months, its reporters had obtained hard-core pornographic pictures, stories, games, and full motion video animations via telephone calls to bulletin boards in Sydney and that highly objectionable material was easily obtainable with a personal computer and a modem by technically savvy teenagers. No proof of age or identity check was required to log on to the various BBSs.[80] Moreover, BBSs were being used to circulate information about how to break into the computer systems of private organizations, including those of the Los Alamos National Laboratory, which was involved in nuclear bomb research.[81] And computer bulletin boards were being used to spread hate speech. In 1985, police disrupted the activities of the Aryan Nation, a neo-Nazi group that communicated using a BBS.[82]

A few months earlier, in November 1984, police had arrested Thomas G. Tcimpidis and seized his personal computer and data storage devices. They found stolen telephone credit card numbers on his BBS, and he was charged with "knowingly and willfully publishing" the numbers with the intent they be used by people to avoid telephone charges. His defense was that somebody else had posted the numbers on the BBS; he was unaware that the numbers were there and he had not authorized anyone to put them there. The question was: who was responsible for the material posted on bulletin boards? If the sysops could be held accountable for everything posted, free speech advocates argued, it would have a chilling effect on this emerging new medium of communication.[83]

Anonymity was the key issue. Computer bulletin board services, both private and commercial, usually allowed users to post messages anonymously. Indeed, one of the distinguishing characteristics of The WELL was that its founder Stewart Brand insisted that posters use their real names.

Unlike with radio and television, however, much of the energy that was animating the growth of online communication was not coming from large corporations such as RCA. The most likely corporate candidate to drive online development would have been AT&T. After all, most of the key technological developments from the transistor to the modem were developed at Bell Labs. But AT&T was hobbled by the antitrust suit it was fighting and the Computer II decision, which sharply constrained it. From the perspective of hardware, IBM could have played a major role in the development in online communication. But not only had IBM been late to the market in developing minicomputers, which

were fast becoming the key computing platforms for online information services, IBM had also been hemmed in by the threat
of antitrust litigation throughout the 1970s. The fight to establish
limits on speech or lack of limits on speech online would often be
left to individuals and small organizations with limited resources.

The appropriate control of content was only one thorny issue posed by the growth of online communication. As early as
1980, the chairman of the FCC, Charles D. Ferris, warned that
as more people went online, it would become increasingly more
difficult to protect their privacy. At a Columbus Day speech at the
Union League Club in New York, he noted that when his children's home is hooked up to a large online network, computers
will know more about them than anyone should know. The legal
questions of censorship, liability, and privacy became only more
acute as the popularity of online services grew and then as the
Internet put millions of people online.

Online services grew steadily throughout the 1980s. By the end
of 1983, The Source claimed 48,000 members, Dow Jones News
Retrieval had 110,000 subscribers, and CompuServe counted
around 100,000 members.[84] By early 1985, when CompuServe
unveiled an aggressive e-commerce effort, it had around 183,000
members. In 1990, Prodigy claimed 460,000 subscribers with industry estimates putting the overall number of subscribers to all
online services at 1.7 million. To put that into perspective, at the
time, an estimated 20 million people owned personal computers.[85]
The online communication network was potentially very large
and as yet largely untapped.

Despite their gains, online services experienced significant
growing pains. CompuServe and others struggled with their per
hour pricing model. Prodigy and GE's GEnie network eventually
opted for a flat monthly rate regardless of the usage time. Changes

in the fees charged by the regional Bell operating companies, the regional telephone companies created with the breakup of AT&T, were always a threat. And although Prodigy was meant to incorporate the graphic prowess of videotex, the online services were still considered tricky to use and had very rudimentary graphics.

Nevertheless, major newspaper publishers were monitoring the success online services were enjoying in gaining new subscribers. In 1988, two years after it ended its Viewtron venture, Knight Ridder purchased Dialog from the Lockheed Corporation for $353 million. Dialog, which Knight Ridder described as the world's biggest electronic information retrieval company, generated $98 million in revenue and had more than 91,000 subscribers in eighty-six countries. It provided access to more than 320 databases. At the time, James K. Batten, then president and chief executive of Knight Ridder, said that the acquisition doubled Knight Ridder's business information services division.[86] In 1993, News Corporation, the international media conglomerate owned by Rupert Murdoch, purchased the Delphi online service, which was the fifth largest with around 100,000 users. The plan was to offer online access to News Corporation's newspapers. "Delphi's leading technology will enhance the News Corporation's role in the rapidly evolving worldwide interactive media marketplace," Murdoch said in a statement announcing the acquisition. "It will provide a series of additional products and services, including an electronic newspaper unlike any other and an electronic version of *TV Guide*."[87]

Computers were first developed to meet a military need to conduct complex calculations at high speed. But even before the first computers were put into production, some visionary thinkers understood that the same technology that served as the basis for information processing could also be used for storing vast amounts of information and making that information accessible to users in ways that were not heretofore possible. While information processing remained the primary driver of computer development, as successive generations made computing technology more affordable and more widely used, efforts to capitalize on the potential of computer networks gained ground.

By the late 1960s and early 1970s, the development of minicomputers led to the first sustained efforts to use computer technology as the basis of a new network to deliver news and information to consumers. Driven by regulated monopolies in France and the United Kingdom, those efforts met some degree of success. In the United States, the leading candidates to promote online access to information—AT&T and IBM—were hobbled by antitrust constraints. Instead, Knight Ridder and other newspaper companies took the lead. Their efforts failed. But as use of the personal computer grew, entrepreneurial companies and hobbyists saw an opportunity to make information available to other computer users. Almost by accident, a new computer-based communications network was emerging.

FOUR

THE NEXT NEW MEDIUM

In October 1957, the Soviet Union, with which the United States was locked in a bitter Cold War, launched Sputnik, a 184-pound man-made satellite the size of a medicine ball equipped with two radio transmitters. It was lifted into space by rockets more powerful than those used in an intercontinental ballistic missile test the Russians conducted the previous August. Its orbit around the earth served as a wake-up call for America. Even though the United States had its own satellite launch scheduled within a few months, with Russia the first to reach space, it seemed that the United States might be losing the technological lead so necessary to maintain military superiority or at least parity. With the critical role nuclear weapons played both in ending World War II and in the ensuing arms race between the Soviet Union and the Eastern European countries on one side of what Winston Churchill had described as the Iron Curtain and the United States and Western Europe on the other, the launch of Sputnik and the prospect of the Soviet Union edging ahead in advanced technology represented a grave threat to the security of the United States and a grave failure of the American scientific establishment.[1]

President Dwight D. Eisenhower responded vigorously. He created the post of presidential science advisor so he could get expert advice on scientific issues, appointing James Killian, the president of the Massachusetts Institute of Technology, to the post. And he approved a suggestion of his secretary of defense, Neil McElroy, the former president of the consumer products company Proctor and Gamble, to create a centralized agency to study the long-term needs for military research and development. The mandate of the newly established Advanced Research Projects Agency (ARPA) was to identify the research needed to support the country's anti-ballistic missile and satellite programs and to ensure the country was not surprised by developments in military technology again.[2] At times in its history, ARPA was also known as DARPA for Defense Advanced Research Projects Agency.

ARPA's mission, however, changed almost immediately. Just two years after it was founded, all civilian research into space programs was transferred to the new National Aeronautics and Space Administration (NASA) and military space programs were assigned to the different military services. Overall, the supervision of military research and development had been assigned to a newly appointed director of defense research and engineering. As Eisenhower shuffled the pieces of the defense research establishment, ARPA was left to concentrate on three areas—nuclear test detection, defense against ballistic missiles, and counterinsurgency research and development. It also launched basic research programs into materials sciences, behavioral sciences, and computer processing.[3]

In 1962, its Information Processing Techniques Office commanded about 10 percent of the ARPA budget. Its first director was J. C. R. Licklider, who was well known in the field not only for his 1960 article outlining a more expansive use for computer technology generally but also for a later paper in which he criticized batch mode processing in computing, which he likened to a dry cleaner. Data came in at 9 A.M. and would be ready at 5 P.M., he wrote, and that wasn't sufficient to meet real-world problems. Managing computer processing rates was tricky. Because humans thought slower than computers calculated, the prevailing wisdom was that computers should not be standing idle while humans slowly went about their business.[4]

Since funding the development of ENIAC, the U.S. military had been deeply involved with the development of computer technology. Licklider, who directed command and control research for ARPA, believed that computers could play much more significant roles in military operations but not if they were limited to batch processing.[5] Computers had to be more interactive and be able to return results more quickly. The obvious solution as Licklider saw it was to invest heavily in time-sharing computers, which gave users the illusion that they controlled the computer. Computer operators working in remote data centers could be eliminated. And instead of working on just one job at a time, time-sharing would allow for the most efficient use of a computer's time by working on multiple problems at once. While it was waiting to return results for one job, for example, the computer could be accepting input for another. Within his first six months, Licklider entered into contracts with computer scientists at the country's leading computer and research centers, dubbing them his Intergalactic Computer Network.

He soon learned that the computers used by his Intergalactic Computer Network all used different programming languages, different control languages, different debugging schemes to solve problems, and different approaches to documentation. He speculated whether or not it would be worthwhile for the disparate systems to be able to communicate with each other in some way, developing the potential capability for all the systems to be integrated into a unified computer network. In Licklider's view, the objective was not to standardize the languages and tools different computing systems used to perform their operations; but he felt it was important to have a common way in which they could communicate with each other. Licklider had a secondary objective for his proposed unified computer network as well. The federal government was one of the largest, if not the largest, customers for computers. Frequently, in funding research at universities or elsewhere, grant recipients would include requests for new or additional computing capability. But computers were expensive. If their processing power could be more efficiently shared, Licklider reasoned, the government perhaps could invest less on funding computers that often stood idle for significant periods of time.

The idea of creating networks of different computers had crept its way onto computer scientists' research and development agendas in the late 1950s and early 1960s. Until that point, most of the attention had been focused on the drive to increase computer processing power and efficiency and the development of information theory. In 1961, Leonard Kleinrock, a graduate student at the Massachusetts Institute of Technology, proposed for his Ph.D. thesis to study information flows in large communications networks. His idea was to look at communications networks generically, defining them as nodes linked to each other by some mechanism, such as the post office, the telegraph system, and, of course, the telephone system. Most of the research on the behavior of networks had been conducted to improve the performance of the telephone network, Kleinrock observed. His argument was that many of the lessons learned in telephony by the early 1950s could be more generally applied.[6]

At the time, the telephone network was a hierarchical, circuit-switched network. When a call was initiated, it traveled a single route to a local routing office, then to a regional center, and then to a national switching center where the call was placed to a recipient outside the local area. Moreover, each call had exclusive use of a single circuit until it was terminated, even if no information was being transmitted.

This system had several drawbacks. If a local switching station was damaged, all the users in that area lost service. If a national switching center malfunctioned, national communications were disrupted. Moreover, circuit-switched technology was inefficient for computing; it generally required companies to lease dedicated lines from the telephone company to ensure that a circuit was available when information would be transmitted from computer to computer.

In 1959, a researcher named Paul Baran, at the Rand Corporation, a think tank that conducted research for the U.S. military, began to explore the challenges involved in building a survivable communication network that would allow military personnel to continue to communicate even if some nodes on the network were destroyed. He conceived of what is called a store-and-forward system, the same kind of system that Kleinrock proposed to study for his thesis. In a store-and-forward system, a message is sent to a node and then stored there until it is passed to another node and so on until it reaches its final destination. Each node could be linked to several other nodes, so potentially a message could travel via several routes to arrive at its destination.

The concept of a store-and-forward messaging system was not new. It is the basic model of the postal system. Letters are sent from post office to post office until they reach their final destination. If one post office is damaged, a letter can be rerouted to another. But at the time, most store-and-forward systems were slow, and messages faced bottlenecks at different nodes. Baran argued that by using available higher speed technology combined with small storage systems, bottlenecks could be eliminated, and it could be made to appear to the user that the communication was taking place in real time. Baran called his approach a "distributed" communication system. Control of the system would be distributed as well, so if one node failed, messages could be automatically rerouted. Baran proposed that messages in the system, which would be transmitted digitally, be divided into standard-sized units called message blocks. Longer messages would be divided into multiple blocks that could be routed independently to their final destination, where the entire message would be reassembled. Message blocks came to be called "packets," and the kind of network Baran proposed came to be called a packet-switched network. The term was coined by Donald Davies, a researcher at the National Physical Laboratory, just outside London, who was developing a similar concept with a focus on interactivity rather than survivability. Packet-switching would allow computers to use their communication links more efficiently.[7] At a conceptual level, a packet-switched network is similar to time-sharing. Time-sharing breaks computer-processing tasks into discrete units that can be more fluidly managed while a packet-switched network breaks messages into smaller units as well.

Baran published most of his suggestions in a 1962 report called "On Distributed Communications Networks." In it, he called for the creation of a national public utility to transport computer data along the same lines that the telephone system transported voice. The system would have no obvious point for command and control. If one node went offline for any reason, the remaining nodes could reestablish links with each other.[8]

The watchword at ARPA was to avoid investing in research and development that the computer industry would undertake itself. But the industry in general viewed computers as calculating machines. ARPA was focusing on computers as communications devices. In a coauthored paper, Licklider and Robert Taylor, who succeeded him as the director of the Information Process Techniques Office (IPTO), wrote, "In a few years men will be able to communicate more effectively through a machine than face to face. . . . When minds interact, new ideas emerge." David Clark, another researcher associated with ARPA, wrote, "It is not proper to think of networks as connecting computers. Rather, they connect people using computers to mediate. The great success of the internet is not technical, but in human impact." [9]

By the mid-1960s, ARPA-supported researchers were actively planning the construction of a packet-switched network to connect universities and research centers already receiving ARPA funding. Technically, they faced two challenges: the first was to build the underlying physical network, including switches and circuits that would be appropriate for transmitting computer data, and the second was integrating the necessary protocols and procedures into the operating systems of the various connected computers so they could share resources over the network. The solution to the second challenge was the creation of what was called an Interface Message Processor (IMP), a minicomputer that could accept information or instructions from one computer and translate it into a protocol that could be understood by a computer using a different set of protocols and procedures. IMPs were installed at the University of California, Los Angeles; the University of California, Santa Barbara; the University of Utah; and the Stanford Research Institute. The IMPs were connected to computers from IBM, Digital Equipment Corp., and other manufacturers, and researchers began to explore the problems they could address collaboratively.

Dubbed ARPANet, the first packet-switched network grew steadily. By early 1971, there were fifteen nodes (or IMPs) and twenty-three hosts (or working computers) on the network. In 1973, there were forty nodes and forty-five hosts, and in 1977 there were 110 hosts on the network. From that point, growth accelerated sharply. In 1983, ARPANet had around 4,000 hosts on its network.[10]

Although ARPANet deployed much of the fundamental technology that served as the basis for the Internet, it was still a single network reserved for use by military researchers and computer scientists. But researchers at ARPA, at that point renamed DARPA, for Defense Advanced Research Projects Agency, making the military orientation of the work clear, had a bigger vision in mind. They anticipated that other organizations would build all kinds of packet-switched networks and those networks would be able to be interconnected. DARPA researchers envisioned packet satellite networks, ground-based packet radio networks, and other packet-switched computer networks. In 1972, Robert Kahn joined DARPA and began to work on a packet radio network.[11] Part of the project addressed the issue of end-to-end reliability of data in the face of the particular problems of radio such as jamming and intermittent blackouts of the signal due to interference. His initial inclination was to develop a unique protocol to address the issues specific to radio transmission and then rely on ARPANet's network control protocol (NCP) to deal with the multitude of different operating systems used by the host computers on ARPANet.

As Kahn investigated the options, he determined that ARPANet's NCP had a number of significant drawbacks. Most notably, it could not address computers further downstream than the IMP nodes, the essential translating computers that powered ARPANet. Moreover, NCP relied on ARPANet to ensure end-to-end reliability. If data were lost, the application using it ground to a halt. Kahn decided that NCP had to be rewritten to create what he called open network architecture—an architecture in which different networks could easily be networked together, or inter-networked. He developed four principles of his new control protocol. Each network had to be able to use the new control program without making any changes to itself. If data did not arrive at its destination, it would be re-sent by the source computer. The technology that connected the networks—routers and gateways—would not retain any information about the data flow; they would, in essence, be black boxes that would manage the complexity of getting different networks to communicate with each other. And perhaps most significantly, at an operational level there would be no global control.

In 1973, Kahn partnered with Vinton Cerf, who was very familiar with the NCP, to develop this new approach. The team came up with two protocols. The Transmission Control Protocol (TCP) provided transport and forwarding services. If a packet was lost, for example, TCP was responsible for its recovery. The Internet Protocol (IP) provided for addressing and forwarding individual packets. Over time, TCP/IP emerged as the key Internet communications protocol, meeting Kahn's goals of allowing individual networks to interconnect with no central point of management operationally. By 1983, all computers on ARPANet were required to run TCP/IP.

As ARPANet grew and computers became more and more powerful, other federal researchers began to clamor for more access to computing power. In 1981, the National Science Foundation's Mathematical and Physical Sciences Directorate started

CSNet, the Computer Science Network for computer science departments that were not linked to ARPANet. CSNet itself was inter-networked with ARPANet. Modest in the beginning, the goal for CSNet was to be self-funding within five years by charging fees to institutions linking to the network. To ensure enough support for CSNet, access to computers and their services on the network would be open to all university researchers, not just computer scientists. The National Science Foundation (NSF) adapted the same tactics in 1986 when it established five university-based supercomputer centers, networked them to both CSNet and ARPANet using TCP/IP, and opened the computing resources available to all academic researchers.[12]

The network linking the five supercomputer centers was called NSFNet, and the backbone for what came to be called first the Information Superhighway and later the Internet was in place. Within a short period of time, usage exploded. In 1987, the NSF awarded a contract to IBM, MCI, and Merit Network, Inc., to upgrade NSFNet, and within a year, seven additional research centers were added to the network. At that time, NSFNet was made up of more than 170 separate networks interconnected via TCP/IP.[13] The growth of the NSFNet resembled a multilevel marketing scheme. In a typical example, in 1988, the State of New Mexico announced the launch of Tecnet, a commercial computer network linking research laboratories, universities, government agencies, and private businesses, with access to 1,000 computers, including Cray-class supercomputers. The network tied together researchers at the Air Force Weapons Laboratory, Rockwell International, the University of New Mexico, Los Alamos and Sandia National Laboratories, New Mexico State University, and the New Mexico Institute of Mining and Technology as well as government offices, private businesses, and high schools, which could subscribe to

Tecnet services. Tecnet, in turn, was linked to Westnet, a regional hub for NSFNet.[14] With that kind of growth model, 4,500 networks were interconnected to NSFNet by 1992.[15] The meteoric gains of inter-networking gave rise to what became known as Metcalfe's law, the insight that the value of a network grows in proportion to the square of the number of nodes on the network. Every new server, every new node, every new user added new potential value to the network.

But despite widespread proliferation of the use of NSFNet, its general use was still seriously constrained. All users of NSFNet had to abide by the NSF's Acceptable Use Policy, which prohibited commercial activity.[16] In 1991, the NSF amended its policy to include use by research arms of for-profit firms when engaged in open scholarly communication and research. By the following January, 7,500 networks were interconnected via TCP/IP and the NSFNet backbone.[17] The Internet was getting ready to open for business.

THE BIRTH OF COMPUTER-MEDIATED COMMUNICATION

In the late 1960s, if companies acquired different computers from different vendors, users needed separate terminals to access each one. Each terminal had to be physically connected to each machine. Pundits at the time likened the situation to having several television sets but only being able to watch a single channel on each one. The situation was exacerbated if a computer was located in a remote location. Then a dedicated data line would have to be leased to connect the terminal. The cacophony of different independent computer technologies was the impetus to figure out how to network computers. The goal of ARPANet was to allow sophisticated researchers to share computer resources.

Consequently, for networking to achieve that goal, two processes were needed. One was to create a general way for any terminal to connect to any computer. That process would allow anybody on the network to log on to any computer, if authorized, regardless of where it was physically located. A second process was needed to move files easily from one computer to another, where the files could be processed locally. Work began on a protocol to achieve the first goal—a general way for any terminal to access any computer either locally or remotely—in 1969, and by 1972 the protocol was largely completed and standardized. It was called Telnet. Work on the second application, called the file transfer protocol (FTP), was also started in 1969 and was largely finished by 1971.

But the need for both Telnet and FTP, which remains a key Internet protocol, were premised on the idea of computers serving mainly as computational engines. With the development of networks, computers were being reconceptualized as communication devices as well. The reconceptualization led to the development of new and unanticipated applications for the new communications network. The first public demonstration of ARPANet took place at the first International Conference on Computer Communications (ICCC) in Washington, D.C., in October 1972. Robert Kahn, working with BBN at the time, installed an ARPANet node with approximately forty terminals attached. Conference attendees could sit at a terminal and log onto dozens of computers around the country. The demonstration lasted for three days of the conference and demonstrated the network's reliability.[18]

As part of ARPANet's public coming-out party, Ray Tomlinson's basic e-mail program was demonstrated. E-mail had been offered as one of the original rationales for building a computer network, but ARPANet's founders did not have a vision of inventing a global messaging system. Nonetheless, between 1972 and 1980, thousands of researchers discovered e-mail and an entire subculture around e-mail emerged. People invented emoticons, rudimentary graphics created using different symbols on the typewriter keyboard, to express their feelings better, and they engaged in long, heated discussions online. According to Katie Hafner, who wrote a history of the development of the Internet, e-mail was to ARPANet what the Louisiana Purchase was to the United States. It greatly expanded the functionality of ARPANet. The availability of ARPANet turned e-mail, which had been first created for time-sharing computers, from being basically a novelty for users sharing a specific computer to a very functional tool. In 1973, an internal study showed that e-mail generated nearly 75 percent of all the traffic on ARPANet.[19]

But e-mail was not limited to one-to-one communication. Very quickly, ARPANet researchers realized that by grouping together lists of e-mail addresses, they could communicate with many people at once. In 1975, Steve Walker, an ARPANet manager, sent a message to participants on a newly formed mailing list called msgGroup. The list was largely made up of researchers with Department of Defense contractors investigating conferencing communication using ARPANet. Walker proposed that they explore establishing a conferencing system or forum through which they could discuss ideas. There were several different commercial options available but since people on ARPANet were working on many different types of computers running many different operating systems, the decision was made to stay with the e-mail functionality already available on ARPANet, called Net Mail. The concept of an e-mail list was warmly embraced by the participants, who recognized that the value of computer conferencing would grow as the number of participants on the list grew. Prior to the birth of the msgGroup mailing list, most of the attention paid to e-mail had been informal. By 1975, the value of e-mail was clear and its development considered worthy of sustained attention.[20] Mailing lists on other topics soon were assembled. Some of the early topics of discussion were a list exploring human factors in computing, a list looking at programming issues, and, hinting at what was to come, a list for science fiction aficionados and a list for wine lovers.[21]

BUILDING COMMUNITIES THROUGH GAMES

E-mail was only one application that began to exploit the ability of the network to link users working on different computers in interactive ways. Starting in 1969, Howard Palmer was part of a group of high school students in a work/study program at the NASA Ames Research Center, located near San Francisco. The research center, whose roots reached back to the early days of government support for aeronautical research, had been reorganized and its research efforts redirected with the creation of NASA in 1958 and the U.S. government's dedication to space in the 1960s.[22] While at Ames, several of the students were using an Imlac PDS-1 time-sharing computer, a machine that was the equivalent of a Digital Equipment PDP-8, a workhorse computer at the time, but with stronger graphics capability. The students programmed several simple games on the Imlac, including a game called Drop, in which players would try to drop a "bomb" on three rectangles moving at different speeds. At the time, one of the more senior members of the team, Steve Colley, proposed developing a three-dimensional mazelike game. Because the graphics involved in a maze were relatively simple, he thought that the Imlac would have the capacity to render the images in 3-D. Colley then had the idea to have the user solve the maze. Initially fun, it soon became very easy to solve the maze. To make the game more interesting, Palmer suggested having two people in the maze. To do that, the group cabled together two Imlac computers using the serial ports to transmit each player's location to each computer. When that worked well, the team wrote the protocols to enable multiple machines on the network to control players in the maze. The result was the first 3-D multiuser networked game. And boys being boys, within a short time they added the capacity for the players to "shoot" each other. They called the game Maze Wars.[23]

Steve Coffey went off to Stanford University and Howard Palmer enrolled at the California Institute of Technology. In 1974, a third member of the group, Greg Thompson, took Maze War with him to MIT's Project Mac DMS lab, which was directed at the time by J. C. R. Licklider, where he enhanced it into a fully networked multiplayer game rewritten for the Alto computer. Developed at the Xerox PARC research center in Palo Alto, California, some observers credit the Alto with being the first fully functional personal computer, complete with a keyboard and a monitor. The Alto was also the first computer to use a desktop metaphor, that is, make the interface on the computer screen resemble a familiar desktop as much as possible.[24] Before long, Maze Wars was being played across ARPANet and, according to a popular legend, at one point DARPA banned the game because half the message packets on ARPANet in any given month were Maze War data flying back and forth between MIT and Stanford.[25]

Online computer games soon became the vehicle to introduce newcomers to the growing network. In 1975, Will Crowther, one

of the original ARPANet engineers at Bolt Beranek and Newman, wrote a computer simulation game called Adventure that
combined his love of fantasy role-playing with his experiences exploring caves with his two daughters. Crowther left the program
unpolished, but the following year Don Woods, working at the
Stanford Artificial Intelligence Laboratory at Stanford University,
discovered the game, which had been left on a university computer by an unknown person, and contacted Crowther via e-mail
(sending the message to crowther@sitename, which went to every host on the Internet), and with Crowther's approval, polished
and expanded the game, adding a dungeon master among other
enhancements. The following year, Jim Gillogly at the Rand Corporation reprogrammed the game to run on the Unix operating
system, enabling it to run on even more computers. From that
point, it spread across the network like wildfire.[26]

Inspired by Adventure, a group of students at MIT created a
game called Zork, which Roy Trubshaw, who would create the
first multiuser domain or MUD, likened to Adventure on ste-
roids. In 1979, as a third-year student at Essex University in the
United Kingdom working on Digital Equipment minicomputers,
Trubshaw was intimately familiar with Adventure, Zork, and a
real-time two-player game based on the science fiction television show *Star Trek*. Trubshaw and his colleagues were inspired
by the multiuser aspect of the *Star Trek* game. They developed a
technique in which multiple users could create rooms and objects
online, as well as ways to save the creations of different users to a
database. When serendipitously he came across the source code for
Adventure, he applied his techniques to rewrite the game, which
was called Multi-User Dungeon 1 or MUD1.[27] At first, MUD1
could only be played on the computer at the University of Essex,
but the following year it was opened up so that people could dial

in via a modem and play. After a flurry of articles appeared about MUD1, both CompuServe in the United States and Prestel in the United Kingdom added similar technology to their services.[28]

Although rooted in gaming, MUDs created and preserved relatively permanent online communities. MUD technology helped to define an entirely new medium through which people could interact. Indeed, as more fantasy role-playing games came online using MUD technology, users found themselves role-playing for many hours of the day.[29]

USENET NEWS GROUPS

Computer gaming had an impact on the development of the online community in two ways. First, gaming steadily attracted university students, particularly young men, to use the network, even if they were not particularly interested in studying computer science. Second, gaming gave the user community a lot of grist about which to communicate. People not only played games, they talked about games as well. Consequently, the demand for improved communication on the network grew.

Throughout the 1990s, the Unix operating system, which had been developed by AT&T in the early 1970s, had become increasingly popular. At the time, Unix represented a next-generation operating system that could support the accelerated development of new computer applications and functionality. Unix was also designed to run on many different kinds of computers from many different vendors. Freely distributed, Unix became very popular in university computing facilities.[30] One of the interesting features of Unix was the Unix-to-Unix Copying Program (UUCP). UUCP was a set of programs that could copy and send files to any system running Unix as well as a way to send commands that could be executed on the files.

In 1979, Tom Truscott and Jim Ellis were graduate students in computer science at Duke University. Familiar with ARPANet and the ARPANet mailing lists, their idea was to use UUCP to create functionality for computer users who were not on ARPANet. Working with Steve Bellovin, a computer science graduate student at the University of North Carolina, they devised a simple method for transferring files over a telephone line using the UUCP utility, which was distributed for free with the Unix operating system. It worked like this: the program would check the "last saved" stamp of files in a specific directory and then send any newly updated files to other computers running UUCP.

The network built on the use of UUCP was called Usenet and the first Usenet connection ran between the computer science departments at Duke University and the University of North Carolina. The Duke University Medical Center Department of Physiology joined the following year. In that year, Truscott and Ellis presented their concept for Usenet at Usenix, a preeminent conference for engineers and others working with the Unix operating system. Established in 1975, Usenix would establish itself as a high-profile venue to unveil new developments to the Unix community.[31] Truscott and Ellis rolled out their program shortly thereafter, calling it Netnews. Since the software had been developed at a university and was based on Unix, by the terms of the Unix licensing agreement Netnews was in the public domain and could be used by anyone. Duke University invited systems administrators at other sites to join the network, thus initiating the first attempt to link what basically were separate computer bulletin board services, that is, a collection of messages posted on a single server used by many users, into a network of multiple servers.

The Usenet news network began to expand dramatically, much more dramatically, in fact, than its creators had anticipated. Truscott and Ellis had designed a program to handle a few messages a day. That number quickly grew to hundreds or more. Mark Horton, a graduate student at the University of California, Berkeley, identified the limitation of the first version of Truscott and Ellis's software, which had come to be called A News, and he conceived of several solutions.[32] But Horton didn't have the time to program the solutions. That task fell to Marc Glickman, a high school student who wanted to devote his spring break to working on a computer project. Glickman consulted with Horton and wrote what came to be called B News, which was demonstrated at Usenix in 1982. In Truscott and Ellis's scheme, it was assumed that all Usenet readers would read all the messages sent all the time. With B News, people could subscribe to specific newsgroups, retain articles for a specific amount of time, skip unwanted articles, track previously read articles, and resume sessions from the last article read. People with varied interests could create newsgroups and then attract like-minded readers. To help organize newsgroups, prefixes indicating the general subject matter were added. The prefix "net," for example, was applied to newsgroups that discussed topics related to the network itself. Eventually nine prefixes were developed. Horton also made a significant nontechnical contribution to Usenet. Because UC, Berkeley was an official ARPANet node, he began forwarding ARPANet mailing list traffic to Usenet newsgroups, significantly raising Usenet's visibility in the online community.[33] In the original Usenet hierarchy, the "fa" prefix stood for "from ARPANet."

In 1983, Rick Adams, a data-gathering specialist with the Center for Seismic Studies, which had a contract with the U.S. Department of Defense to develop technology for nuclear testing violation detection, and consequently a link to ARPANet took over responsibility for B News. He added the ability to moderate groups, that is, the capability to screen postings before they were distributed through the Usenet network. Two year later, Phil Lapsley of UC, Berkeley, and Brian Kantor of the University of California, San Diego, developed the Network News Transport Protocol (NNTP), which would allow Usenet traffic to be transmitted using TCP/IP, the ARPANet/NSFNet standards, rather than UUCP. In 1987, Adams recognized the burden that Usenet traffic placed on sites that were not part of ARPANet. Those sites relied on modems to connect to other Usenet servers, dialing out periodically. In response, Adams convinced Usenix to lend him money to establish UUNet, a nonprofit network running TCP/IP, making it possible for organizations ineligible to link directly to ARPANet or NSFNet to realize the benefits of TCP/IP. In 1988, UUNet, by then an independent operation, began offering access to commercial companies as well, becoming one of the first Internet service providers.

Usenet represented a radically new kind of mass media. The content was completely generated by individuals yet could be transmitted to a large audience. For people with access to Usenet through an organization with which they were affiliated, often a college or university, the service was free both to receive Usenet postings and to transmit comments, observations, ideas, and news. The same principles that supported Usenet came to inform many of the later developments in online journalism.

As more people subscribed to Usenet newsgroups, they became sites of discussion for early intelligence about technology and trends. For example, in June 1981, there was a posting drawn from an ARPANet e-mail list about Microsoft developing an operating system for the personal computer IBM was going to offer.

In 1982, a thread about AIDS was initiated. And in 1985, a long discussion about the threat that the year 2000 potentially posed to the operations of legacy computer systems was kicked off in the group net.bugs.[34]

Over time, Usenet newsgroups formed around almost every conceivable subject. Unlike traditional e-mail in which the user typically knew to whom a message was being sent, with Usenet messages were sent to the entire newsgroup, the make-up of which was generally unknown to the sender. The interactions on Usenet were often heated and rude. People were willing to post messages to newsgroups that they would never say one to one, using language that was not acceptable in polite company. Participants would also sometimes vigorously criticize another poster in nasty and insulting ways, a response called a "flame." Flame wars would break out when entire discussion threads became consumed in a volley of flames. As more people began to subscribe to Usenet newsgroups, an entire etiquette defining polite behavior in the use of Usenet was developed.[35]

In 1987, the issue of free speech on Usenet erupted. At the time, there were three prefixes that described newsgroups: "net" for unmoderated groups, "mod" for groups that had moderators, and "fa" for groups coming from ARPANet. Systems administrators could choose to subscribe or not subscribe to groups with specific prefixes. By 1987, the tone, intensity, and direction of the discussions on religion and race taking place in the "net" hierarchy made some systems administrators uncomfortable and they refused to subscribe to those groups. In response, under the leadership of Gene Stafford, the Usenet administrator at the Georgia Institute of Technology, a group of administrators dubbed the "backbone cabal" proposed reorganizing Usenet into seven hierarchies. Controversial topics would be identified with the "talk" prefix.[36]

This solution, however, raised widespread protest. Although in unmoderated Usenet newsgroups, users could post whatever they wanted, the establishment of newsgroups themselves and their propagation throughout the Usenet network was controlled by network administrators and systems operators, who would vote to see if there was enough interest to create a new group on a specific topic. Some Usenet users felt those votes were not fair or not honored.[37] As a joke to show how easy it was to set up a new newsgroup on Usenet, Richard Sexton, a computer technician in Baldwin Park, California, accidently sent a message to the talk.bizarre newsgroup proposing a new newsgroup called talk .fucking. Although Sexton wasn't serious, the participants in talk .bizarre thought it was a good idea but that the group should be renamed rec.sex. After two weeks of discussion, systems administrators voted and rec.sex was not allowed. That vote did not sit well with Brian Reid, who was already upset because a newsgroup he had been running had been renamed when the Usenet hierarchies had been reshuffled. Reid created a new Usenet hierarchy called alt, where users could establish Usenet newsgroups on their own and not be bound by a vote by systems administrators. Alt.sex and alt.rock-n-roll were the first two groups established in the alt hierarchy. Before long, the alt newsgroups were the most widely read on Usenet with newsgroups discussing issues like bondage and sadomasochism proliferating quickly.[38]

As Usenet flourished, it became clear that computer-mediated communication was different from other forms of communication. Usenet was distinct from bulletin boards as messages were distributed throughout a network; there was no central location for distribution or control. Anyone posting had no idea exactly where a message might go and who might read it. Computer-mediated communication opened new possibilities and with the new possibilities, new risks.

Usenet was not the only one-to-many computer-based communication network to develop in the 1980s. In 1981, Ira H. Fuchs, vice-chancellor of university systems and formerly executive director of the computer center at the City University of New York, and Greydon Freeman, the director of the computer center at Yale University, decided protocols already within their IBM mainframe computers made computer-based communication between their facilities possible and practical. They leased a telephone circuit for communication between New York and New Haven and initiated what they called Bitnet. The "bit" stood for Because It's There, and, later, Because It's Time.[39] Although Bitnet did not run TCP/IP, like Usenet, it was a store-and-forward system that used a tree structure to send messages that did not require a lot of bandwidth. Within a year, twenty institutions had signed on with Bitnet. In 1984, IBM gave Bitnet a grant to develop centralized network support services. The facility was called the Bitnet Network Information Center.[40]

Bitnet proved to be enormously popular with educational institutions that were not linked to ARPANet. At its peak, Bitnet linked more than 500 institutions with 3,000 nodes. And, as has been the rule with the nascent networks, Bitnet had an impact in ways that were not necessarily anticipated by its founders. In 1984, the first international Multi-User Dungeon game was initiated on a Bitnet node at the École Nationale Supérieure des Mines de Paris, and in 1985, a young French university student named Eric Thomas offered a large computer center his services in creating a better security infrastructure for its IBM mainframe computer in exchange for a computer account, which was linked to Bitnet.[41] At the time, one of the most popular Bitnet features was its mailing list, which was supported on the IBM mainframe. To subscribe, however, a user would send a message to the Bitnet Network Information Center, where an actual person would have to sign the user up for the list.

The system had two main drawbacks. First, because a staff person had to enroll each name, it took a long time to get onto the list. Second, the communication process itself was very cumbersome. Once a name was added to the list, a message sent to a central address would be redistributed to the entire list. Replies had to be sent to the central address as well. If a user simply hit the reply button, the message would be discarded.

The Bitnet Network Information Center ran its mailing list in an account called LISTSERV, and the central mailing address was listserv@bitnic. As the mailing list grew in popularity, LISTSERV's limitations became glaringly apparent, particularly for European users, whose messages had to travel across the ocean at relatively slow speeds. Thomas decided to rewrite the LISTSERV electronic mailing program to eliminate both the need for manual intervention and the centralized processing of the messages. His solution was "peered" mailing lists. An administrator could set up two or more lists and then "peer" them. Any message that was posted on one list would automatically be posted on the other. This approach allowed other Bitnet sites to create their own mailing lists. By 1986, forty-one sites were running Thomas's electronic mailing program. Over the next several years he added additional features, including database functions that made it possible to archive and search messages. Like Usenet, LISTSERV lists, as well as lists maintained by similar software called listproc and Majordomo, could be either moderated or unmoderated. Unlike Usenet, which required separate software, listserv messages were delivered to the subscriber's mailbox. Hundreds and then thousands of electronic mailing lists were soon in operation, and popular lists could have hundreds or even thousands of subscribers and generate tens of messages a day.

COMPUTER NETWORKS IN THE OFFICE

Large-scale networking like ARPANet and Bitnet, as well as the development of new methods of computer-mediated communication, were taking place largely in the military, academic, and research communities, not in the traditional world of media or in the consumer arena. In terms of online services, the public was more aware of commercial efforts such as CompuServe and, later, America Online. But starting with the release of the IBM PC in 1981, personal computers became the hot new product in consumer electronics. Companies began to invest heavily in equipping many of their employees with personal computers. Individuals were snapping up personal computers for their homes as well.

As more and more companies equipped more and more employees with personal computers, the same sorts of problems that confronted military researchers in the 1960s began to confront businesses. Staff created word-processing documents and spreadsheets, but it was difficult to share them. People had to save the information on floppy disks and walk them around to other stakeholders. Different versions of the same program could produce output that was incompatible, and fully loading every application a person may need onto a personal computer was costly, inconvenient, and impractical.

If the problems were similar to those faced by military researchers in the 1960s, the solution was similar as well—networking not networks designed to connect big powerful computers in remote locations but networks connecting computers in a single building or department. These kinds of networks came to be called local area networks (LANs).

Local area networks were not invented by accident or serendipity. In 1969, Robert Metcalfe, a recent graduate in electrical engineering, took a part-time job building hardware to connect his alma mater, MIT, where he had worked on Project MAC, to ARPANet. At the same time, he pursued a doctorate in mathematics at Harvard, but when he presented his dissertation on ARPANet, it was rejected for not being grounded enough in theory. In the meantime, Metcalfe accepted a job at Xerox's Palo Alto Research Center, where he worked on Alohanet, a random-access, radio-wave networking technology developed at the University of Hawaii. That work served as the basis for a successful dissertation.[42]

The Palo Alto Research Center (PARC) had been founded by the Xerox Corporation in 1970. Xerox had gathered a world-class team of information and physical scientists and charged them with establishing the "architecture of information."[43] As could be expected, PARC was jammed with computers of all kinds, including the Alto, a personal computer developed by Xerox in 1973. Company executives felt the Alto was too expensive to win broad acceptance, but it was distributed widely within PARC and to select government agencies.[44]

Metcalfe, who had connected PARC's minicomputer to ARPANet, was given this assignment: how could the hundreds of personal computers in the building be connected? This was a new problem because in most places at the time, there were only one, two, or three computers in operation. Metcalfe's network also had to be fast enough to allow the computers to share a new laser printer that Xerox had recently developed. Working with the same concepts he used in his work on Alohanet, Metcalfe wrote a memo to his supervisors describing the potential of networking computers locally.[45]

Metcalfe knew that the approach to networking used by ARPANet, with its dedicated interface message processing (IMP) machines doing the translations between different computer systems, was too costly and not practical for local area networks. The key breakthrough was an algorithm that could control the message traffic through the network. In 1976, Metcalfe and his assistant, David Boggs, published a paper titled "Ethernet: Distributed Packet-Switching for Local Computer Networks," in *Communications of the ACM*. He called it Ethernet because messages could be sent to every node on the network in the same way that "luminiferous ether" was once thought to propagate electromagnetic waves through space.[46]

In the late 1970s, Xerox convinced Digital Equipment and Intel to produce hardware to run Ethernet. The three companies also agreed to open the specifications, making them available to other companies who might want to build networking products. In 1979, Metcalfe left Xerox PARC to establish the 3Com Company, entering the commercial networking arena. With the availability of higher speed coaxial cable, by the early 1980s, it was clear that local area networks would be an efficient route for companies of all sizes, and eventually homes as well, to get better value from their investments in personal computing by allowing computer users to share resources like printers, storage, and communication gateways.[47]

The spread of local area networks in business mirrored the spread of personal computer use in general. According to the market research company Dataquest, in 1980, approximately 500,000 computers costing less than $5,000 were sold worldwide. With companies large and small ranging from IBM to Apple to new entrepreneurial start-ups introducing computers for both the business and home markets, with some costing as little as $300, Dataquest forecast that the number of personal computers sold would climb to 3.7 million annually by 1985.[48] In 1989, Dataquest estimated that 21 million personal computers would be sold worldwide.[49]

Despite the rapid growth throughout the 1980s, most personal computer industry analysts argued that computers were still too hard for average people to use. IBM personal computers and others that used the same operating system were predominantly text-based. When a personal computer was initially turned on, all that would be displayed would be a C>, which was called the C prompt, and a command-line interface. Users needed to develop some degree of expertise to enter the commands needed to run application programs such as spreadsheets and word processors as well as store and retrieve files. To many, operating a standard personal computer seemed too challenging for nontechnical people.

Making computers easier to use had long been an industry dream. Even when Vannevar Bush first proposed Memex as a way to access all human knowledge, he envisioned users sitting at keyboards with graphics terminals that would allow them to follow trails of information. In the early 1960s, Bush's article "As We May Think" inspired Douglas Engelbart, a researcher at the Stanford Research Institute, to think about broader applications for computers. In 1962, Engelbart published a report for the U.S. Air Force's Department of Information Science in the Office of Scientific Research called "Augmenting Human Intellect: A Conceptual Approach." In it, he argued that with new methods and concepts, the computer could provide direct, online assistance and presented the best near-term opportunity to improve the "intellectual effectiveness of the individual human being." Engelbart suggested several features that could help computers augment human intelligence, among them Bush's concept that knowledge could be linked in associative trials. Engelbart also proposed the idea of an interface in which a user would point at something on a computer screen and the computer could take a specific action determined by where the user was pointing.[50] That basic concept came to be known as the point-and-click interface.

Based on the report, Engelbart obtained the funding to pursue several of the ideas he had sketched. In 1968, he presented a rudimentary system to one thousand computer professionals. The demonstration was a landmark event. Working with three input devices, including a point-and-click device his team had named a "mouse," Engelbart created several different windows on the screen. He clicked on one piece of information and jumped to another piece of information—a demonstration of hyperlinks. And he communicated in real time with another user—an example of instant messaging. The demonstration also included e-mail functionality. Engelbart later added database capabilities, and the system ultimately was used to store data generated through ARPANet.

Of course, the system shown at the demonstration did have some limitations. Because of memory constraints in the IBM mainframe on which it ran, only uppercase characters could be displayed. And although the system supported multiple onscreen windows, there was no easy way to delineate where one window stopped and another started. Nevertheless, with its hypertext, network document collaboration, and full-screen editing, the NLS, which stood for oN-Line System, clearly pointed in the direction that a human interface for computing should take. Engelbart's ideas were vigorously pursued at Xerox PARC.[51]

The main obstacles to implementing Engelbart's ideas were

computer processing power and memory. As the technology in both these areas improved, different commercial computer manufacturers began to explore how to bring Engelbart's concepts to fruition on relatively inexpensive personal computers. The first company to succeed was Apple Computer. In 1979, Apple founder Steve Jobs toured Xerox PARC, reportedly in exchange for shares of Apple stock, and was convinced that Engelbart's ideas, which were described as a windowing graphical user interface or GUI, was the next step for personal computers. The Apple engineering team incorporated the concepts into the Apple Lisa computer, the company's next generation computer aimed at the business market. The Lisa's interface featured windows, icons, and a mouse that made it easy for users to perform tasks by pointing a cursor at them and clicking. As dynamic as it was, however, the Lisa proved to be too expensive and the business world was simply not ready for the radical departure it presented. It flopped in the market. But in one of the most memorable advertisements in television history, during the Super Bowl in 1984, a slimmed down version of the Lisa called the Macintosh was introduced to the world. The advertisement, based on an Orwellian vision, showed a young woman symbolically smashing the monotone world of IBM-based personal computing.[52]

The Macintosh established the windowing graphical user interface as the new bar to reach in personal computing. However, when the Macintosh was released, Apple was in corporate disarray. The founders Steve Wozniak and Steve Jobs had been pushed aside in favor of John Scully, the former president of PepsiCo, who was supposed to bring professional management to the company. Moreover, Apple refused to license its technology to any other computer companies. This meant it would have to fend for itself not only against IBM but against every company that built computers running the same operating system as IBM, which was known as MS-DOS. So while Apple promoted the Macintosh as the "computer for the rest of us," targeting it specifically for novice users, it was relegated to a small niche of the market.

The corporate market, which was growing even faster than the home market, was dominated by IBM, the leading computer company since the 1950s. IBM had entered the personal computer market by setting up a separate organization to quickly assemble a product. As part of the process, instead of developing its own operating system, it licensed a system from a small start-up company called Microsoft. Microsoft retained the rights to license MS-DOS to other vendors as well, which it did. Given the credibility that IBM had in the corporate marketplace and the vast number of other companies marketing IBM-compatible computers—that is, computers running the MS-DOS operating system, it was positioned to set the dominant standards for personal computing.

As was the case at Apple, Microsoft's leadership was fully aware of the advantages of a graphical user interface. In fact, Steve Jobs had visited Microsoft in 1981 and showed them an early version of the Macintosh, and Microsoft agreed to develop application software for it. The deal gave Microsoft an intimate knowledge of Macintosh's design. In November 1983, Microsoft announced that it was developing a graphical user interface as well, which it called Windows. Windows 1.0 was released two years later. But there were very few applications that ran on it and it performed slowly, so it was not widely accepted. Microsoft's next attempt, Windows 2.0, was released in 1987. It took advantage of the improved computer processing power available and Microsoft released its own spreadsheet application, Excel, and its own word-processing program, Word, to run under Windows 2.0. The "look and feel" of Windows 2.0 was so close to the look and feel of the Macintosh that Apple sued Microsoft for violating its copyrights on its visual displays. The suit discouraged applications developers from creating software for Windows 2.0, fearing that if Microsoft lost the suit, other developers would be liable as well. In 1989, a federal judge threw out most of Apple's complaints, ruling that many of the displays could not be copyrighted. The following year, Microsoft issued Windows 3.0, which looked almost exactly like the Macintosh interface. Running on a faster computer than before, Windows 3.0 and Windows 3.1, which came out shortly thereafter, proved to be very popular. The graphical user interface would dominate personal computing from then on.

As local area networks became more commonplace on desktops throughout corporate America as well as nonscience departments in colleges and universities and elsewhere, the demand for access to the national and international networks like ARPANet and NSFNet grew. In 1985, NYSERNet was founded by a consortium of public and private institutions in New York to provide high-speed networking capabilities to the state's educational and research institutions. Meeting at Cornell University, participants agreed to a proposal to build a network that would link institutions across the state with the supercomputer facilities at Cornell, which served as a key hub for NSFNet. With the enthusiastic backing of corporate sponsors like IBM, AT&T, and Xerox, a plan was put in place and fourteen universities and the Brookhaven National Laboratory joined as the initial member institutions. By 1987, the network was in place, making it the first non-U.S. government organization to offer connectivity to a TCP/IP network to transfer data.[53]

Others saw an opportunity to provide commercial customers access to TCP/IP networks. UUNet Technologies, founded in 1987 by Rick Adams, first served as a gateway between UUCP mail (the Unix program that served as the technological basis for Usenet at the time) and e-mail being transported using TCP/IP compatible protocols. Adams created the serial line Internet protocol, which allowed personal computers to connect to the emerging Internet.[54] He repaid the loan to Usenix and converted UUNet into a for-profit company, providing Internet access to commercial companies. In 1989, the original NYSERNet network was spun off into a commercial company called PSINet. In 1991, commercial providers like UUNet and PSINet formed the Commercial Internet Exchange (CIX); this would allow companies that did not adhere to the NSFNet usage policies to still transmit data over the Internet. By 1995, there were 160 commercial Internet access providers.[55]

The Internet was opening up to commercial activities and Metcalfe's law, that networks gain in value as more users join the network, was clearly in operation. The TCP/IP networks were becoming more available, and as more people got access, more people wanted access. Nonetheless, even as NSFNet increasingly opened up to traffic from people who were not scientists or researchers, the policies set by the scientific and research community governed its use. This meant that although institutions paid for access to the network, the data available via the network was free. Unlike the commercial online services, which had both free data and premium data, which cost money to obtain, people who had access to NSFNet or any of the secondary TCP/IP networks inter-networked with NSFNet had access to all the information made available by other users and institutions at any of the network nodes.

Accessing remote files across the network was one of the fundamental applications for ARPANet. The file transfer protocol (FTP) allowed large files to be transferred from remote computers and Telnet allowed users to log onto remote computers. But as the Internet grew, the problem of locating files of interest or making files available to others became more complex. In 1989, Peter Deutsch at McGill University created the Archie protocol, an index of all publicly available FTP sites. If a user stored a file on an FTP server that allowed for anonymous access, Archie could index it; then, using Archie, other users could find and retrieve the file. At one point, half the Internet traffic going into and out of Canada was being generated by Archie users. At the same time, Brewster Kahle, then at Thinking Machines Corp., a developer of supercomputers, created what he called a wide area information server (WAIS). WAIS indexed the full text of files in a database and allowed users to search for those files. At its peak, WAIS indexed more than 600 different databases.[56]

In the early 1990s, the University of Minnesota created Gopher. Like WAIS, files stored in directories on a Gopher server could be located by two subsidiary programs called Veronica and Jughead. Gopher had a relatively simple user interface and anybody with Internet access could Telnet to the Gopher server at the University of Minnesota and search for information. Archie, WAIS, and Gopher signaled an important new direction for the network. Users across the network could make files on their computers publicly available, and other users around the world could locate and access files of interest. The network could be seen as the underpinning of a distributed repository of information created by people around the world and accessed by people around the world. There was no central point of management. No specific government could control or constrain the users on the network. And access to the information was free to the user.

Throughout the 1980s, several independent trends were beginning to converge. The United States government was funding the creation of a national computer network with a standard communications protocol called TCP/IP. As the network developed, young computer scientists were creating new and often unanticipated applications to run over the network—applications such as games that put interactivity in the foreground and applications like Usenet, which put the spotlight on the uncontrolled distribution of information. At the same time, the technology associated with personal computing was improving rapidly, putting sophisticated, intelligent, general purpose computers on people's desks at their offices, where they were often linked in local area networks. Personal computers were also finding their way into people's homes. As the use of graphical user interfaces became ubiquitous, the market for personal computing expanded tremendously. Finally, online services like CompuServe and Prodigy were promoting the advantages of accessing information online.

Then, in 1988, Vinton Cerf, who had been instrumental in creating the TCP/IP protocol, arranged for MCI Mail, the e-mail service supported by MCI's online services, to be interconnected with NSFNet's e-mail service on an experimental basis. The following year, CompuServe interconnected its e-mail services as well. By interconnecting with NSFNet, suddenly a CompuServe user could send e-mail messages to anybody at a college or university, for example, who had an e-mail account, as well as to users of the MCI network. Over the next couple of years, other commercial online service providers also interconnected with NSFNet. These interconnected networks formed an integrated global e-mail network where users of commercial service providers and NSFNet users could send e-mail to each other. The growth of an integrated e-mail network proved to be another strong enticement for people to get online.

ONCE BURNED, TWICE WARY

Media companies were not unaware of the growth of online services but, having stumbled badly with videotex services, many companies eyed the developments warily. Some newspapers, like the *Fort Worth Star Telegram* and the *Atlanta Journal-Constitution,* continued to support small videotex operations. In 1991, the *Kansas City Star* purchased a videotex system with the idea of launching a news service. Publishers felt that the videotex market could rebound and being early in the market would give them an advantage, particularly if deep-pocket competitors like the regional Bell telephone operating companies entered the market.[57]

Others went in a different direction. In 1986, the *Middlesex News,* a 36,000-circulation daily in Framingham, Massachusetts, launched a computer bulletin board service to allow readers to preview the next day's headlines, check calendar and club listings, look up movie and restaurant reviews, and search a database of answers to readers' questions on various subjects. Framingham is located in the thick of the Route 128 corridor, Boston's equivalent to the Silicon Valley, and the goal was to build a closer relationship with the high-tech workforce in the area. The bulletin board was initially set up by a reporter whose beat was technology, and when she left, it was taken over by Adam Gaffin, a senior reporter covering planning and public works in Framingham. The project was not terribly ambitious; according to Gaffin, he spent about 10 to 15 minutes a day uploading material to the bulletin board.[58]

There were a few other relatively low-key experiments that attempted to use the budding national computer-based network to deliver news and information to readers. In 1990, the *Albuquerque Tribune* set up a service it called the Electronic Trib, which allowed users to access information via personal computers. According to Dave Carlson, who set up the E-Trib for $5,000—the cost of an inexpensive IBM personal computer, customized bulletin board software, and four telephone lines—it was the first multi-line, personal computer-based online newspaper. Users could read full texts of news wire services, old restaurant and movie reviews, drunken driving court records, and information on local landlord-tenant disputes. There were no graphics. According to Carlson, on the first day of service, 400 people logged in. The *Tribune* ultimately charged people an annual $50 subscription fee for access for three hours a day.[59] "I'm going to be No. 1 in my city in providing information, so nobody else can come in and take this away from me," said Tim Gallagher, editor of the *Albuquerque Tribune,* who described the the E-Trib as an "electronic supplement" in 1993.[60]

In addition to some intrepid newspaper companies, there were a few entrepreneurial ventures underway. In 1988, Brad Templeton, who was a moderator of a popular Usenet newsgroup called rec.humor.funny, decided there was a business opportunity to distribute news and information via Usenet, which at the time was not integrated with NSFNet and therefore not bound by its use policies. After being turned down by the Tribune Company to carry the column of the humorist Dave Barry, Templeton inked a deal with the United Press International wire service to carry their news feed. Templeton converted the UPI feed into the Usenet format and with that, he launched ClariNet, which Templeton claims ultimately became the first "digital" newspaper and later the first commercial company on the Internet.[61]

By the early 1990s, ClariNet reached 30,000 subscribers using the Usenet message-interchange format. Subscribers paid $35 and received content from wire services, syndicates, computer industry sources, newsletters, and other services categorized by priority and subject and organized according to keywords that corresponded to geography and story content. Most of the content was prepared automatically by computers, but a small team of editors reviewed and corrected the material as needed. According to Templeton, in 1993 ClariNet had been profitable for four years.[62]

While a few publishers and entrepreneurs were nibbling around the edges of the potential of the Internet, reporters were becoming alert to the new sources of information available to them online. In 1989, Bill Dedman, a reporter for the Associated Press, won a Pulitzer Prize for investigative journalism for a series about discrimination in mortgage lending practices in middle income neighborhoods that ran in the *Atlanta Journal-Constitution*. As part of the report, Dedman analyzed a computer database of thousands of mortgages. As well as the ability to analyze huge amounts of information in databases, reporters were learning that they could use online services offered by governments and private companies to do research for articles. Instead of being reliant on a newspaper morgue or clipping library, they could easily discover what had been published in other newspapers and magazines on almost any subject. Online services provided access to trade magazines and commercial databases. And computer bulletin boards, LISTSERV discussion groups, and Usenet newsgroups could put enterprising reporters in contact with a new class of human sources made up of regular people interested in specific issues and topics.[63]

THE COALESCING OF THE WORLD WIDE WEB

Throughout the 1980s, an increasing amount of information came to be stored in databases around the world and an increasing amount of information was accessible online. But the increase in information and its availability only exacerbated the same old challenges. The information was hard to find. It was stored in incompatible systems. Personal computers were hard to use. Commercial online services often were costly, particularly for users who spent a lot of time online. And specialized content providers not infrequently looked to charge a premium for their information.

Once a person had access to a network that interconnected to NSFNet, there were often no additional time-based usage charges, but there were other problems. Information was difficult to locate and access. While WAIS and Gopher services were designed to help users locate the information they wanted, those services covered only a small fraction of the material stored on computers linked to the network. Moreover, like most programs at the time, WAIS, Gopher, and other Internet applications were command-line driven. They were not intuitive and thus were difficult for nontechnical people to discover and learn.

In the technical community, it was a different story. As early as 1980, Tim Berners-Lee, a software engineer working at CERN, the European particle physics laboratory in Geneva, Switzerland, speculated about the possibility of linking all information found on all computers everywhere. In his spare time and for his own use, he wrote a program called Enquirer, primarily to help him remember the connections among people, computers, and projects underway in the laboratory. Berners-Lee reasoned that if information could be labeled with an address, other computers could then retrieve it. Then, by being able to reference yet other information, associations among pieces of information that on the surface might appear unrelated could emerge.[64] The lineage of this idea could be traced back directly to the thinking of Vannevar Bush and Ted Nelson, who had promoted the term *hypertext* to reflect creating links among different pieces of information, and Douglas

Engelbart, who had demonstrated a rudimentary system along those lines more than a decade earlier.

Keeping track of documents was a significant problem at CERN. Although it supported a permanent staff, many other researchers, scientists, and contractors worked there for short periods of time and then moved on. There was a relatively short-term fellowship program, and many scientists stayed at CERN only long enough to collect their experimental data before they returned to their own institutions. As could be expected, a huge number of different computers were in operation, and as time went on, more and more small personal computers were being added. While most people documented what they did, it was very difficult to keep track of the documentation. A great deal of information was simply being lost.[65]

After a stint in private industry, Berners-Lee returned to CERN and the research community in 1984. His first project was to create a technology to perform remote procedure calls (RPC). An RPC would allow a user to write an application on one kind of computer but "call" a specific procedure or process from a different computer even if the second computer ran a completely different operating system or the procedure was written in a completely different programming language. RPCs helped improve the communication between disparate computers. After he completed his work on the RPC technology, Berners-Lee turned his attention to managing the documents being produced at CERN. He knew that he wanted easier access to technical papers, minutes of meetings, notes, and experimental data as well as the sort of functionality that his earlier Enquirer program had provided in tracking relationships among people, projects, and computers. The challenge was to devise a system in which documents could be used without modification by all of the diverse computer systems. The solution, Berners-Lee decided, was hypertext, which could provide a common format with which to display information. Several companies had already developed hypertext technology to run on specific computers, most notably the hypercard developed by Bill Atkinson of Apple Computer in 1987. Berners-Lee reasoned that if he could combine the Enquirer program with external hypertext links and the interconnection schemes he had developed for RPC, he could build webs of information linking both internal and external computers.[66]

In late 1988, Berners-Lee began to work on the concept. Enquirer provided a method for linking documents and databases. Hypertext provided a common format to represent documents. The challenge was to get the system to work on disparate computers. CERN had been a late adopter of TCP/IP and the Internet, in part because it had been a leader in developing an alternative networking protocol. But as more computers running the Unix operating system came online at CERN, the more convinced Berners-Lee became of the effectiveness of TCP/IP in allowing different computers to communicate with each other. The TCP/IP protocol was routinely bundled with Unix computers. The final piece of the puzzle was an addressing scheme to allow information to be located easily. For that, Berners-Lee adapted the addressing scheme he had used in developing RPCs.[67]

For several reasons, Berners-Lee's proposal to create a global hypertext database received very little support at CERN. In essence, CERN's central focus was physics, not information technology. After purchasing a new computer in 1990, however, Berners-Lee pushed forward on his hypertext experiment. He decided that he would begin every program associated with the effort with "HT" and, after some deliberation, decided to call the entire system the World Wide Web.[68]

With the support of Robert Cailliau, Berners-Lee first wrote a Web browser, the program for the user. He determined a way for the program to distinguish between text and links to another piece of information. He developed the hypertext markup language (HTML) to format pages with hyperlinks and created the hypertext transport protocol (HTTP) to communicate over the Internet. He settled on the way that the browser would decode what he called the universal resource identifier, ultimately renamed the uniform resource locator (URL), so the program could know where to retrieve information. The final step was to create the Web server software for the computers that would store the documents that would be accessible via the Web. But to make sure there was interesting information available from the start, Berners-Lee and Nicola Pellow, an intern at CERN who was assisting him, decided to enable the browser to retrieve documents using the file transfer protocol (FTP) as well. By Christmas Day 1990, the CERN Web server info.cern.ch was up and running. Two users, Berners-Lee and Cailliau, were communicating with it.[69]

When Berners-Lee first started demonstrating the technology, it did not create a great stir. Its first use was to access telephone numbers from different directories at CERN. But the system had certain compelling underlying principles. It was universal and could be accessed by any computer. There was no central point of management. All documents were on the same footing. It was simple. Once an organization began storing information in a Web server, it could link to and display documents stored in Web server directories anywhere else. Once a document had a URL, it could be stored on a server and displayed by the browser. That universal functionality represented a profound, fundamental shift in computing.[70]

In 1991, Berners-Lee and Cailliau made the World Wide Web

available to a few other researchers at CERN and word of the technology began to spread through the high energy particle physics community. Paul Kunz arrived for a visit to CERN from the Stanford Linear Accelerator (SLAC) in Palo Alto and used the Web. On his return to SLAC, he shared his experience with the librarian there, who saw it as a way to make the center's extensive catalogue of online documents available to physicists around the world. SLAC soon set up the first Web server outside of CERN. Berners-Lee then posted the browser and the server software to selected Usenet newsgroups, including alt.hypertext, and immediately began receiving e-mail from hypertext enthusiasts trying to install the program. He created a Telnet port to info.cern.ch that allowed people immediate access to the line-mode browser—a browser that used and displayed only text—opening the Web to people who did not have a browser on their own machine. The Web server at info.cern.ch included instructions on how to download a Web browser.[71]

By 1993, there were approximately fifty Web servers operating around the world. The growth of the Web was being limited in part by the primitive nature of the browser, which Berners-Lee had kept simple to ensure that it could work on all computers. A more sophisticated browser, Viola, had been developed by Pei Wei, a recent graduate of the University of California, Berkeley, for Unix computers, which were used primarily by scientists and engineers. A group at the University of Kansas had created Lynx, which was text-based like the original browser. A more robust browser for the Macintosh computer was completed at the end of 1992.[72]

In early 1993, a group made up mostly of students at the National Center for Supercomputing Applications at the University of Illinois created Mosaic, a point-and-click graphical browser.

The first release was for Unix machines but within the year, Mosaic was available for the Macintosh, Commodore Amiga, and Microsoft Windows computers. The browser was distributed freely throughout the Internet. One of the creators, Marc Andreeson, promoted Mosaic vigorously through Usenet newsgroups, incorporating the comments he received into subsequent iterations of the browser.[73] With Mosaic's graphical user interface, surfing the World Wide Web was simple even for nontechnical users. In August 1993, O'Reilly and Associates, a technical book publishing house, officially launched the Global Network Navigator, which the company claimed was the first commercial Web site.[74] From that point on, the rush to set up Web sites was fast and furious.

MEDIA COMPANIES EYE THE INTERNET

In the early 1990s, Knight Ridder was still feeling bruised from its failed foray into videotex. Nonetheless, Robert Ingle, president of the company's New Media group, was worried that Knight Ridder would miss an opportunity when the time for a videotext-like service was ripe. Based in San Jose, he had served for fourteen years as the executive editor of the *San Jose Mercury News,* the chain's paper in Silicon Valley at the heart of the computer industry. Ingle was aware of analysts' forecasts for explosive growth in the use of personal computers and modems. With that in mind, he wrote a memo proposing that Knight Ridder start an experimental electronic service integrated with the *Mercury News.* Originally, the plan was to make a wide range of information available, but not current news.[75]

In 1992, Ingle got corporate approval to pursue the project, and in May 1993, just about the time that the Mosaic Web browser was beginning to circulate in earnest around the Internet, Knight Ridder launched the Mercury Center, which it described as a series of "electronic extensions" to the *Mercury News*. The service was available via fax, telephone, and the commercial online service America Online and included online copies of the newspaper, news updates, transcripts of news conferences, raw news releases, and archival material going back to 1985, when the newspaper's database went online. There was also a classified advertising section, twenty-five message boards on different topics, and the ability to communicate with *Mercury News* reporters and editors via e-mail. From time to time, readers would have the chance to "interview" elected officials and others online and also get access to supplemental information. The Mercury Center offerings were heavily promoted in the newspaper.

The Mercury Center immediately raised concerns in the newsroom and elsewhere. Some staff members wondered if it would feed unedited, self-serving information to its readers in the form of raw news releases, for example, or if the fifteen-person staff would still filter the news. The Center had both business and editorial staff, and the line between them did not seem as sharply drawn as was typical at the time in the newspaper business. The newspaper had to get specific permission from the Newpaper Guild for editorial workers to participate in the project.[76]

At the project's launch, Knight Ridder officials and personnel seemed to have mixed opinions about the Mercury Center. At a conference about newspapers and telecommunications opportunities just prior to its launch, Chris Jennewein, general manager of the new venture, said the Center's first goal is to "strengthen the newspaper by extending the franchise."[77] Several months after the launch, when the Mercury Center still had only a little over 5,000 subscribers, Robert Ingle said, "The idea is to use the newspaper as a bridge to point to a great deal more than we can deliver in the traditional way."[78]

Still, executives were convinced that newspapers had to continue to experiment with the online delivery of the news. "A new medium will be born, and newspapers can be programmers in it," William R. Hearst III, editor and publisher of the *San Francisco Examiner,* said at the same conference at which Jennewein spoke. "We already know about arranging information, about technology. We have capital. We know how to create and sell advertising. We have regional franchises and, most importantly, we have a newsroom—a place where information is gathered, tested, and put into packages," he added.[79]

Less than seven months later, Jennewein and Mike Delco, a programmer at the *Mercury News,* gave Ingle a demonstration of Mosaic. Ingle quickly saw that the Internet was the future. All the work that had been done to get the Mercury Center up and running had to be redone. Ingle flew to Miami to confer with Knight Ridder's top executives, telling them that the old days of a few companies owning the online "pipelines" were over. For $50,000 Knight Ridder signed on to become the first content provider for Netscape, the commercial company that had been set up to market Mosaic, renamed Netscape Navigator. Knight Ridder also took an equity position in Netscape, an investment that ultimately produced a profit of $40 million. At the time, Ingle said, most newspapers "were not even conscious of the Web or its implications."[80]

FIVE

THE AVALANCHE OF ONLINE NEWS

By the late 1980s, the newspaper industry realized that its read-ership had been eroding for at least a generation, if not more. As watching television and television news became a national habit in the late 1950s and early 1960s, a steady stream of news-paper readers disappeared. Between the end of World War II and 1965, four hundred newspapers merged or closed. The number of newspapers overall remained constant because smaller newspa-pers serving suburban communities replaced larger urban dailies, but newspapers were clearly under pressure. With the move to the suburbs and changing demographics, afternoon newspapers were the most vulnerable. In 1962, Times-Mirror, owner of the *Los Angeles Times,* closed its afternoon paper, the *Evening Mirror,* leaving the afternoon market to its competitor, the *Los Angeles Herald Examiner.* Since its founding in 1948, the *Evening Mirror* lost more than $25 million, according to Norman Chandler, the publisher of both the *Times* and the *Mirror.* A 114-day strike in New York in late 1962 and early 1963 by the International Ty-pographical Union led directly or indirectly to the demise of the *New York Mirror,* the *New York Journal American,* the *New York*

World-Telegram and Sun, and ultimately, the venerable *New York Herald Tribune.*[1]

Newspaper closings were only one symptom of the challenges newspapers faced. Almost from the end of World War II, fewer and fewer markets were able to sustain competitive newspapers. As early as 1933, the *Albuquerque Journal* and the *Albuquerque Tribune* had entered into what was called a joint operating agreement (JOA). In an effort to keep two independent editorial voices alive, struggling newspapers would combine their back-office business operations while maintaining two independent editorial offices. After World War II, JOAs became more commonplace. Four JOAs were made in the 1940s and eight involving sixteen newspapers in the 1950s. After four more JOAs came into effect in the 1960s, the federal government challenged the renewal of a JOA between two newspapers in Tucson, Arizona, stating that the JOA represented a restraint of trade. The U.S. Supreme Court agreed, and in 1969, the JOA was struck down. But the U.S. Congress stepped in. In 1970, it passed the Newspaper Preservation Act protecting the JOAs then in operation and established a mechanism for newspapers in competitive marketplaces to apply for a JOA if needed.[2] In supporting the passage of the Newspaper Preservation Act of 1970, publishers argued that it was essential if more than one newspaper was to survive in many major metropolitan areas. By the late 1970s, there were twenty-eight JOAs in operation.[3] But JOAs were not panaceas for failing newspapers. In 1983, for example, the *St. Louis Globe Democrat,* which had been in a JOA with the *St. Louis Post Dispatch,* announced it was closing. Analysts at the time estimated that more than twenty other newspapers that were the second paper in their respective cities were facing a similar end.

As the number of competitive newspaper markets declined,

the trend toward consolidation and development of large news-paper chains picked up. Newspaper chains were nothing new. Joseph Pulitzer had owned multiple newspapers in the 1880s, and in the decades that followed, William Randolph Hearst and E.W. Scripps along with Roy Howard built large chains of news-papers. In the 1960s and 1970s, the trend toward consolidation accelerated. Perhaps the most prominent example was the growth of the Gannett Company. At the end of the 1960s, Gannett, which had been founded in 1918, had a stable of thirty-three daily and twelve weekly newspapers, six radio stations, and two television stations. In 1967, the company went public, and it was listed on the New York Stock Exchange in 1969. Ten years later, the com-pany owned seventy-eight daily newspapers in thirty-three states and Guam, twenty-one weekly newspapers, a national news ser-vice, seven television stations and fourteen radio stations, outdoor advertising operations in the United States and Canada, and the research firm of Louis Harris & Associates.[4] During its growth, Gannett newspapers were routinely criticized for being nonde-script, superficial, and more geared to turning a profit than sup-porting good journalism. Even when the company initiated one of the last successful entrepreneurial efforts with the creation of the country's first national daily newspaper, *USA Today,* in 1982, the effort was blasted for being shallow and flimsy.[5]

The picture for television news was very different. Throughout the 1960s and 1970s, television news continued to expand both at the network and local levels. By the 1970s, news programming was generating 40 to 60 percent of revenue at many local sta-tions, which in turn were expanding the number of hours they devoted to local news. At the network level, while long-form documentary programming was becoming less frequent, weekly news magazines, sometimes airing several times a week, became commonplace. ABC even devoted its 11:30 P.M. time slot, long the domain of entertainment-oriented talk shows, to a news program. While television viewership climbed, newspaper readership sank 16 percent. The drop in readership was particularly sharp among younger people. Newspaper executives were also troubled because television had emerged as the most credible source of news, displacing newspapers.[6]

The 1980s, however, were not kind to network television news. Viewership for the networks' flagship nightly news broadcasts began to drop precipitously and the networks' overall share of the viewing audience during primetime viewing hours dropped from 81 percent in 1982 to 64 percent in 1990, due to increasing competition from cable and home video. The networks' news divisions were under pressure to present news in a more entertaining fashion to hold on to their audiences.[7]

EDGING ONLINE

Although healthy newspapers continued to generate strong profits, in the late 1980s even senior newspaper executives, having lived through decades of newspaper closures, joint operating agreements, declining readership, and fierce competition from television, knew that they had to change. It was clear that emerging new communications technologies could play an important role in at least augmenting print and broadcast media. When Chinese students organized large-scale protests in Tiananmen Square in the middle of Beijing in 1989, they communicated with the outside world via fax machines and e-mail even after the Chinese authorities pulled the plug on broadcasters.[8] The fax and, to a lesser degree at that time, the laptop computer had become instruments of democratic and cross-border communication. As the headline on an editorial comment about activists' use of new communication technology put it, even in 1989 it was a "Wired, Wired World."[9]

The question was how could newspapers capitalize on the possibilities offered by new communication technology? Fax technology seemed like it could be a dynamic new delivery mechanism for news. Although it had been around for decades, in the mid-1980s the use of facsimile machines, which could transmit exact duplicates of documents via the telephone line to other fax machines which could print them, was exploding in popularity. Hoping to capitalize on that development, several newspapers, including the *Hartford Courant,* the *Chicago Tribune,* the *Minneapolis Star Tribune,* and the *New York Times,* launched fax services. The *Times*'s initial fax product was four-to-six letter-sized pages with a synopsis of the news sent to travelers in Asia. The goal was to send *Times* information to places where the newspaper itself was not available.[10] The drawbacks to fax services were obvious. They were costly, slow, and did not provide a great deal of information. At best they would appeal to an affluent niche market that would put a high value on the information received.

Audiotext seemed to be another attractive alternative. In the early 1990s, around one third of newspaper companies were offering some form of audiotext service. People could call a central number and by punching a few buttons on their touchtone telephones, they could access news and weather, classified ads read by a computerized voice, stock-market information, loan rates, race results, lottery numbers, and soap opera updates. Cathleen Black, president of the Newspaper Association of America, suggested at the trade organization's convention that the move toward audiotext signaled newspapers' efforts to expand beyond their traditional purview. In a typical system, the phone call itself would be free but callers would also have to listen to a 15-second commercial. At the time, the *Washington Post*'s Post Haste audiotext system was receiving 800,000 calls a month.[11] In 1993, the Evansville Courier Company in Indiana (made up of the *Evansville Courier* and *Evansville Press*) reported that one of its audiotext services alone, Homework Hotline, generated $60,000 in advertising revenue for 1992–93.[12]

Audiotext had its limitations. First, it was curiously disconnected from newsroom operations. At best, the editorial staff saw audiotext as the domain of the sales and marketing departments. At worst, audiotext represented extra work for reporters.[13] Perhaps most worrisome, audiotext played to the strength of the regional Bell operating companies (RBOCs), the regional telephone systems that had been established with the breakup of AT&T. The regional Bell systems were still viewed as the primary threat to newspapers in delivering information online. While the FCC's Computer II decision had raised significant barriers to telephone companies entering what was called the enhanced services market, by the mid-1980s, following the actual dismantling of AT&T, those obstacles were no longer seen as appropriate. In 1985, the FCC began work on the Computer III decision. While the objective was still to prevent basic ratepayers from subsidizing the RBOCs' ancillary business initiatives, the requirement that RBOCs establish separate subsidiaries was seen as too onerous and hampering innovations beneficial to the public. Instead of a structural safeguard to prevent the RBOCs from using their quasi-monopoly positions unfairly, the FCC opted for a new, nonstructural solution. It mandated that the telephone system develop what it called an open network architecture. The open network architecture required the RBOCs to break their networks into basic building blocks and then make those blocks available to all companies providing enhanced services, allowing them the same opportunity to innovate. Once an RBOC filed a plan for its open network architecture, it could enter the enhanced services market as well. In 1987 and in 1991, Judge Harold Greene, who was presiding over the breakup of AT&T, gave his permission for the RBOCs to enter the enhanced services market.[14]

That ruling, as well as the Computer III decision in general, was not well received by the RBOCs' competitors, including the Commercial Internet Exchange, whose leadership felt it would be impossible to enforce. Newspaper publishers also vigorously resisted the entry of the RBOCs into the enhanced services market. They voiced their objections so loudly that in 1992, Allen Neuharth, the former chairman of the Gannett Company, blasted the American Newspaper Publishers Association for leading the charge to block the entry of the RBOCs into the electronic distribution of information, arguing that the First Amendment applied to the telephone companies as well as newspapers. In turn, the RBOCs lashed out harshly at newspapers, arguing that newspapers often had a monopoly on classified advertising in a specific city, and when they did, they sharply raised classified advertising rates. Competition in the local market was needed, the RBOCs asserted, and they could supply just that.[15]

Clearly, both fax services and audiotext services had serious shortcomings as alternative platforms for the delivery of news. But newspaper companies continued to invest in them for several reasons. In 1993, according to a survey conducted by the Kelsey Group, the historic rationale for investing in audiotext was to remain the predominant provider of local news. But that goal was fading by the early 1990s. The second goal was to increase advertising opportunities. But it was rapidly becoming even more important for newspapers to invest in audiotext and fax services to gain experience with the electronic delivery of the news. The Kelsey Group had conducted the survey since 1990, and the number of respondents indicating the importance of gaining experience with electronic delivery had jumped sharply.[16] Newspaper executives knew that they had to identify a vehicle to take advantage of the growing potential in the electronic delivery of news.

But if plunging into audiotext meant working with companies who may soon turn out to be fierce competitors, signing deals with online services also had the potential for becoming problematic. First, there was little evidence that people who accessed online services had any interest in accessing news electronically. To drive home the point, after the conclusion of the CompuServe test providing access to newspaper content online in the early 1980s, a cartoon ran in the trade magazine *Editor & Publisher* in which a figure labeled "The Press" is standing tall in a boxing ring, his arm raised as he is proclaimed the "winner and still champ" over a sprawled figure labeled "CompuServe Electronic News Test."[17]

And there were several potential obstacles to working with online services. In late 1993, Jonathan Tasini, Mary Kay Blakely, and several other freelance writers sued the *New York Times, Newsday,* and Time, Inc., for including their articles in the Lexis/Nexis database and, in the case of the *New York Times,* on two CD-ROM products—the *New York Times* OnDisc (NYTO) and General Periodicals OnDisc (GPO)—produced by University Microfilms International. Tasini and the others claimed that licensing their articles to Lexis/Nexis and University Microfilms had violated the authors' copyrights to their work. Eventually the case, which pitted Jonathan Tasini against the *New York Times,* made its way to the United States Supreme Court, which decided in 2001 that in fact the publishers had violated the freelance authors' copyrights.

In the early 1990s, it was clear that if publishers moved vigorously to the online delivery of the news, they would have to redefine their relationships and rework their contracts with their freelance writers as well as the Newspaper Guild, the union representing reporters at many major newspapers.

Like the telephone companies, online services were seen largely as potential competitors. As David Easterly, president of Cox Newspapers, told *The Quill* magazine at the close of 1993, "As journalism . . . is going to be practiced in the twenty-first century, there's a real question about who's going to own it, whether it's the Coxes, Gannetts and the *New York Times,* or whether it's H&R Block [CompuServe's then parent] and Microsoft. So my view is at this point, we need to get really busy proving we can put compelling services up on electronic platforms."[18] Newspapers had to be in the game.

The game changer, however, was America Online. America Online was a relative latecomer to the online service provider arena. It had been founded in 1982 under the name Control Video Corporation with the idea of developing a console, using a telephone line and a modem, on which anybody could download games for the Atari home video player. In 1983, Steve Case, the brother of one of the investors in Control Video, joined the company as a marketing consultant after seeing the module at the semi-annual Consumer Electronics Show. Although Control Video received thousands of orders at the annual show, the video game market slumped, and the company teetered on the edge of bankruptcy. The investors forced the founder of the company out, and the company was relaunched as Quantum Computer Services, offering an online service for Commodore 64 computers. At the time, Commodore 64 computers were the most popular home computer. Called Q-Link, the service started up in 1985.

Over the next few years, Case signed deals to create proprietary online services for Apple Computer, Radio Shack computers, and IBM. In 1989, the company renamed its service for the Apple Computer from Apple-Link to America Online (AOL), and in 1992 the company turned down a $50 million offer to be bought by CompuServe and instead went public. Shortly thereafter, Case was named CEO.[19] In 1993, AOL, with approximately 285,000 subscribers, was still dwarfed by CompuServe, which had more than a million members, and Prodigy, the joint venture between IBM and Sears. But it had several advantages. Like Prodigy, AOL was aimed from the beginning at the home market and to very nontechnical users. Its interface was graphical and easy to use. Second, AOL was the first service to be compatible with Microsoft Windows, which, by 1993, was well on its way to becoming the dominant operating system in computing. Third, AOL launched a very clever and massive marketing campaign that made it easy for people to sign up for the service (and somewhat difficult to get off the service for those who wanted to discontinue). Fourth, AOL had an innovative feature in interactive chat, where volunteer subscribers could conduct chat sessions with other users on specialized topics. And fifth, and probably most important for newspapers, AOL aggressively signed deals with content providers to make their information accessible via AOL.

In one of its first deals, AOL entered into a joint venture with the *Chicago Tribune* to create Chicago Online. As part of the deal, the *Tribune* purchased 10 percent of the company. Shortly thereafter, AOL inked a deal with the *San Jose Mercury News,* which was owned by Knight Ridder, to create the Mercury Center, also in return for a stake in AOL. By this point, the attraction for newspapers to climb on board with AOL or another online service was clear. Kenneth Paulson, a former executive editor of *Florida Today,* who engineered the deal to put his newspaper up on Compu-Serve put it this way: "They've got the infrastructure, they've got the hardware and the customer service, and I recognized that this was not going to be a huge profit-making operation for the newspaper, so I needed to find a way to be able to develop an electronic newspaper at minimal cost." It was not practical, he added, for newspapers to set up their own computer bulletin board services. "The biggest thing is that a daily newspaper doesn't want to be in the business of explaining to people how to hook up their modem," he said. "This was the least expensive, hassle-free way I could come up with to do two things: to provide an electronic service to our readers and to have the reach of the newspaper go beyond our circulation area."[20]

In the wake of the Tribune Company and Knight Ridder deals with AOL, the fastest growing online service at the time, and Gannett's deal with CompuServe, the largest online service, Cox Newspapers and Times Mirror announced that they had signed up with Prodigy, perhaps the best capitalized of the group, to offer local newspaper services. It was the beginning of a trend, newspaper executives opined, in which national networks would carry "brand name" newspaper services.[21] The strategy was clear. AOL, CompuServe, and Prodigy could partner with and help guide news companies as they developed the long-awaited electronic newspaper. Online service providers would help newspapers learn their way around the online world, or so newspaper executives thought. And newspapers were not alone in this approach. In 1994, CNN signed up with CompuServe to offer interactive forums for CNN programs, including Larry King Live. CNN Online, as the service was to be called, would also provide extensive background material and produce CD-ROMs that could link to CompuServe.[22]

RAMPING UP THE INFORMATION SUPERHIGHWAY

On the surface, the deals that media companies were signing with the commercial online service providers did not seem to hold a great deal of potential. After all, even CompuServe, the largest online network, had only around one million subscribers. Any specific city, of course, would have only a small percentage of the total number of subscribers. Moreover, even though the use of personal computing was growing rapidly, the use of modems, which were needed to connect home computers to the telephone network, trailed overall personal computer growth significantly. CompuServe had developed a format called the Graphic Interchange Format (GIF) that allowed graphics to be sent more easily over the network, but information was still transmitted very slowly. Newspapers' efforts with online services were clearly ancillary to their main line of business.

Even as newspapers began to make more extensive and significant forays online in conjunction with the commercial online services, the landscape was shifting rapidly. During the 1992 presidential campaign, candidates Bill Clinton and Al Gore had pledged to build a national data network that would lead to the proliferation of new digital information services. In February 1993, the Clinton-Gore administration released its first policy paper about the National Information Infrastructure (NII); the final report, released that September, ultimately envisioned a seamless web of communication networks, computers, databases, and consumer electronics devices that would make vast amounts of information available to people everywhere, both at work and at play. With the NII in place, people could live anywhere and telecommute to work on the "electronic highway." Regardless of where they lived, students could access top-rated schools, teachers, and learning. Health care information and other important social services could be delivered via the NII as well.

While the report acknowledged that private companies were already active in building an infrastructure along the lines envisioned, it argued that government had an important role to play too. Borrowing a concept from the telephone system, the government had to guarantee universal service, ensuring that everybody would have access to the NII at a reasonable cost. Conceived of as a "network of networks," the government would require that information could pass easily among networks and that the NII was "user-driven." The government had to foster innovation and set the right tax and regulatory policies that encouraged the private sector to continue to invest in the development of the NII. Finally, the federal government had a role in protecting the security and reliability of the network, the privacy of the users, and intellectual property rights.[23]

After the release of the first report in February, which generally urged greater U.S. investment in technology research beyond basic science and mission-oriented military research, John Markoff, a technology reporter for the *New York Times,* suggested that while the public waited to see if the Clinton-Gore administration would fulfill its promise to build a national data network, businesses could sample the NII not through commercial online services such as CompuServe, Prodigy, and AOL, which, he noted, were based on computer technology from the 1960s and 1970s and connected people via telephone lines to a central system, but through the Internet, which he described as a "web of networks with shared software standards, allowing users on one network to reach anywhere into the global thicket." Once the domain of government officials and academic and corporate researchers, by that point many commercial and nonprofit organizations were offering access to the Internet, and many companies both large and small were benefiting.[24] Markoff himself had deep experience with the emerging Internet. Fifteen years earlier, while a news service reporter in the Silicon Valley, Markoff had first logged onto ARPANet. In 1988, he had a front-page story in the *New York Times* about Robert Morris, a student at Cornell University who one night inadvertently released a computer virus that caused the failures of more than 6,000 computers at companies, universities, and military facilities across the United States.[25]

Both the first and second NII reports triggered a flurry of media attention to what was then called the information superhighway. In the first half of 1992, twenty-five articles referring to the information superhighway appeared in selected major newspapers and national news magazines. In the second half of the year, while the presidential campaign was underway, seventy-one articles appeared. In contrast, from January 1993 to August 1993, 562 articles about the information superhighway were published, and after the release of the final NII report in September 1993, through February 1994, 2,873 articles appeared.[26]

The concept of the information superhighway climbed onto the national agenda and into public consciousness, even if nobody knew exactly what it meant. Perhaps the first use of the term *electronic highway* was in a special issue about cable television in *The Nation* magazine in 1970, and subsequently in a book published in 1972 called *The Wired Nation, Cable TV: The Electronic Communication Highway,* in which the author, Ralph Lee Smith, suggested that the cable television system could serve as an kind of electronic highway system that would enable the exchange of ideas and information. For his part, Vice President Al Gore claimed that he coined the term *information highway* at a meeting with computer executives in 1978.[27] Nobody was quite sure if the term *information superhighway* referred to the proposed interactive cable network that could support 500 viewing channels, enhanced services from the regional Bell operating companies, the commercial, governmental, and nonprofit computer networks, or all of them taken together. In 1994, Vice President Gore gave a speech at the Television Academy in Los Angeles during what was called the Superhighway Summit, where he observed that cable, local telephone, long-distance telephone, television, film, computers, and others were headed toward what he called a "Big Bang" of their own. In its wake, the old divisions between different communications companies would be eradicated and everybody would be in the information business. Gore anticipated that there would be information conduits, information providers, information appliances, and information consumers. The role of government, he added, was to ensure that everyone was able to compete with everyone else for the opportunity to provide any service to all willing customers; that the new marketplace reached the entire nation; and that the new infrastructure delivered on the promise of education, economic growth, and job creation. He also pledged to have every classroom, library, hospital, and clinic connected to the National Information Infrastructure by the year 2000.[28]

While nobody knew exactly what the information superhighway was or might become, the race to start traveling down it was on. According to the market research company Jupiter Communication, the number of subscribers to online services jumped more than 28 percent in 1993 and was projected to grow more than 30 percent in 1994. After racking up annual losses of $40 million a year, Prodigy received a new infusion of capital from IBM and Sears and launched a nationwide advertising campaign complete with television commercials. In the face of that vote of confidence for online services in general, AOL scrambled to maintain its position as the fastest growing service with the most aggressive marketing. The online services were looking to build links to the Internet and trying to figure out how to use the higher speed cable network instead of the lower speed telephone network to connect to the home. The online services were positioned as on-ramps to the information superhighway. Hot markets attract new competitors, and the online market was no exception. AT&T, Ziff-Davis, and Apple announced online services, and rumors were flying that Microsoft was thinking about jumping in as well. While the numbers were still small—of the thirty-one million personal computer owners in the United States, only four million used modems—the information superhighway was on a lot of people's minds.[29]

INVESTING IN ONLINE

As the image of an information superhighway facilitating easy and inexpensive access to the world's information gripped the popular imagination, newspapers accelerated their online efforts. In early 1994, the *Washington Post* announced that its subsidiary, Digital Ink, which had been set up to explore online and new media opportunities, had signed a deal with Ziff-Davis Interactive, a division of Ziff-Davis Publishing, to use Ziff-Davis technology to create an electronic version of the *Post,* which would also be available on Ziff-Davis's new online service called Interactive Online. At that time, Ziff-Davis was primarily known as a publisher of computer magazines. *Post* officials explained the agreement with Ziff-Davis by pointing out that it was the only online provider that enabled the publisher to create its own "look and feel" for the electronic edition, preserve the company's direct business relationship with *Post* readers, and use delivery and interface technologies that best served content. The electronic edition would use the *Post*'s logo and design elements and offer more content than appeared in the print edition, including neighborhood news, texts of speeches and press conferences, and a Washington-area entertainment guide.[30] At the end of that year, the *New York Times* announced that it planned to invest $1 billion in electronic media in an effort to reduce the percentage of its revenue stemming from its print publications from 90 percent to around 25 percent. The bulk of the investment was aimed at buying local television stations, but $30 to $40 million was earmarked to fund online services and publishing using CD-ROM. It also announced that the *Boston Globe,* which it owned, would start a computer-based online service within the next six months. The plan was for a subsidiary, Boston Globe Electronic Publishing, to develop interactive news and advertising services in such fields as local entertainment, regional travel, local news, shopping, and real estate.[31]

While most big media companies were still looking for partners to bring them onto the information superhighway, the *Raleigh News and Observer* took a different route. In the spring of 1994, the company set up its own Web site, calling it NandO, as well as offering its customers Internet access. Within fourteen months, NandO had 2,500 household and 10,000 individual subscribers and was providing direct Internet access to 650 households. Frank Daniels III, executive editor of the *News & Observer,* argued that newspaper companies were "missing the boat" by not offering Internet access directly. "You have to have relationships with your customers. They have to have a way to get on the Internet. Do you want them to use UUNet or any of the other local access providers or Microsoft? They can use that and still get to your product. But . . . you provide Internet access because your readers want it," he argued. Moreover, he felt that by setting up his own

Web site, NandO was able to establish its own brand recognition, beyond the awareness of the newspaper itself.[32]

Although different newspapers and magazines were taking different routes to get onto the information superhighway, it was clear throughout the news industry that companies had to gain experience with the online world. A 1995 survey of newspapers and magazines conducted by Steven Ross, a professor at the Columbia University Graduate School of Journalism, and Donald Middleberg, a public relations professional, found that 54 percent of the respondents had plans for online editions in the following year. In 1996, 77 percent indicated they were planning to stake out a position online. At the time of that year's survey, about 15 percent of the daily newspaper respondents and 29 percent of the magazine respondents had some sort of online edition of their publications.[33]

But if newspapers and magazines understood that in some way they had to embrace the online world, in many ways they did so grudgingly. In fact, newspaper and magazine executives worried that online publishing clearly presented a number of serious threats and challenges for newspapers. If they provided too much of their content for free via an online service, would readers still be willing to pay for the newspaper? Would the newspaper's content be cannibalized? Could enough revenue be generated either through revenue sharing with an online service provider (newspapers at the time received about 10 to 20 percent of the time charged for viewers looking at their material) or through selling advertising to make it profitable? There was no model for pricing online advertising. Was there really a big enough opportunity online to make it worthwhile to invest the time, money, and personnel? Some analysts believed that even in 2000, six long years away, online revenues would account for no more than 5 percent of overall revenue for most newspaper companies.[34] Despite the hype, some observers believed as late as 1996 that the future of online news was hardly certain.[35]

The challenge and confusion the explosion of the Internet and online services presented to newspapers in particular can be seen in a speech Arthur Sulzberger Jr., the publisher of the *New York Times,* gave at the Columbia University Graduate School of Journalism breakfast meeting discussing the newspaper of the future and future of newspapers. Sulzberger was agnostic on delivery systems for journalism: "As long as our customers want it on newsprint, I'll do all I can to give it to them on newsprint. If they want it on CD-ROM, I'll try to meet that need. The Internet? That's fine. Hell, if somebody would be kind enough to invent a technology, I'll be pleased to beam it directly into your cortex. We'll have the city edition, the late city edition, and the mind-meld edition."[36]

But, Sulzberger said, the *New York Times* didn't have to be the first newspaper to solve every problem. It just had to be ready to jump when a new technology proved itself. At that moment, Sulzberger did not see an economic model that supported online delivery of journalism. "Right now, I see lots of ways of losing a great deal of money very quickly," he added.

But if news media executives thought they could take a measured approach toward integrating online delivery systems into their work, others disagreed. Computing and networking had stepped up the pace of change and were on the verge of being the catalyst for one of the great entrepreneurial binges in the history of the United States. If newspapers did not adjust, they would die. This was the argument of Michael Crichton, author of best-selling science fiction novels, including *Jurassic Park,* a story in which dinosaurs are cloned back into existence and then run amok. In a widely read and quoted article in *Wired*—a start-up magazine and Web site that had brought a very hip sensibility to the emergence of "digital culture"—Crichton argued that the media's concept of news was outmoded. The media's product is information and the product quality is low, he wrote. It is not reliable, has too much glitz, and is sold without a warranty. Worst, the media had failed to recognize the changing needs of its audience. "Who will be the GM or IBM of the '90s?" he wrote. "The next great American institution to find itself obsolete and outdated, while obstinately refusing to change? I suspect one answer would be the *New York Times* and the commercial networks."[37]

Several trends were leading to the demise of traditional media, according to Crichton. Technology was putting more information in the hands of consumers, so they were demanding higher quality information. Second, technology provided for direct access to information; no longer were consumers dependent on second-hand accounts for events. Third, technology would break traditional media's monopoly on information. He imagined artificial intelligence agents roaming databases and assembling personalized front pages on which the reader could click for more information. How could newspapers compete with that, he wondered. The existing media was too incompetent and superficial to meet the needs of its audience. The title of the essay was "Mediasaurus." The news media were dinosaurs. They would soon be dead.

Crichton's vision of software agents crawling the Web to pluck the information he wanted was not entirely science fiction. At the News in the Future program at the MIT Media Lab, engineers were working on creating just that. Sardonically, they called their electronic newspaper prototype "FishWrap," after the journalist's proverb, "Yesterday's news wraps today's fish." The goal was to provide the kind of personalization Crichton felt was necessary.[38]

Crichton's indictment and dour forecast for the established media was far from extreme. In 1994, Bill Gates, the chairman of Microsoft, opined that with the development of the Internet, "if your business has anything to do with information, you are in trouble."[39] The next year, Michael Conniff, a columnist for the trade magazine *Editor & Publisher,* wrote, "Newspapers are going to get blown away by any Tom, Dick, or Jane Soave Bolla with a computer and an address on the Internet. They'll be lucky if they're still around to write their own obituaries."[40] In 1999, Andy Grove, chairman of Intel, the leading manufacturer of the microprocessors that powered personal computers, told the American Society of Newspaper Editors that if newspapers didn't change rapidly, they would be out of business in three years.[41]

The reasons for their skepticism about the future of newspapers were twofold. First, computer technology traditionally appealed primarily to men, particularly young men, and young people were the demographic group least interested in newspapers.[42] But newspaper readership was aging, and if newspapers could not capture new readers through online delivery, the attrition in readership would accelerate.

Second, while the news media wanted to move cautiously and prudently online, trying to determine how to turn a profit before investing too heavily, nobody else was taking that approach. Even before NSFNet was officially turned over to a private consortium in 1995, America and rest of the world were gripped in one of the greatest entrepreneurial frenzies in history. The dot-com boom was underway. Fortunes would be made, and lost, overnight.

DOT-COM

To a large degree, the dot-com frenzy was kicked off in 1994 when James H. Clark partnered with Marc Andreessen, who had played an instrumental role in developing Mosaic, the Web browser with a graphical user interface, to form the Mosaic Communications Company. Clark was an experienced and successful technology entrepreneur. While an assistant professor at Stanford University, he had devised a way to create extremely vivid graphics on desktop computers and parlayed that idea into a $1.5 billion company called Silicon Graphics. Silicon Graphics was one of the hottest computer companies in Silicon Valley, deeply entrenched in both the research and engineering and the entertainment communities. Mosaic Communications planned to offer a commercial version of the Mosaic Web browser. The concept was provocative, if not without its challenges. At the time, an estimated 20 million people had access to the Internet, and the number of Web sites had jumped in one year from 50 to 7,000. For most people, accessing the Internet and the Web was still challenging. Mosaic made it fun and easy to use even for nontechnical people, particularly as they became more familiar and comfortable with the Microsoft Windows graphical user interface.

There was one catch, however. Created at the National Center for Supercomputing Application (NCSA) at the University of Illinois, as was the custom with development of software in a research setting, Mosaic was already available for free. By 1994, more than 600,000 copies of NCSA's Mosaic had been downloaded and 100,000 copies were being downloaded monthly. And those copies could be freely passed along to anyone who wanted a copy.

Undeterred, Clark invested $3.3 million of his own money in

addition to lining up investments from venture capitalists and hired Andreessen and others to write a new, commercial version of the browser called Mosaic Netscape. Available for Windows, the Apple Macintosh, and Unix computers, Mosaic Netscape ran ten times faster than the academic version of the program. Clark also had a strategy to deal with the idea that a version of Mosaic was available for free: he planned to make Netscape available for free also. The goal was to establish Netscape as the industry standard in the browser market in the same way that Windows had emerged as the industry standard for operating systems. If Netscape was the standard browser, Clark would generate revenue by selling Web server software to companies that wanted to open businesses on the Web. He could include programs that would, for example, make sure credit card information transmitted over the Internet was secure.

Becoming the industry standard would not be easy, however. Ten other companies had also licensed Mosaic from the NCSA.[43] In many ways, Clark's approach defined the culture for businesses that would try to take advantage of the Internet. The consumer software was free. Access to Web sites was free. To the end user, the Internet seemed free for all.

By early 1995, the landscape of cyberspace was clear. Millions of people could log onto online services or the Internet and do virtually anything. All they needed was the software to let them find, access, and do what they wanted to do, and everybody from the largest corporations in the world to computer-savvy teenagers with an Internet account sitting in their bedrooms was in a rush to do just that. Oracle, the maker of the leading commercial database, planned to build software to enable everything from video on demand to home shopping to information searching. Larry Ellison, Oracle's CEO, wanted to beat Microsoft, which had announced plans to invest $150 million to develop software for information and entertainment networks.

The key was making the Internet easy to use, and the World Wide Web was quickly emerging as the laboratory for the most interesting experiments in that regard. The ability to link information found in different files and different computers that could then be accessed by clicking on a highlighted word proved intoxicating to many as they spent hours surfing the Web. Companies large and small began to create their own Web sites, staking their claim to a piece of the Internet. According to Sun Microsystems, in February 1995, there were 27,000 Web servers online and the number was doubling every fifty-three days. Millions of copies of Mosaic were in circulation.[44]

The World Wide Web unleashed a torrent of creativity as companies explored countless ideas about how to profit from the Web. Not surprising, some of those ideas cut directly into newspapers' revenue. For example, the Internet quickly became a medium for companies to post job listings and for job seekers to post their resumes. Not only did individual corporations recruit via the Internet, starting in 1994 with the launch of Monster.com huge job-oriented Web sites with names like HotJobs, JobWeb, CareerMosaic, and others listed hundreds and even thousands of jobs across the country. One Web site, The CareerPath, aimed at people who wanted to relocate, listed the classified help wanted ads from twenty-one newspapers, including the *New York Times,* the *Los Angeles Times,* and the *Chicago Tribune.* In most cases, job listings scheduled to run in the Sunday newspaper were available at The CareerPath on Saturday.[45] The advantages of searching for appropriate job openings online rather than scanning a newspaper were eminently obvious. Job seekers could search listings by key words, salary levels, location, and other criteria. The sites often offered advice about cover letters and resumes and even facilitated the initial application process. As with so many Web services, they were free to users.

In 1995, eBay launched what it called an electronic classified advertising service. People could post items for sale and buyers could bid for them online. After a specified period of time, the item would go to the highest bidder. As with most good ideas, eBay was not the only company that saw the Internet as a more effective platform for classified advertising than what existed. By 1998, there were at least 150 World Wide Web sites running auctions of various sorts, auctions that competed with the classified advertising in newspapers.[46]

Internet start-up companies in this period were different from traditional start-up companies. Since the Internet was so new, it was hard to judge just how big these companies would ultimately grow. Consequently, many of them were able to go public, raising enormous amounts of money and making their founders wealthy beyond belief. For example, in 1998, just three years after it was founded, eBay completed a successful initial public offering, selling 3.5 million shares at $18 each, raising $63 million. The offering placed a value on the whole company at $715 million. The stake retained by the company founder, Pierre Omidyar, who was thirty-one years old at the time, was estimated to be $274 million.[47]

The potential riches offered by a successful Internet start-up did not escape enterprising journalists either. With an active tradition of entrepreneurial activity reaching back to the very first news publications and continuing through hardy one-person operations like I. F. Stone's news weekly in the 1960s and 1970s, independent news operations were venerated in the industry. Creative magazine-like publications, conceptually linked in many ways to fanzines—small publications generally produced by one or a few people geared to a small community devoted to a particular topic and often photocopied or otherwise inexpensively produced— had circulated through the Internet long before the Web was created. Net Audio Bits, which contained reviews of compact discs and other music-related material, began circulating through the Internet in 1987. Athene: the Online Magazine of Amateur Creative Writing was first published in 1989, the same year Quanta, a science fiction and fantasy e-zine appeared. Before the advent of the World Wide Web, there were perhaps a hundred or so e-zines being circulated through the Internet. As with all Web-related activities, however, as the Web grew, so did the number of e-zines.[48]

By the mid-1990s, however, more ambitious publishing projects were launched. After working without a contract for a year, in November 1994, the employees at the *San Francisco Chronicle* and the *San Francisco Examiner* walked out on strike. The *Examiner,* the newspaper with which William Randolph Hearst had launched his career, was the weaker newspaper in a joint operating agreement. David Talbot and several of his colleagues decided it was time to leave the newspaper. With $100,000 seed money from Apple Computer, in 1995 they launched Salon Magazine, a biweekly online compendium of political and social commentary, cultural criticism, and coverage of the arts. Over time, Salon began to build an audience and build a business. It worked to answer the question: would educated, relatively high-brow readers—the kind who might subscribe to *The New Republic* or *The New York Review of Books,* return regularly to read a Web site?[49]

Unlike e-zines, Salon attracted high-profile writers, publishing online diaries by James Carville, who had masterminded the election of President Bill Clinton in 1992, and the gothic fiction writer Anne Rice. Carville also agreed to participate in a chat session with Salon readers; Rice answered e-mail queries as she toured America promoting her latest book.[50] At the end of 1996, *Time* magazine tabbed Salon as the best Web site of the year. In making the award, *Time* called Salon a "refuge" in the "wastelands of the Web," adding that, "while many have tried, few have succeeded in building a truly compelling magazine (or 'zine) on the World Wide Web ... [Salon] does almost everything right. It looks fresh and dramatic. It loads fast, even on pokey dial-up modems. And it features first-rate writers."[51]

But the reading habits of Web surfers were different than the reading habits of magazine subscribers. Over time, Talbot noticed, updating the site biweekly just didn't work. Viewers would only return when new information was available. Salon became less like a magazine and more like a newspaper, with new content posted every day. Readership began to climb from 400,000 unique visitors a month, to more than one million visitors a month when the site published a high-profile story. By mid-1999, Salon was attracting over 800,000 unique visitors a month.[52]

Building a Web site that could generate high traffic was only one piece of the plan. Besides being a magazine, Salon was also an Internet start-up company. In June 1999, Salon went public, selling 2.5 million shares at $10.50 a share. The deal valued the company at approximately $100 million. When Salon, which was producing ten Web sites at the time, reported its first quarter revenues as a public company, the company stressed that it was promoting itself through radio and print ads and had a television advertising campaign planned, and that it was demonstrating that an online publication could do things a print publication could not. Among other deals, Salon announced it had completed an agreement with AvantGo to distribute Salon.com's content on PalmPilots and other personal digital assistants popular at the time. It signed an e-commerce agreement with CultureFinder.com to offer their arts and entertainment ticketing engine and content to the Salon audience. The company noted that it had revenues of $1 million for the quarter, but its net loss on an operating basis for the period had grown to $4.6 million, with a one-time dividend payout driving the overall net loss to $16 million or $10.10 per share.[53]

Salon was not the only Internet start-up publishing effort that went public. The financial news Web site, TheStreet.com, which was spearheaded by James Cramer, a former trader for Goldman Sachs and a well-known financial journalist, went public in May 1999, offering 5.5 million shares at around $19 a share. The stock jumped to $75 a share on the first day of trading. That year sales reached $14 million and the company lost $28 million.[54] Perhaps the most dramatic Internet start-up involved *Wired* magazine and the Hotwired Web site. *Wired* was launched in 1993 with the idea that far from being the domain of techies, the digital world was trendy, hip, and cutting edge. It soon caught the imagination not only of computer aficionados but the public just waking up to the possibilities offered by personal computing and the Internet. Among the coterie of people around *Wired* magazine were Nicholas Negroponte, the director of the MIT Media Lab and a prominent spokesperson for the revolutionary potential of computing; the science fiction writer William Gibson, who is given credit for coining the term *cyberspace* and much of the other argot associated with the online world; and Stewart Brand, well known from *The Whole Earth Catalogue* and The WELL. A line attributed to Gibson—"the future has arrived, it is just unevenly distributed"—became one of *Wired*'s guiding principles. In 1996, *Wired* tried to complete an initial public offering that would have valued the company at $400 million, even though its magazine and

Web site had combined revenue in the range of $20 million and it was losing $500,000 a month. Nonetheless, *Wired* and HotWired were considered to be very hot.[55]

The valuations put on these Web sites put pressure on established news media to move more aggressively into online ventures. Why couldn't traditional media—the dinosaurs, in Michael Crichton's essay—realize the same kind of value if they moved onto the Web? The stock market did not seem to care if the Web sites made money or not. Profitability, or even revenue, were not the metrics by which companies could be evaluated. The number of "eyeballs" a Web site could attract and how long users spent on the site, a measure known as "stickiness," were considered more important. But Salon, TheStreet.com, and even HotWired were small and could be easily snapped up by larger media companies. In fact, the *New York Times* invested $15 million in TheStreet .com and Rupert Murdoch's News Corp. invested $7.5 million in TheStreet.[56] Perhaps irrationally overvalued, start-up Web publishing companies posed no real threat to the established media.

The company that did pose a threat to media companies was Microsoft. In the mid-1990s, Microsoft moved aggressively into the online world from four different directions. It launched MSN, the Microsoft network that provided Internet access to individuals as well as online content. It created a portfolio of city directories serving up local information. It partnered with NBC to create MSNBC, a combination cable and Internet news channel. And it launched Slate, a Web site of ideas and politics. Even before Microsoft launched MSN in August 1995, its plans were under scrutiny by the U.S. Justice Department. Microsoft's strategy was to integrate the software necessary to connect to MSN, which would provide Internet access as well as other online services, with the next release of its operating system, Windows 95. Then, when using Windows 95, a single click on a screen icon automatically connected a user to MSN. The process would be much easier than dialing into other online services, which usually required a specialized program that online services company distributed for free either through the mail or through deals with computer hardware vendors. In early June, the Justice Department requested information from CompuServe, Prodigy, and AOL about the impact of Microsoft's approach on competition in the online services arena. Analysts anticipated that Microsoft could sell as many as 20 million copies of Windows 95 within the first three months of its release so that even if only a small percentage of the users opted for MSN, it could leap ahead of AOL's 2.5 million subscribers within a short period of time. At that point, Microsoft had already been investigated twice on antitrust issues. For its part, Microsoft argued that it would simply be a new player in an emerging market and its entry would enhance competition.[57]

In early August, the Justice Department announced it would not block the release of Windows 95 and the launch of MSN with it. Prior to the launch, MSN revealed that it had already enrolled more than 70 content providers ranging from newspapers to special-interest magazines and online shopping merchants. More ominously for the news media, it had also staffed a newsroom with sixty journalists to produce a worldwide news service.[58] Journalists immediately wondered how Microsoft, which made so much news, would be able to cover itself objectively. Moreover, as a technology company, journalists worried that technologists and marketers would dominate the editorial decisions at MSN, leading all of journalism on a race to the bottom in terms of quality, at least quality journalism as defined by professional journalists.[59]

On a more fundamental level, many industry observers believed that Microsoft was trying to use its control of the Windows operating system to monopolize the Internet. In addition to MSN, it bundled Internet Explorer, a Web browser and a direct competitor to Netscape, with Windows 95, in what Netscape claimed was an effort to drive it from the marketplace. Moreover, Microsoft was accused of incorporating technology into the Web page editor Frontpage so that it would create pages that would only display properly on Web sites running on the Internet Information Server, Microsoft's Web server technology. If Microsoft could monopolize the Internet, the thinking went, it could also control the news flow on the Internet as well. With that in mind, on May 18, 1998, the U.S. Department of Justice and twenty state attorneys general sued Microsoft for engaging in anticompetitive and exclusionary practices. Among the complaints, the suit alleged that Microsoft entered into anticompetitive agreements with virtually all of the nation's largest and most popular online and Internet service providers, requiring them to use Microsoft proprietary standards and tools that would make their sites more effective when viewed through Internet Explorer than when viewed through competing Internet browsers.[60]

Microsoft's moves with MSN raised fears reminiscent of an AT&T-like monopoly which had so worried the news media in the early days of the availability of online information. But there was no Computer I decision on the books to restrain Microsoft from creating content. In July 1996, the joint venture with NBC called MSNBC went live. MSNBC was an experiment linking network television, cable television, and the Internet. With a staff of two hundred journalists, MSNBC had a cable operation in Fort Lee, New Jersey, and an interactive Internet site on Microsoft's campus in Redmond, Washington. The goal was to create synergy between television and the Internet and to figure out ways to get viewers and users to interact with the news.[61]

With both partners having very deep pockets, MSNBC represented a long-term commitment to fostering the synthesis of the Internet and broadcasting. But in some ways, a more limited project marked a major turning point in the perceived maturation of online journalism. In July 1996, Microsoft launched Slate, an online journal of politics and ideas, a sort of Web version of *The New Republic* or, in the beginning, *The New Yorker.* For its editor, it recruited Michael Kinsley.

The choice shocked many people. The forty-four-year-old Kinsley was considered something of a wunderkind in the journalism axis that ran from Boston to Washington, D.C. He had been named editor of *The New Republic* at age twenty-eight, writing the magazine's celebrated TRB column, which was syndicated nationally. Also, while in his early thirties, he had been the editor of *Harper's,* one of the nation's most prestigious magazines of arts, culture, and ideas. In 1989, Kinsley had assumed the "liberal" chair on the CNN news analysis show *Crossfire.* Columnist, former Nixon administration aide, and future presidential candidate Pat Buchanan sat in the "conservative" seat. The guests sat in the middle.

Kinsley had approached Steven Ballmer, the executive vice president of Microsoft, who Kinsley knew from their days together at Harvard University, about the position when Kinsley heard that Microsoft was looking to hire a "big time" editor. Eventually, Kinsley turned down a competing offer at a higher salary to work for Slate, becoming the most prominent journalist to cross over from traditional print and broadcast media to the world of online publishing. Not only did Kinsley join Slate, he relocated from Washington, D.C., to Seattle. The move signaled that online journalism must be taken seriously.[62]

The established media were not idly standing by. In late 1994,

Time Warner created the Pathfinder Web site, a portal for four-teen of the company's magazines, and within six months the site was receiving three million hits, described as "requests for infor-mation," a week. In May 1995, Condé Nast launched CondeNet, a subsidiary charged with getting fourteen of its magazines onto the Web. Another large publishing company, Hachette Filipacchi Médias, said that it would have twenty of its magazines online by the middle of 1996.[63] By spring 1995, some Wall Street analysts argued that Pathfinder, which had not yet earned any revenue, would be worth $1 billion as an independent company. That pre-diction did not prove to be accurate, and three years later the author Michael Wolff chronicled the high cost of Time Warner's spectacular failure with Pathfinder in his book, *Burn Rate.*

THE RULES OF THE GAME

When Michael Kinsley moved to Slate, he told the *New York Times,* "The thing that I really love doing is editing a magazine, and this seemed to me to be an interesting new way to do it."[64] A new me-dium is often understood in terms of the medium that preceded it—television was radio with pictures and early phonographs were described in terms of talking books—but as participation in on-line services and the Internet grew, it became increasingly clear that an entirely new communications medium had emerged, a medium that could not be likened to any other. Decentralized by design, the Internet had no official governing body. The two organizations with the most influence over the Internet's actual operation, the Internet Engineering Task Force (IETF) and the Internet Corporation for Assigned Names and Numbers (ICANN), were both nongovernmental agencies. The IETF worked in conjunction with the World Wide Web Consortium (W3C) and the International Standards Organization (ISO) to set the standards and protocols for the infrastructure itself. ICANN managed the assignment of domain names to new Web sites. The Internet was not like newspapers, which emerged in a period of great social upheaval and led to a regulatory scheme anchored in the freedom of speech protected by the First Amendment. Nor was the Internet like broadcasting, which was regulated by national governments from shortly after its inception. Whose rules would govern speech on the Internet was not clear.

This issue was complicated by two novel factors. The Internet was a global network. Generally speaking, people in the United States could access information on servers in Finland just as easily as they could access information on servers in Philadelphia. So even if the United States banned material in Philadelphia, that content could still be only a mouse click away from virtually anyone. Second, the culture of what can be called speech on the Internet had always been rough and tumble, often spilling over the edges of what might be considered generally acceptable. Not surprising for a communication network heavily used by young men at the time, there was a considerable amount of pornographic material to be found in Usenet newsgroups and other nooks and crannies in the online world. There was no shortage of extreme images online, including child pornography, graphically violent sexual pornography, and bestiality.[65]

The availability of pornography and what should be done about it and by whom was only one of many questions raised by the growth of online services. When Vice President Gore described the Clinton administration's vision for the National Information Infrastructure at the Superhighway Summit in 1993, he argued that the free flow of content could not be subjected to "artificial constraints at the hands of either government regulators or would-be monopolists." [66] But Gore's visions of an unregulated communication medium anchored in the tradition of free speech raised several tangled issues. Traditionally on LISTSERV discussion groups, on computer bulletin boards, and in Usenet newsgroups, discussions were robust, uninhibited, and not infrequently vituperative. Sometimes comments crossed the line into libel and defamation. Was the Internet going to be regulated more along the lines of a common carrier, required to transmit anything, or more along the lines of a newspaper, where editors selected the material to be published?[67] The concern was that if online service operators exercised judgment and only carried certain approved information, bottlenecks would emerge. Ironically, common carriers were generally regulated by governmental agencies while newspapers enjoyed greater First Amendment protection from governmental interference.

As vexing, if libelous or defamatory information was posted on a computer bulletin board, was the operator of the board responsible? That question was addressed in the 1991 case of *Cubby, Inc. v. CompuServe, Inc.* At that time, online services like CompuServe routinely contracted with outsiders to manage their online forums. CompuServe supported a forum about journalism, with one section called Rumorville, managed by an outside contractor named Don Fitzpatrick. Rumorville contained information, or rumors, about broadcast journalism and journalists. Fitzpatrick would upload information to the Rumorville computer bulletin board daily, and then, without intervention from CompuServe staff, the information would be immediately available to CompuServe subscribers. CompuServe did not receive any payment from Fitzpatrick, and Fitzpatrick did not receive compensation from CompuServe.

In 1990, Robert Blanchard and Cubby, Inc., launched an online bulletin board service called Skuttlebut, which was designed to compete with Rumorville. In April of that year, Blanchard alleged that Rumorville had made the claim that individuals at Skuttlebut gained access to information first published by Rumorville "through some back door" and that Blanchard had been fired from his previous employer, WABC. It also described Skuttlebut as a "new start-up scam." Blanchard and Cubby sued for libel, business disparagement, and unfair competition. The legal question was whether CompuServe had "published" the offending statements or had acted merely as a "distributor." While libel law holds that if people repeat a libelous statement, they are as liable as the person who first uttered it, the idea that a distributor must have an idea about the content of a publication before it can be held liable was untested as far as online distribution was concerned. CompuServe, the U.S. District Court of New York ruled, functioned more like a for-profit electronic library or book store. Once it provided access to a publication, it has no way of knowing its own content, particularly if the publication was part of a forum managed by a company unrelated to CompuServe. "CompuServe," the court wrote, "has no more editorial control over such a publication than does a public library, bookstore, or newsstand, and it would be no more feasible for CompuServe to examine every publication it carries for potentially defamatory statements than it would be for any other distributor to do so. . . . A computerized database is the functional equivalent of a more traditional news vendor, and the inconsistent application of a lower standard of liability to an electronic news distributor such as CompuServe than that which is applied to a public library, bookstore, or newsstand would impose an undue burden on the free flow of information."[68]

Indeed, if CompuServe had lost the case, an employee would

have had to read every posting to every forum and perhaps open and read every piece of e-mail, Kent Stuckey, CompuServe's general manager, contended.[69]

Although in theory the Cubby decision seems to protect online service providers, and later Web sites, that allow viewers to post their opinions against libel and defamation charges, in practice the situation was still not clear cut. In October 1994, several anonymous messages appeared on the Money Talk bulletin board hosted by Prodigy with derogatory statements about a Long Island stock brokerage called Stratton Oakmont. It referred to the company's president as a "soon to be proven criminal" and labeled a recent underwriting deal the company had completed as fraud. The posts remained on the bulletin board for two weeks. After researching the matter, Prodigy determined that the messages had been posted from an account of a former employee who had left the online service three years earlier. The employee denied posting the messages. Stratton Oakmont sued for $200 million in damages and, to expedite the settlement, asked for a ruling as to whether Prodigy was a publisher or a distributor. Much to the surprise of the legal community, acting New York State Supreme Court Justice Stuart Ain decided that Prodigy was not a distributor. Since the company used filtering software to prescreen messages for racial slurs and obscenities, and because Prodigy marketed itself as a "family-oriented computer network," Prodigy exhibited editorial control and could be sued as a publisher, the judge reasoned. Although the case was settled out of court, the ruling in the Stratton Oakmont case posed a serious threat to free speech on the Internet.[70] Kent Stuckey's dire forecast became a distinct possibility.

The limits of, and the liability for, speech on the Internet was only one of a raft of sticky legal issues that had to be addressed. The whole concept of linking, the central technology driving the

World Wide Web, raised significant intellectual property issues. In 1997, the *Washington Post* and other news organizations sued Total News, Inc. Total News had created a frame around their Web page on which they could display advertising. Inside the frame, they displayed content from the *Post* and other newspapers. The plaintiffs argued that Total News diluted and detracted from their trademarks. The suit was settled when Total News agreed to remove the frame and link to the newspaper sites using standard hyperlinks. But even simple linking raised questions. It wasn't until the year 2000, in a case involving Ticketmaster and a competitor called Tickets.com, that a U.S. district court ruled that linking to material on another Web site without authorization in and of itself did not constitute a violation of the copyright act.

Virtually every aspect of the online world appeared to be fraught with legal peril. The basic address for a Web site is known as the domain name. For example, the domain name for Fox News is www.foxnews.com. Of course, the name Fox News is trademarked. If somebody registered a domain name containing the name of a trademarked company, would the domain name automatically receive trademark protection? On the flip side, could somebody register the domain name of a trademarked company and demand payment as compensation, a process that became known as cyber squatting? The Internet made it easy to copy music, computer games, and other digital content and make that available to anybody who wanted it. How could copyright holders' interests be protected? How much privacy could participants expect online and how much could they get? What was the liability for defamatory material that was archived? Did Web site and computer database companies have to go back into their archives to correct errors?

As lawsuits generated by these questions and others worked

their way through the American legal system, there were international questions to be resolved too. Well before the World Wide Web connected servers around the world in unpredictable ways, it was obvious that regulating the Internet would be challenging if not impossible via national press laws. In a dramatic example of the problem, in June 1991, the body of a young girl was found encased in seven blocks of concrete at the bottom of Lake George in Ontario, Canada. The following spring, 15-year-old Kristen Dawn French's naked body was found in the brush on the side of a road two weeks after she had been kidnapped. The following year, Paul Bernardo and his wife Karla Homolka were charged with these heinous crimes. Homolka quickly pleaded guilty and was sentenced to prison. Bernardo, however, who also faced fifty-three other related and unrelated charges, had not yet been tried. Fearing that Homolka's trial would jeopardize the integrity of Bernardo's trial, the judge closed the proceedings to all but accredited Canadian journalists, families of the accused and the victims, and a few court officials. He also forbade publication of any of the details of Homolka's trial until after Bernardo's case ended.

But even though the Canadian media generally adhered to the judge's order, the ban could not be enforced. As word about the trials circulated, several computer bulletin boards were set up to publish information as well as a Usenet newsgroup called alt .fan.karla-homolka, established by Justin Wells and Ken Chasse at Chasse's Sonic Interzone BBS, a public access bulletin board in Toronto. Placing the newsgroup in the alt.fan hierarchy was meant as a wry comment. During the course of the trial and throughout the publication ban, rumors and facts about the trial as well as spirited discussion about the actions of Bernardo and Homolka and about the publication ban itself were carried in Usenet newsgroups and on computer bulletin boards.[71]

While the Internet could be used to disseminate information in violation of national press rules, it also potentially made U.S. publishing companies vulnerable to press laws in foreign countries. Despite the complexity of the task, some countries tried to regulate the flow of information into their countries. For example, for months in the mid-1990s, China blocked the Web sites of the *Wall Street Journal* and other Dow Jones publications. The ban may have been in part because articles in the *Wall Street Journal* suggested that the Internet could be a forum for dissent in China.[72] China wasn't the only country attempting to police the Internet. In 1995, Singapore had only one Internet gateway into the country. Its government promised that it would prosecute people who posted subversive material.[73]

The Internet truly was like the Wild West. Torrents of people were rushing into a space where there were few laws and those laws were hard to enforce. Starting in 1995, the United States Congress made an effort to define the contours of free speech on the Internet. That year, Senator James Exon, a Democrat from Nebraska, and Senator Slade Gorton, a Republican from Washington, introduced a bill to "protect the public from the misuse of the telecommunications network and telecommunications devices and facilities."[74] Titled the Communications Decency Act of 1995, the bill had several stipulations. Perhaps most important, the bill proposed to make commercial online services, the Internet, and computer bulletin board services liable for messages, files, or other content carried on its network including the private conversations or messages exchanged between two consenting individuals. The most visible target of this section of the bill was pornography, which was rampant and freely available throughout the Internet and had been for many years. Wading into the thickets of obscenity regulation, the law would subject anyone who "makes, transmits, or otherwise makes available any comment, request, suggestion, proposal, image, or other communication" which is "obscene, lewd, lascivious, filthy, or indecent" using a "telecommunications device" to a fine of $100,000 or two years in prison.[75] By including the word "indecent," Exon and Gorton were proposing to deal with the Internet using the same kind of regulatory approach taken in broadcasting, rather than the approach taken with print publications. In a seminal case, *FCC v. Pacifica Foundation* in 1978, the United States Supreme Court ruled that the Federal Communications Commission could regulate "indecent" speech in broadcasting. In other forms of media, governments could only ban "obscene" speech that met the three-part definition laid out in *Miller v. California* in 1973.

Civil libertarians and free speech advocates immediately viewed the Communications Decency Act as a serious threat to free speech on the Internet. Given the interactive nature of online communication, free speech advocates thought that it should be the responsibility of parents and others to protect children from inappropriate online material. But the argument was not solely about safeguarding children. Free speech advocates argued that institutions, organizations, agencies, and individuals with small budgets could not afford to put the technology in place to ensure that children could not access material that might be deemed "indecent." With these regulations, providing content on the Internet could be restricted only to parties with significant financial resources. The Internet's promise to provide ordinary citizens a medium to communicate well beyond their immediate circle of friends and families would be destroyed.[76]

The Communications Decency Act was passed as part of the Telecommunications Act of 1996, which represented the first sweeping reform of the telecommunications system since 1934.

The reform touched virtually every aspect of the telecommunications industry, and it was intended, in the words of President Bill Clinton, who signed it into law in February 1996, "to stimulate investment, promote competition, and provide open access for all citizens to the Information Superhighway."[77] Among its more notable components was the elimination of many of the barriers placed on telephone companies during the breakup of AT&T in the 1980s, including allowing telephone companies to enter the cable television market. In return for enabling open access and competition in local telephone service, regional telephone companies could reenter the long-distance telephone arena. The restriction on the number of local television stations the television networks could own was lifted. And the act criminalized the intentional transmission of "any comment, request, suggestion, image, or other communications which is obscene, lewd, lascivious, filthy, or indecent. . . ." and established an "anti-flame" provision, prohibiting any computer network transmission for the purpose of annoying or harassing the recipients of messages.[78]

A coalition led by the American Civil Liberties Union immediately filed suit challenging the constitutionality of the Communications Decency Act (CDA). The case quickly made its way to the Supreme Court, and in 1997, the Court ruled that the CDA violated the First Amendment. Online communication, the Court ruled, should be afforded the same broad First Amendment protection enjoyed by newspapers and other print publications, and the CDA unconstitutionally imposed a ban on specific content. The CDA had failed to define the banned content specifically enough to pass constitutional muster and consequently suppressed speech that adults had a constitutional right to send and receive.[79]

The Supreme Court ruling was an important victory for the protection of free speech on the Internet in the United States.

But another unchallenged section of the CDA was also significant. Addressing the conflict in rulings raised by the Cubby and Stratton Oakmont cases, Section 320 of the CDA stated that providers and users of interactive computer services should not be treated as publishers or speakers of any information provided by another information content provider. In terms of information posted by third parties, Internet service providers and Web site operators were to have the stronger safeguards afforded to distributors of information, such as libraries and book stores.[80] That year, an anonymous user of AOL posted messages on a bulletin board advertising T-shirts with tasteless slogans referring to the bombing of the federal courthouse in Oklahoma City in 1995. The messages listed a telephone number to call. The posting was a malicious hoax, and the victim, Kenneth Zeran, was inundated with derogatory and threatening telephone calls. Zeran demanded that AOL remove the message, which it did. But in accordance with its policies, it refused to publish a retraction. When Zeran continued to receive harassing telephone calls as often as one every two minutes, he sued AOL for negligence, contending that distributors of information are liable for the distribution of material which they knew or should have known was of a defamatory character. The court, however, ruled that holding AOL liable would contradict Section 320 of the CDA, which intended for service providers to regulate themselves.[81]

WHAT KIND OF JOURNALISM IS IT?

While the legal issues intertwined with the emergence of online communication were being sorted out, a more pressing issue confronted the news media. The Internet and online access to information and online communications were already having a dramatic impact on news reporting, but the role the Web and other online services would play in delivering the news to an audience was still uncertain. Despite the millions of people signed up for online services and jumping on the Internet, the actual audiences accessible at any one time were relatively small. On its largest night in 1996, AOL had 70,000 users online at once. In that year, ABC World News Tonight averaged 13 million viewers a night.[82] Could Web sites actually reach television-sized audiences? With the proliferation of information providers setting up on the Web, how would users determine what information was credible and what wasn't? Should many of those information providers even be considered journalists or were they better described as something else? Perhaps most important, as early as 1994, Marshall Loeb, the managing editor of *Fortune* magazine, and others had argued that it was the content that would ultimately determine the future of the information superhighway.[83] With online distribution of information, how could newspapers and news broadcasts safeguard their most valuable asset—their content?

News events themselves set in motion the processes that would provide answers. One of the first events occurred on Wednesday, April 19, 1995, at 9:02 A.M., when a rented truck packed with more than two tons of explosives exploded in front of the Alfred P. Murrah Building in Oklahoma City. The nine-story structure housed offices of the U.S. federal government as well as a day care center on the second floor for the children of employees, who were arriving to start their workday at the time. The blast, set off by Timothy McVeigh, claimed the lives of 168 people, including nineteen children, and wounded 500 others. It was the worst incident of domestic terrorism on U.S. soil in history.

As could be expected, after the blast the news media rushed

to provide coverage, looking for answers for the most basic questions—what had happened; how did it happen; and who was responsible for this heinous crime? But reporters from the nation's leading newspapers and television networks were not the only people providing information to the public as fast as possible. As the event unfolded, the telephone lines into and out of Oklahoma City quickly jammed. At that point, IONet, an Internet service provider, began receiving e-mail messages asking for details about the blast. "We realized they could get to us through the Internet. So it dawned on us that we were an information provider, and we'd better get information out of the city for people who were trying to find out what's going on," Phyllis Johnson, a co-owner of the service, told Newsbytes, an online news service, two days later. Johnson sent a team to cover the explosion and over the next two days, the number of visits the company's Web site received jumped from an average of fifty a day to 19,000. IONet also posted a live video feed from a local television station via CU-SeeMe, an early Internet video-conferencing technology, and lists of hospital survivors, composite drawings of the bombing suspects, and links to other information services and providers.[84]

IONet was not the only online effort. Journalism students at the University of Oklahoma quickly created a Web page providing coverage of the event. That page linked to the National Institute for Computer-Assisted Reporting, which posted first-person accounts by blast survivors and a gallery of photographs taken at the scene.[85] Aaron Dickey, a contributor to *Wired* magazine, established a LISTSERV e-mail discussion group to share information and thoughts about the events. Twenty-four hours later, 500 people had signed up.[86]

AOL, CompuServe, and Prodigy also worked diligently to get the most updated information to their users, creating forums for discussions and links to computer bulletin boards around Oklahoma City. Much of the coverage was text-based. Nonetheless, "watching what happened online in this case convinces me we're looking at a fourth medium, a new kind of newsroom," Ann Brill, director of the Digital Missourian, part of the University of Missouri School of Journalism, told the *Toronto Star* less than two weeks after the event.[87]

Providing a medium to report on the events of Oklahoma City was only one part of the equation. The Internet also offered a platform to discuss the events as well. Discussion rippled through Usenet newsgroups, where there was no shortage of conspiracy theories. The Federal Bureau of Investigation was accused of orchestrating the blasts. An incorrect report that the suspects were of Middle Eastern origin circulated widely online. As law enforcement officials and journalists began to troll Usenet and the Web for information about the blast, it became very clear that militant militia groups like the one to which Timothy McVeigh belonged used the Internet to recruit members. Moreover, there was no shortage of information about how to construct explosives like the kind McVeigh used. In fact, discussions of bomb-making jumped significantly after the blast.[88]

The Oklahoma City tragedy was an early example of both the strengths and weaknesses of online journalism. Breaking news was published quickly and news could be gathered from nontraditional sources. The Internet also provided a vehicle for ordinary citizens to get involved in "reporting" information and discussing the story. But as more information from more sources could be accessed virtually around the world, the issue of how to judge the credibility of information found online became increasingly acute.

It was another tragedy that raised the heat generated by the issue of online credibility to the boiling point. On July 17, 1996, TWA Flight 800, a Boeing 747 jumbo jet bound for Paris, exploded minutes after taking off from New York's John F. Kennedy Airport. All 230 people on board were killed. The airliner had shown no signs of duress nor had the pilot radioed a need for help prior to the explosion. The FBI was called in to determine the cause of the blast. While rumors abounded that the plane had been accidently shot down by a missile fired by the U.S. military during a training exercise, both the FBI and the National Transportation Safety Board had ruled out that possibility.[89]

On Friday, November 8, 1996, Pierre Salinger, a longtime correspondent for ABC News, the former press secretary for President John F. Kennedy, and at that point vice chairman of Burson-Martsteller, a very prominent Washington-based public relations firm, called a press conference to make a shocking revelation. He had obtained a document that showed that the U.S. Navy had, in fact, inadvertently shot down TWA 800. The Navy had been testing missiles in the area and had been told that planes would be flying at 21,000 feet or higher. TWA Flight 800 was flying at 13,000 because another plane was above it. Salinger had obtained the document from French Intelligence sources in August, and the document had been posted to the Internet in September, he said. Salinger held the news conference at an aviation conference on the French Riviera. "The truth must come out," he said.[90]

U.S. officials vigorously denied the charges, and within a day, Salinger admitted that he had relied on old Internet postings. The document he had shown at the news conference matched a posting on an Internet site called Cloaks and Daggers on September 19. It was a letter written by Richard Russell, a former United Air Lines pilot, which had circulated on the Internet for months. At that point, the coverage of the event shifted focus to the credibility problem of information on the Internet and how journalists should treat that information. CNN had apparently seen the same information as Salinger in August but discounted it. But information on the Internet had its own sort of cachet and credibility, even if it was undeserved. Information on the Internet, "has been blessed by the computer, and sprinkled with techno holy water," Clifford Stoll, something of a celebrity in the computer community for unmasking one of the earliest versions of computer fraud, told the *New York Times*. "The gossip that comes across the Internet comes in precisely the same format as does professional news, Wall Street reports, and important other factual information." The *Times*'s reporter, Matthew Wald, concluded, "Thus ordinary scuttlebutt at the watercooler (a redundancy; a scuttlebutt was the small barrel on ships where sailors got their drinking water) is now for the whole world to read and believe."[91] As a news source, much of the information on the Internet was discredited in the eyes of the community of professional journalists.[92]

Despite the issues professional journalists had about the credibility of much of the information on the Internet, people continued to flock online and news was among the most popular content. A study by the market research company FIND/SVP, Inc., predicted the number of online users would grow from 31.3 million in 1997 to 45 million before the start of 1999. Sixty-six percent of the survey respondents went online for news, the most popular category. Sixty percent looked for news online every day.[93] Another study in 1998, this one commissioned by MSNBC, reported that 20.1 million U.S. residents used the Internet as a source for news, a little more than 53 percent of the 38 million people in the U.S. thought to access the Internet. In fact, Internet users were perceived as a community hungry for news. In the MSNBC study, 82 percent of Internet users regularly read newspapers, 74 percent regularly watched broadcast TV for news, 71 percent said they watched cable news shows, and 57 percent read news-related magazines. "The Internet news usage behavior pattern is shaping up similar to broadcast television in terms of weekday use and is used more than cable television, newspapers, and magazines during that same period of time," Merrill Brown, editor in chief of MSNBC on the Internet, told *Editor & Publisher.*[94]

Established newspapers and magazines as well as start-up companies accelerated their creation of Web sites to meet that perceived need. As with the early days of radio and television, some venues did not want to issue reporting credentials to reporters working for online publications. For example, when Legi-Slate was first created, it was a news database and online document delivery service. In the mid-1990s, it expanded its news-gathering capabilities. But when Legi-Slate applied to the Standing Committee of Correspondents, which issues credentials for covering Congress, it required significant cajoling for its reporters to obtain press credentials. The fact that Legi-Slate was owned by the *Washington Post* did not help a great deal.[95]

The problem was not only with Congress. At the Final Four of the NCAA college basketball championship tournament, reporters from USA Today Online were not credentialed. The NCAA explained that it retained the rights for videotex, audiotext, and online reporting. For a time, the NFL did not allow news photographers to post their photographs on the Web, and reporters for the ESPN Sportszone Web site, which claimed 250,000 daily viewers, were denied credentials to the Summer Olympic games in Atlanta in 1996.[96]

The organizations refusing to credential journalists working for online publications gave several reasons for their decisions. Since audience figures were hard to measure, it was difficult to assess the importance of a particular Web site. Since virtually anybody could set up a Web site, it was sometimes difficult to separate real operations from hobbyists' sites or even shams. Many Web sites did not have original reporting, so they did not need to be credentialed for entrance to specific venues. In many other cases, the quality of reporting on Web sites was low. Journalists working for online publications were treated like second-class citizens, the argument went, because the journalism they produced was second class.

The specific nature of the content and the quality of the content were probably the most vexing issues that traditional news media faced as they tried to come up with a strategy to integrate online media into their news delivery systems. In 1994, Jon Katz wrote an influential article in *Wired* magazine subtly titled "Online or Not, Newspapers Suck." After decades of resisting change, Katz wrote, newspapers finally understood that moving online was imperative, noting that a Prodigy user broke the news about a major earthquake in California before CNN and long before any newspaper could get the story. But watching sober, proper newspapers online, he opined, "stirs only one image: that of Lawrence Welk trying to dance at a rap concert. Online newspapers are unnatural, even silly." There were several problems, Katz said. On the one hand, online newspapers had not fully embraced the interactivity of the Web. When the editor of *Time* magazine went online to respond to charges that the magazine had darkened a cover image of O. J. Simpson, the defendant in a trial that had gripped the imagination of the nation, and faced 70,000 complaints, it was like "watching elephants learn to fly," Katz said.[97]

What newspapers really needed to do, Katz wrote, was to change their content. Newspapers had little original or distinctive writing. They were cautious and tepid. They had become irrelevant, and their online versions only replicated what was in print. Much of Katz's criticism struck a chord. Newspaper Web sites were often just rehashes of the articles that had already appeared in print. Newspapers editors did not want to break news on their Web sites, fearing not only that they would tip off their competitors but that they would, in essence, be scooping themselves. If their exclusive articles appeared for free, why would anybody buy the newspaper? Furthermore, consumers resolutely refused to pay for online news. In experiment after experiment, newspapers had to back away from their efforts to charge a subscription fee for their news Web sites. For example, in 1997 the *St. Paul (Minn.) Pioneer Press* dropped all fees and made its online version available for free; only 3,500 people had signed up for the site when the paper charged $4.95 a month.[98] Shortly thereafter, the *San Antonio Express-News* dropped its subscription charge after a three-year trial; it too had attracted only around 3,000 subscribers. Only the *Wall Street Journal* seemed to be able to charge for its site.[99]

But the ability for traditional news media to hold back stories so they did not scoop themselves was about to change. On January 18, 1998, thirty-one-year-old Matt Drudge published an item on his Web site, The Drudge Report, stating that *Newsweek* had just killed an article by its reporter Michael Isikoff that asserted that President Bill Clinton had been conducting an affair with an intern named Monica Lewinsky. A day earlier, President Clinton had given a deposition in a sexual harassment suit that had been filed against him in which he denied that he had had sexual relations with Lewinsky. Two days after Drudge posted his 400-word story quoting unnamed sources, the story was in the *Washington Post,* setting off a chain of events that propelled Drudge to fame. That year, *Time* magazine named Drudge as one of the one hundred people who shaped the world. Drudge agreed. In June

1998, speaking at the National Press Club, Drudge said, "Now, with a modem, anyone can follow the world and report on the world—no middle man, no Big Brother. And I guess this changes everything."[100]

Matt Drudge was not a journalist by training. He had held various jobs in the retail industry, including a stint at the gift shop at CBS in Hollywood. While there, he picked up tidbits of gossip and began posting them on different Usenet newsgroups as well as on a Web site. As people visited his site, he began to build a mailing list. His site slowly gained a reputation as a source for journalists to go to for breaking news, and he eventually signed deals with *Wired* magazine and AOL to carry his material. Drudge never did any actual reporting. Instead, he and a friend constantly monitored other news sources and created links to those sources. After he broke the piece about *Newsweek*'s story on the Clinton affair, he also began to receive a steady stream of leaks from political operatives and others. In May 2003, The Drudge Report was typically getting about 6.5 million visitors a day. Drudge's total cost: a computer and Internet access.[101]

The way the Clinton-Lewinsky story broke fundamentally changed the practice of journalism. News organizations began tripping over each other to break the next piece of news in the affair. There was no holding back.[102] The Internet had become the medium for breaking news. If traditional media did not report a story, a lone individual sitting in an apartment in Los Angeles would. As if to signal the new role the Internet would play in the delivery of the news, when Kenneth Starr, the independent counsel who investigated President Clinton for much of his presidency, released his 445-page report on September 11, 1998, it was posted directly to a congressional Web site, and readers rushed to access it. It was read by twenty million people online within forty-eight hours of its release.[103] Two weeks later, tens of millions of viewers logged onto CNN.com, MSNBC.com, and other Web sites to view the videotape of President Clinton's grand jury testimony and to access three thousand supporting documents that were also released by Congress. "Journalistically, while the Starr report was the turning point for the Web, this report was a trial by fire," Leah Gentry, new media editorial director at the *Los Angeles Times* told *Editor & Publisher.* "Again, there was information that we could not come near touching in our print edition, not only because of the nature of the content, but also because of the sheer volume."[104]

The 1990s witnessed the birth of a new platform for journalism. The Internet and the World Wide Web had begun to take shape as a multipurpose mass medium. As the cost of computing continued to plunge, the software became increasingly easy to use, and the speed at which material could be downloaded improved, millions of people from all age groups got online. Companies large and small scrambled to understand how to incorporate this new medium into their operations.

The news media were no exception. The potential of the Internet both as a reporting tool and as a delivery vehicle for news was self-evident. How to integrate the Internet with traditional news operations was another matter entirely.

====================◇====================

SIX

NEWS FROM ANYONE
AND ANYWHERE

In August 1995, Victoria's Secret, the leading retailer of sexy woman's lingerie, decided to preview the new collection for its fall catalogue with a fashion show at the Plaza Hotel in New York. The goal, said Ed Rezik, vice president of merchandising for The Limited, Inc., which acquired Victoria's Secret in the early 1980s, was "to illustrate the fact that lingerie is fashion, too. Just like fashion designers, we bring out a new collection every three to six months, so it makes sense to preview the new styles." The company more than achieved its goal. Although only the media were invited to the show itself, sneak peeks of supermodels like Stephanie Seymour parading down the runway in lacy undergarments were broadcast on the Jumbotron screen in New York's Times Square. The result was a positive frenzy, with reams of media coverage and men from around the country begging their journalist friends to get them tickets to the next event.[1]

In the wake of its success, the fashion show became a fixture in Victoria's Secret marketing program. To increase its exposure, in the winter of 1999, the company spent $1.5 million to run a commercial during the Super Bowl and then spent $4 million to advertise in newspapers internationally to announce that the next lingerie fashion show would be broadcast over the Internet. Victoria's Secret inked a deal with Broadcast.com, which added 120 extra servers to handle the expected traffic.[2] They weren't enough. In the hour after the Super Bowl commercial, more than one million people logged on to the Victoria's Secret Web site. More than two million people logged on to watch the show itself, overwhelming the servers. Potentially, millions more people tried to watch but could not get the Web site to respond. While critics complained that even more people could not access the Web site and those who did experienced sputtering video and audio that cut out, a bigger point was not missed.[3] The Victoria's Secret fashion show was one of the first large-scale live video events on the Internet. Given the right content, the Web could attract an audience, a huge audience.

The Victoria's Secret fashion show put to rest any lingering doubt about the Web as a potential medium for mass communication. But evidence of the possible reach of the Web had been steadily building for years. In March 1997, in a mansion in Rancho Santa Fe, California, an extremely upscale area near San Diego, thirty-nine bodies were discovered lying on their backs neatly in rows and on bunk beds. Each body was dressed in black pants, a black shirt, and a pair of black Nike running shoes, with a purple cloth covering the face. The victims were members of a cult called Heaven's Gate, led by the sixty-five-year-old Marshall Applewhite. It was the largest mass suicide in the United States, triggered in part by the appearance of the Hale-Bopp comet. The members of the cult felt that their bodies were only "containers," and by leaving their containers behind they would ascend to the "kingdom level above human."[4]

But the members of the Heaven's Gate cult did more than

just commit suicide; they left behind a virtual press kit announcing their deaths as well as an elaborate Web site explaining their philosophy and what they had done. As soon as news of the suicide began to circulate, the staff of SignOnSanDiego, the Web site of the *San Diego Union-Tribune,* copied the entire Heaven's Gate Web site. That turned out to be a major coup. When the server that housed the Heaven's Gate Web site became inaccessible, traffic at SignOnSanDiego nearly tripled as online viewers logged on to read the material directly. Moreover, SignOnSanDiego created a special section on the Web site, which at that time required users to register, to archive all the Heaven's Gate materials as well as the news articles that had been written about the cult. A month later, the material was still available. The plan, the editor of SignOnSanDiego said, was to keep the material online for as long as viewers showed interest.[5] The Washington Post.com reported the Heaven's Gate story prior to the story running in the newspaper and also posted original materials and documents about the cult.[6]

The Heaven's Gate episode was evidence of two emerging trends in the use of the Internet and the Web for news. First, when big news broke, people were increasingly willing to go online to get the information. Second, as readers and viewers turned to the Web first, newspapers and television news organizations had to decide if they were going to make the news available on their Web sites before it is available through their traditional outlets. A 1997 report from the market research group Jupiter Media documented that online users were going to the Web for headlines and news updates. In response, online news media Web sites began to grapple with the idea of producing shorter news stories updated more frequently. This approach seemed to pit all online news sites in competition with the news wire services like the Associated

Press and United Press International. Each new development in a breaking news story would lead to a spike in Web site traffic, which was good. During the height of the Clinton impeachment scandal, the traffic on the Web site at Fox News doubled. But neither newspapers nor broadcasters had experience publishing on an "always-on" schedule.[7]

Like the Victoria's Secret webcast, the Heaven's Gate story demonstrated that providing source material—unfiltered, unpackaged, and unedited—could also attract a large audience. This trend was driven home a few months later when NASA's Pathfinder spacecraft approached its destination and prepared to land on Mars. On July 4, 1997, NASA prepared to bring Pathfinder, an unmanned exploratory vehicle equipped with a robot explorer called Sojourner, to rest on the red planet. As part of its preparations, NASA had created twenty-five Web sites that would transmit the images Sojourner was sending back to earth. People around the world would be able to see the same pictures that NASA scientists were seeing at the same moment the scientists saw them.[8]

When Pathfinder actually touched down, activity on the Web sites, which mirrored each other, reached record levels. NASA officials estimated that fifteen million visitors watched the Pathfinder land without a glitch. It proved that Web technology could scale up to handle a mass audience without problems. Moreover, by putting the information on the Web, users were free of the constraints of the traditional media. "The news coverage has been great, but you can't turn on the TV at any time and get updates on the mission," Richard A. Pavlovsky, a programmer at NASA's Jet Propulsion Laboratory who helped design NASA's Pathfinder site, said at the time. "With the Internet, any time you want to find out something, you can." NASA was able to place images themselves within an appropriate context, including virtual reality simulations and maps of the landing site in addition to the technical data on the Web site. And it didn't take a great deal of human resources to make a significant impact: the NASA Pathfinder Web sites were created by three programmers.[9]

Clearly, online news was an important factor that had to be reckoned with both by the established news media and by those interested in news. On September 16, 1998, the online magazine Salon, which was then three years old, published an article based on an eyewitness account accusing Henry Hyde, a staunchly conservative member of the U.S. House of Representatives and a leading voice in the Right-to-Life antiabortion community, of having had an extramarital affair thirty years earlier. The report set off a firestorm of criticism directed toward the online magazine, and included the resignation of its Washington bureau chief, who asserted that the magazine should not have run the story because there was no public policy issue involved. Salon editor David Talbot defended the piece, arguing that as the chair of the House Judiciary Committee, Hyde was slated to preside over the impeachment trial of President Bill Clinton, where the primary charges were from accusations that he lied about an extramarital affair he had with White House intern Monica Lewinsky.[10] Hyde ultimately admitted to the affair and issued a public apology, characterizing it as a "youthful indiscretion," even though he was more than forty years old when the events took place.[11] The Salon article demonstrated that online news media could put issues on the public agenda even if they were initially ignored by the more traditional media.

By the mid-1990s, online news sites had periodically been able to attract large audiences. They could offer viewers news and information in ways that neither print nor broadcast could—access to unfiltered content and timelier updates on breaking news—and they could break stories of national importance. As a result, many more newspapers began to explore the move online. According to one study, the number of newspapers with online editions jumped from 745 in July 1996 to 2,059 in 1997.[12] Newspapers and television news organizations were not the only ones lifting off into cyberspace. The number of World Wide Web users hit 30 million in 1996, up from 10 million in 1995. In that year, Web use was projected to double again by the end of 1997 and reach 120 million users by the end of the decade, according to IDC, a technology-oriented market research company. Moreover, e-commerce—commerce conducted over the Internet—was expected to climb from $600 million in 1996 to over $3 billion in 1997.[13] By the end of 1998, e-commerce was exceeding expectations, with analysts estimating activity at over $5 billion.[14] As for Web servers (computers that actually hosted Web sites), more than 150,000 were running by early April 1996.[15] By 1998, there were more than 2.6 million Web sites in the world and by 2000 there were more than 7.1 million.[16]

WHO CONTROLS THE INTERNET

The proliferation of the World Wide Web coincided with several other tectonic shifts in telecommunications. The ramifications of the breakup of the former telephone monopoly AT&T into a long-distance carrier and seven regional Bell operating companies (RBOCs) was still reverberating and working itself out in a series of acquisitions, mergers, and divestitures. Cable television was also in a process of consolidation and change. Cable was poised to compete with telephone systems in delivering Internet access to homes and businesses. At the same time, cable companies and telephone companies were seen as potential merger partners. Further churning the cauldron, the development of digital broadcasting sparked the possibility of increasing the number of television stations exponentially as well as the dream of video on demand. Consumers were on the brink of being in a position to watch what they wanted, when they wanted it. And, at the same time, the use of cellular telephone technology and direct broadcast satellite was ramping up. In theory, anything that could be done on the wired network, including access to the Internet, could be done on the wireless network.

It seemed to many people that the Communications Act of 1934, which was still the primary framework for regulating broadcasting and telecommunications, and the Federal Communications Commission were both obsolete, and the U.S. Congress began to consider an overhaul of telecommunications regulation. In the mid-term elections in 1994, the Republican party swept to power in both houses of Congress, gaining control of the House of Representatives for the first time in forty years. The House Republicans were led by Newt Gingrich of Georgia, a self-styled visionary animated by an ideology that strongly favored deregulation. In 1995, Speaker Gingrich opined that he favored completely deregulating telecommunications within three to five years, perhaps abolishing the FCC.[17]

What emerged from the regulatory and deregulatory crosscurrents at work was the Telecommunications Act of 1996. The Telecommunications Act of 1996 did not abolish the Federal Communications Commission or completely deregulate the telecommunications industry. Passed with overwhelming support from both political parties and in both houses of Congress, the act was touted as an effort to eliminate outmoded restrictions on telecommunications companies and to spur competition to benefit consumers. Underlying the act was a vision of a network of interconnected networks made up of complementary components providing both competing and complementary services.[18]

For the development of the Internet, one of the most important aspects of the Telecommunications Act of 1996 was not only what it contained but what it did not contain. The act required that telephone companies continue to provide nondiscriminatory access to their underlying networks—a stipulation that had been in place during the breakup of the AT&T monopoly. It did not, however, require cable companies to provide nondiscriminatory access to their networks. As cable became the preferred method for consumers to access the Internet, the cable companies did not strike a single deal with third-party Internet service providers. By 2001, cable companies controlled 75 percent of the market for residential Internet access.[19]

The most prominent features of the Telecommunications Act of 1996 were the removal of many of the barriers to expansion of telecommunications companies. The act lifted the number of radio and television stations a single company could own; it deregulated cable television rates, eased cable-broadcast cross-ownership rules, and gave broadcasters rights to valuable new frequencies in the broadcast spectrum. Instead of spurring competition, however, the act led to a round of significant consolidations. Within seven years, five companies—Viacom, Time Warner, News Corp., the Walt Disney Company, and General Electric—controlled 75 percent of all prime-time television and 90 percent of the top fifty cable stations. Cable rates soared.[20]

As the industry consolidated, the cable companies began to lobby for the right to provide different levels of access to their Internet infrastructures. In the deregulatory spirit, cable companies wanted to be allowed to charge more to companies that sent a lot of information over the Internet, and otherwise negotiate prices with information providers using their networks. Cable companies wanted to be able to provide higher quality service to companies that paid more. Already at a disadvantage because cable companies did not have to provide nondiscriminatory access to their networks, at first AT&T and other telephone companies resisted the cable companies' efforts to implement what was called "quality discrimination." But as the industry continued to consolidate, all of the major Internet access providers began to lobby for the right to differentiate their pricing for different customers. The issue crystallized into the term *net neutrality,* meaning that all Internet content providers would receive the same quality of service regardless of size or other considerations. In June 2006, the FCC dropped its rule mandating net neutrality.[21] However, the requirement for net neutrality in the late 1990s and early 2000s meant that the smallest news-oriented Web site—even one-person operations like Matt Drudge—could compete on equal footing with the biggest corporations in the world. At that point, the cable telephone companies—the providers of the underlying infrastructure itself—were not able to control the Internet.

The cable and telephone companies were not the only corporations with nearly monopolistic power that might attempt to control the Internet. As early as 1990, Microsoft, which would soon become the biggest software manufacturer in the world, had been investigated by the Federal Trade Commission concerning its marketing practices for its computer operating systems, which controlled the basic operations of most personal computers in the world. After the commission deadlocked twice on investigations, the probe was picked up by the Department of Justice, and in 1994, Microsoft signed a consent decree forbidding it to use its dominance in computer operating systems to gain an unfair advantage in other areas of the software market.[22] In the early 1990s, after the release of the Windows 3.0 operating system, Microsoft had come to dominate not only the operating system market but the market for personal productivity software such as word processors and spreadsheets. Before the release of Windows 3.0, the Microsoft products in the personal productivity software market had often been second or third in their category and many competitors and critics at that time argued that Microsoft had used its intimate knowledge of the operating system, including undocumented features, to boost its products ahead of its competitors. Microsoft also bolstered its position through aggressive licensing and bundling requirements. The 1994 consent decree forbid Microsoft from requiring a customer to buy one product as a precondition to being allowed to buy another product; from bundling products into the operating system, and from offering products at no charge.[23]

In early 1995, Netscape, the company that had been formed by Jim Clarke and Marc Andreessen to commercialize the Mosaic Web browser, controlled about 60 percent of the Web browser market, with online services like Prodigy and other smaller companies holding the remainder of the market. Like the original code, Mosaic was given away for free to stimulate demand for Netscape's Web server software. Netscape, however, was only one of several companies that had licensed the original code from the NCSA. Microsoft had purchased rights to the original Mosaic as well.[24]

On July 14, 1995, Microsoft began to manufacture Windows 95, the new version of its operating system, and momentum began to build toward the late August release of the product. The company announced that an icon for the Microsoft Network, but no other commercial online service, would appear on Windows 95's opening screen. It also said that it would bundle its Web browser,

Internet Explorer, which was based on the NCSA Mosaic code, with the version of Windows 95 loaded onto new computers. Netscape and other competitors in the industry immediately cried foul. Microsoft, they claimed, was in violation of the 1994 consent decree by giving Internet Explorer away for free as well as forcing personal computer manufacturers to include Internet Explorer if they wanted to load Windows 95 onto new computers prior to selling them to the end users. As Windows held an overwhelming share of the market, the personal computer manufacturers had little choice.

Launching a Web browser was only the first step in Microsoft's Internet initiative. In the fall of 1995, the company announced plans to release a Web server, the software used to create Web sites, as well as a Web editor, software that could be used to create Web pages more easily. Shortly thereafter, Microsoft's strategy became clear. The essential underpinnings of the World Wide Web were the hypertext transport protocol (HTTP) and the hypertext markup language (HTML)—the protocols all Web servers and Web browsers everywhere used. These protocols were considered international standards and controlled by the nonprofit World Wide Web Consortium run by Tim Berners-Lee, who had created the Web, and the International Standards Organization. When Microsoft began showing early versions of the next release of Internet Explorer, it contained nonstandard enhancements to HTML, which Microsoft officials called state-of-the-art innovations.[25] The problem was this: if Web designers wanted to take advantage of the new features, they would have to redesign their Web sites. But even then, those using other browsers, including Netscape, would only have limited access to Web sites tailored to Internet Explorer. Over time, with its market power, Microsoft could potentially control as large a share of the Web browser,

Web server, and Web editor markets as it did the office productivity market. With control of the HTTP and HTML protocols, it would be easy for Microsoft to cripple competitive companies' Web sites. Microsoft could conceivably control the Web.[26]

In late October 1997, the U.S. Department of Justice sued Microsoft for violating the 1994 consent decree by forcing computer vendors to bundle Internet Explorer with Windows 95. The motivation for the suit, however, was the growing unease about Microsoft's efforts to dominate the Internet.[27] Later, the European Commission also sued Microsoft for anticompetitive behavior. Both suits dragged on for several years, and in April 2000, the judge hearing the case, Thomas Penfield Jackson, ruled that Microsoft had violated antitrust laws. In June of that year, he ordered the breakup of Microsoft. That ruling was overturned the following year, but during the four years that the case was under litigation, Microsoft was effectively restrained from attempting to assert its dominance over the Internet and the Web in the same fashion that it had dominated the desktop software industry.

The Justice Department's antitrust suit was only one of the results of Microsoft's fierce competitive tactics. From the beginning of computer networking, there had always been a culture of sharing in the computer community. Some people trace this culture back to the release of the IBM 704 mainframe computer in 1954. The 704 represented a radical departure from the IBM 701, which had preceded it. When the 701 was released, IBM called a meeting of systems operators to train them on the new computer. The interaction was so fruitful that some of the participants formed a permanent group for the ongoing exchange of information. In 1955, they formed the first computer users group. Its name, tellingly, was SHARE. IBM funded the SHARE meetings and also made a library of three hundred software programs available to them. IBM provided the basic code—the source code—to the participants and invited them to modify and improve the programs.[28]

In the 1960s and 1970s, as computers became less expensive and more commonplace, companies began to develop software but retained the rights to the source code, providing a version of the program that would run but could not be modified by end users. The source code was said to be closed to the end users. A flourishing proprietary software market emerged.

In the early 1980s, a programmer named Richard Stallman, troubled by the move toward closed, proprietary software that users could buy but not modify, set out to create an operating system that would work with Unix, an operating system from AT&T intended to run on computers from many vendors, but with open source code so that anybody could modify it.[29] He believed that software should be "free" in the same way that speech should be free. Afraid that companies would grab software in which the source code was free and make it their own, Stallman also created a license that prohibited anybody from restricting the use of open source programs.

Stallman's approach appealed to many hard-core computer enthusiasts and programmers, including a student in Finland named Linus Torvald. In the early 1990s, Torvald wanted to create an operating system, and, working with Stallman's development tools, he succeeded in making an operating system that worked the same way as Unix but with open and free source code. Lacking a graphical user interface and other attributes of mass software at the time, he thought it would interest only a few people.

The open source approach to software development had always been used by some of the researchers integral to the development of computer networking and the Internet. These researchers would develop games or a small piece of useful code and then make it available to the entire community. The first Web browser and the first Web server software were released freely to the community. As the Internet developed, it became easier and easier for software developers to collaborate. In 1998, in response to Microsoft's attempt to collar the Web, Netscape introduced an open source version of Netscape. An open source Web server named Apache was already the primary competitor to Internet Information Server, Microsoft's Web server software. Other open source programs—like sendmail for e-mail and bind, which tracked Internet domain names—became very popular. Around that time, a programmer named Eric Raymond wrote an influential article called "The Cathedral and the Bazaar," explaining why software developed by the open source community was often more powerful and reliable than proprietary software created by companies. The reason, he argued, was that really great software could best be developed by harnessing the brainpower of entire communities.[30]

Raymond, along with Bruce Perans, with whom he founded the Open Source Initiative, argued that open source software represented a better software development strategy than the typical corporate engineering process. For their part, many companies saw open source development as a way to resist pressure from Microsoft. An entire open source movement emerged, a community in many ways enabled by and dependent on the Web. Projects were posted to and coordinated from the Sourceforge Web site, among others. Not surprisingly, in part in reaction to the efforts of Microsoft and others to try to control the Web, open source applications that provided exciting new functionality began to appear.

When the Web began to grow exponentially in the mid-1990s, it was an open question as to how it should be regulated, if at all, and by whom. It emerged at a moment in time when the pendulum was swinging toward governmental deregulation, which could have left the field open for large corporations to control the Internet. But the legacy regulations against quality discrimination in telephone service, a throwback to the period when telephone service was highly regulated and then systematically deregulated, prohibited the Internet service providers from asserting control over the Internet. The Justice Department antitrust suit prevented Microsoft from using its dominance in the personal computer market to capture the Web. The open source reaction to Microsoft ensured that there would be innovative, low-cost tools to run Web servers and create content. The Web was the first mass medium with access for all.

MANY QUESTIONS, FEW ANSWERS

At the turn of the century, online journalism was at something of a crossroad. The major news organizations had gone online and were making increasing investments in creating original content for the Web. News organizations were beginning to understand that they would not be able to hold back news to publish or broadcast first in their newspapers or evening news broadcasts. On the other hand, it was not clear at all that online journalism would ever consistently attract the same kinds of audiences that urban newspapers and the nightly news, both national and local, could attract. For example, in a study of the Sydney Olympics in 2000, the Pew Internet and American Life Project found that the official Olympic games Web site received 8.7 million visitors, and more than 370,000 messages were sent by fans of Olympic athletes. Measured by the number of hits, Web site traffic increased seventeenfold over the 1998 Winter Games in Nagano, Japan, and nearly sixtyfold over the 1996 Summer Olympic Games in Atlanta. Nonetheless, television was still the medium of choice for Olympic news. On a typical day, 57 percent of Americans got some Olympic news from network, cable, or local television and 12 percent read some Olympic news in newspapers. Only four percent of Americans accessed Olympic news online.[31] Indeed, network news divisions never seemed busier. As network news executives figured out how to make network news profitable, they were filling their prime-time broadcasting hours with news magazine of all kinds.[32] While online news had joined print journalism and broadcast news outlets as a credible source of information, online news was nonetheless a supplementary source of news.[33]

The question was whether an economic model that would support online journalism would emerge. News, it seemed, had become a commodity, and a free commodity at that. It was widely available and few news Web sites had been able to charge subscriptions for their content. News media were not only competing with each other but with sites that aggregated news headlines, like Yahoo!, as well as with direct providers of content like the United States government. It was not clear that Web site users really wanted the in-depth information that the Web promised to deliver or that they wanted links to source documents. When they did want to read source documents, those documents were often already online. Nor was it obvious how to build a "community" around a news Web site and to interact effectively with viewers in a positive way.[34]

The issues were just as daunting on the business side of the house. The number of people who visited a given news Web site regularly was often too small to charge a significant amount for display advertising, and even in 1999, the number of people willing to click on a banner ad was dropping. Just as troubling, advertising on the Web could easily blur the once sacred line between advertising and editorial content. For example, in 1999, the CNNfn.com travel page blended CNN travel articles with reservation services, and some leading Web site operators felt that there was really no need to distinguish between objective and paid content.[35] Complicating matters, classified advertising was migrating to sites like Monster.com and eBay. In short, media companies were throwing money down what Don Logan, the chief executive officer of Time, Inc., called a black hole, with no certain return.[36] Within this muddled mix, a new application appeared. Blogging started out as disjointed personal online diaries with daily updates, but it would dramatically change the equation.

THE RISE OF THE BLOGOSPHERE

The impact of Matt Drudge's post stating that *Newsweek* was withholding a story about President Clinton's affair with Monica Lewinsky underscored one of the long-term phenomena of the Internet and the Web. Like lonely pamphleteers in colonial times, individuals could gather and publish information and, with the right combination of skills, Internet savvy, and luck, gather an audience. In the early 1990s, for example, Brock Meeks, who wrote for the computer magazine *Byte*'s online bulletin board, launched CyberWire Dispatch, a self-styled effort in personal journalism, which circulated through The WELL and other online services before the Web was a mass medium. Meeks claims that the CyberWire Dispatch was named by users after a story that he had published was apparently picked up, without attribution, by the *New*

York Times. A writer with a very sharp edge, Meeks, who went on to work for MSNBC, was also the target of one of the first libel suits aimed at an online publication.[37]

New-style reporters like Drudge and Meeks were hardly alone. By 1997, sites maintained by Jim Romenesko called mediagossip.com and www.obscurestore.com had become must-reads for many journalists. Romenesko would get up at 5 A.M. to cull newspapers, magazine, and gossip Web sites for gossip about the media as well as obscure and offbeat stories. By 8:30 A.M., he would head off to his day job covering the Internet for the *St. Paul Pioneer Press.* Romenesko received no pay for maintaining the site, which received steady traffic from journalists working at National Public Radio, CNBC, and scores of other media outlets, and he had competition from people like Steve Knopper, who wrote The Daily Buzz, another compilation of stories with a "twist" to them.[38] Romenesko characterized his work as an "online do-it-yourself" project. He said that he was not interested in expanding or generating revenues. He wanted to maintain a one-person operation.

The do-it-yourself impulse was deeply embedded in online culture. In 1997, Dave Winer had launched Scripting News as part of his Web site, DaveNet. Scripting News had an eclectic collection of industry and technology news. In December 1997, Jorn Barger launched what he called RobotWisdom.com. Barger, who first started using computers in the 1960s, was a programmer and one-time researcher in artificial intelligence. He had devised a theoretical methodology in which a hypothesis could be expressed as a computer simulation and the simulations then refined by analyzing literary descriptions of human behavior. He called the methodology "Robot Wisdom." Barger actively promoted his ideas through Usenet newsgroups in 1990s. RobotWisdom.com was Barger's effort to log the Web as he surfed it. He described it as a "weblog."[39]

Others embarked on similar kinds of projects. Jesse James Garrett began compiling a list of sites similar to his own and eventually sent his list to Cameron Barrett, a Web site designer, who published it on his Web site, Camworld.[40] In one section of Camworld, Barrett published what he called "rants." In January 1999, he reported he had heard the term *Weblog* a few months earlier and when he wondered if Camworld was a Weblog, the response he received was yes. He stepped back to consider what a Weblog was and concluded that they had several common elements: the sites were regularly updated, often daily; they had simple designs and user interfaces; there was generally a theme; and there was a way for readers to interact with the site and readers were respected.[41] His musing became the working definition of a Weblog, a term later shortened to *blog*.

None of these ideas were new. Like Garrett and Barger, people had been compiling lists of interesting or related Web sites since the beginning of the Web. Others had begun creating daily posts of their lives, creating online diaries. For example, in 1994, while an intern at *Wired* magazine and encouraged by the editors at Suck.com, a new start-up Web magazine like Salon, Justin Hall, a sometime student at Swarthmore College, began posting intimate details of his life online daily.[42] Over the next ten years, Hall posted 5,000 pages online about his alcoholic father, his stepfather, his travels, his work, and his love life, including his making love with twenty-six different partners ranging in age from 16 to 38. Sex was always the topic that generated the most interest, Hall later recounted.[43]

When Hall first started posting about his life, the site on which he posted was called a personal Web site. Later it was called a Web diary and only after the blog phenomenon started to gain momentum was it identified as a blog. Under different names, blogging was a defined, if small, often relatively underground domain populated by Web aficionados and technologists. Several open source software applications that circulated through the Web in the late 1990s, however, turned blogging from what was basically a cult activity into a publishing platform for everybody. In 1999, Andrew Smales, a programmer in Toronto, wanted to develop a tool that would allow him to update his personal Web site more easily and to facilitate what he called an "online blogging community." Personal sites like his were not easy to find, and he felt it would be nice if he could just click on what other people had written rather than blindly surfing the Web. As he worked on the program, he posted updates on his Web site and became aware of the nascent blogging community. In response, he created Pitas. com, an easy-to-use tool to create blogs, and launched his own blog, Diaryland.com.[44]

As with many open source projects, Smales was not the only person to see the need for an easy way to create blogs. The founders of Pyra Labs were working on a software project that would include a project manager, contact manager, and to-do list. As part of the project, they created a program that allowed them to collaborate more easily by blogging. Evan Williams, one of the founders of Pyra Labs, liked the blogging format and the script he had developed and thought that others might appreciate it, so he released it to the community.[45] Like Pitas.com, the Pyra Labs application, which was called Blogger, was completely free to use, as were Groksoup, EditThisPagePHP from Dave Winer, Velocinews, WordPress, Moveable Type, Open Diary, and Live Journal, among the other platforms that supported blogging. The original blogs usually consisted of links to other Web sites and the author's commentaries on those links; they required the blogger to know at least a little HTML and other Web-related technology. The new, free blogging applications meant that people with absolutely no technical knowledge whatsoever could set up a blog with about three clicks of a mouse. Posting and maintaining the blog were just about as easy. Moreover, with just a little technical sophistication, anybody could create a blog using these platforms under an individual domain name.

Creating an easy-to-use platform was an important step in the emergence of blogging. Perhaps as important, however, was the development of a technology called RSS, usually spelled out as "really simple syndication." RSS was created in 1997 by integrating technology created by Dave Winer with Rich Site Summary, a function created by Netscape that allowed users to create custom Netscape home pages with regularly updated data flows. Netscape lost interest in the technology, which was then promoted by Winer. RSS gave subscribers the option to receive updates from their favorite blogs. While by definition blog pages are continually and dynamically changing as they are updated, RSS created a permanent link to each post. RSS allowed readers a way to stay in touch with blogs of interest easily and helped distinguish blogs from other Web pages. Blogs also had a feature called the blogroll, which consisted of a series of links to other blogs selected by the blogger. If one blog was entered in the blogroll of a popular blog, traffic often would climb as readers surfed from blog to blog.[46]

Another piece of the puzzle came in November 2002 with the launch of Technorati, a Google-like search engine geared specifically for blogs. With Technorati, users could more easily find blogs of interest to them. Moreover, the astronomical growth of what came to be called the blogosphere could be more easily tracked.[47]

In 2000, a friend told Rebecca Mead, a reporter for *The New Yorker* magazine, that she should look into this interesting new activity on the Web called blogging. Mead wrote a story about Meg Hourihan, one of the founders of Pyra Labs, and her relationship with Jason Kottke, a Web designer, and their blogs.[48] Blogging had hit the mainstream.

JOURNALISTS DISCOVER BLOGGING

While many of the early blogs were truly personal diaries and other attempts at personal expression, as usual journalists were also among the early adopters. Andrew Sullivan had joined *The New Republic* in 1986, and in 1991, he was named the magazine's editor in chief, the youngest person ever named to the post. In 1995, Sullivan, a devout Catholic who described himself as a libertarian but was largely seen as a conservative politically, published *Virtually Normal: An Argument About Homosexuality,* in which he discussed his own homosexuality and defended same sex marriage.[49] Not surprisingly, the book received a controversial reception. By the year 2000, Sullivan had become a freelance writer, and he felt that he needed an online presence. At first, a friend posted old columns and essays on a Web site for him, but when the process became tedious, his friend introduced him to Blogger.com. Sullivan, in his own words, was completely clueless technologically. But he realized that he could post new writing directly on Blogger. He had written for online publications before, both a LISTSERV for gay writers and for Slate. He decided to try combining a British style of crisp, short commentary with a more personal, essayistic, first-person form of journalism. He found the experience an "exhilarating literary liberation."[50]

Sullivan was not the first prominent journalist to launch a blog. Mickey Kaus, who had written for the *Washington Monthly, Newsweek,* and once again *The New Republic,* had written the blog-like Chatterbox column in Slate magazine in 1997. In 1999, he launched the Kausfiles as a private blog, which was often written as interior monologues and conversations with a nonexistent editor.[51]

A handful of other established journalists began to experiment with blogs. But the breakthrough moment came with the terrorist attack on the World Trade Center on September 11, 2001. Although the traditional news media gave round-the-clock coverage to the events, the thirst for news simply could not be satisfied and the traditional media's Web sites could not handle the rush of traffic.[52] In addition to the coverage itself, the normal political commentary seemed unable to address the enormity of the situation and the impact it had on so many people adequately. In response, established bloggers deviated from what they normally did to provide coverage. Blog pioneer Dave Winer, for example, began posting one-line news flashes, clips from webcams, and links to other blogs from eye witnesses.[53]

Many journalists also felt they needed a personal outlet to express their feelings. In a typical example, Jeff Jarvis, a former columnist of the *San Francisco Examiner* and the founding editor *of Entertainment Weekly,* was actually trapped in the cloud of dust generated by the collapse of the Twin Towers. A few days later he started a blog. "I had a personal story that I needed to tell," he said later. As soon as his blog launched, other bloggers started to link to him. He found that he had "joined this great conversation."[54]

Blogging was the quintessential democratic medium. Anybody could do it. After the events of 9/11, eye witness accounts flooded the Internet. The left-wing documentary film maker Michael Moore blogged about telephoning a friend in the World Trade Center and having the phone go dead when the building collapsed. Jon Katz posted his account of watching the towers collapse as well. While many of the accounts were posted on personal blogs, Katz posted his on Slashdot, which was known for its coverage of technology.[55] All sorts of people started posting both what they saw and how they felt about the event in blogs, newsgroups, forums, and chat rooms. Shortly after the event, the blog www.worldnewyork.org was set up to capture people's stories and provide links to other information sources. Blogs were also used to host survivor registries. The sheer volume of the output of blogs was captured in archive sites like NYC Bloggers and, later, the September 11 Digital Archive Project. The chaos was "a galvanizing point for the blogging world," said Dan Gillmor, director of the Center for Citizen Media, who for ten years served as a columnist for the *San Jose Mercury News* and wrote a blog for Silicon Valley.com.[56]

From that point, blogging spread like wildfire. From fewer than one hundred Web sites that might be called blogs in 1999, it was estimated that there were close to 500,000 blogs by 2002, and a blog was being started every 40 seconds.[57] By 2004, according to Technorati, there were more than four million blogs. That year, blogs were being added at the rate of 12,000 a day, or one every 7.2 seconds.[58]

Blogging was one salvo in the move to create user-generated content on the Web. In 2001, Jimmy Wales and others established Wikipedia, an open-content encyclopedia in which anybody could contribute information and edit articles. The inspiration for Wikipedia came directly from the open source software movement and was based on the premise that a large community of people could create better content than a smaller group of professionals. By September 2001, Wikipedia had attracted about one hundred volunteers who had written about 10,000 articles in what was intended to be a comprehensive encyclopedia of the world's knowledge. The software tool used to create Wikipedia was known as a wiki, free software that could be downloaded by site administrators. With a few clicks, users could modify each entry. One person could start an article on a subject of interest and write a few paragraphs. Another reader could then add a few more paragraphs and a third could then correct the mistakes that the first two made. Wales called the process "self healing."[59]

From its modest beginning, by July 2004 the site had more than 300,000 articles on a vast array of subjects. In comparison, the *Encyclopaedia Britannica* had only 65,000 articles. Moreover, Wikipedia had more than 1,200 volunteers reviewing articles for accuracy. As with so much content on the Internet, Wikipedia was free for all to use.[60] And the growth was accelerating: in November 2004, Wikipedia had more than 350,000 articles. More than 1,800 volunteers had made more than one hundred contributions to the site and more than 8,000 volunteers had made five or more contributions.[61]

Other approaches to consumer-generated content were initiated. In 2003, Friendster, an application designed to help people meet new friends and stay in touch with old friends, was unveiled. Friendster enabled users to generate "profile pages" and then link those pages using different communication technologies. People could share content such as photos, videos, and messages. Friendster was followed quickly by MySpace and Facebook, which operated along the same lines. In February 2005, Chad Hurley, Steve Chen, and Jawid Karim, three friends working for PayPal, a site that managed electronic payments over the Internet, saw an opportunity to share user-generated videos over the Web and registered the domain name YouTube. In May, a public test of the site was launched, and it quickly attracted an average of 30,000 viewers a day. The founders promised to give away one Apple iPod per day to people who uploaded videos. When the comedian Jon Stewart castigated the traditional media for falling down on the job on the CNN show *Crossfire,* more people watched the clip on YouTube than on television. By November 2005, YouTube had over 200,000 registered users and claimed to have shown more than two million videos a day. The site made its official debut on December 15, 2005. By January 2006, users were watching 25 million videos per day.[62]

Taken together, blogging, Wikipedia, Facebook, and YouTube were elements in what came to be called Web 2.0. The emphasis in Web development was moving away from creating static information that could be accessed from anywhere by anybody to generating content as the basis for collaboration and communication. Collaborative and social media were growing forces. In 2003, Google bought Pyra Labs for an undisclosed sum and renamed it Blogger.com. At the time, Pyra Labs had 1.1 million users.[63] In 2004, blog posts began to be indexed by the Google search technology, making the posts easier to find. In 2005, News Corp. bought MySpace for $580 million.[64] The next year, Google bought YouTube for $1.65 billion. "This is the next step in the evolution of the Internet," Google chief executive officer Eric Schmidt said during a conference call after the purchase was announced.[65]

The drive toward user- and consumer-generated content posed significant problems for journalism and journalists. Individual bloggers began to gather significant followings of their own. Glenn Reynolds, a law professor at the University of Tennessee, had launched InstaPundit the month before the events of 9/11.

His site traffic jumped from 1,600 visitors a week to over 4,200 after the terrorist attack. By 2003, his blog was drawing 100,000 visitors a week.[66] The Daily Howler, launched by the standup comedian Bob Somersby in 1998 and considered by some to be one of the first, if not the first, political blogs, also gained traction. Offering trenchant criticism of the performance of the Washington, D.C., press corps, The Daily Howler was particularly popular among other press critics.[67]

But if virtually anybody could create a blog, how could users assess the credibility of any individual blogger? And in the age of blogging, was everybody now a journalist? If so, who should receive press credentials to cover specific events and who should be excluded? And if anybody could cover any event and then post reports that the whole world could access, would blogging eventually kill the need for paid reporters and the established news media?[68]

Credibility was a serious and ongoing issue for online journalism. Since the days when heated discussions would take place on Usenet and Pierre Salinger erroneously claimed that TWA Flight 800 had been shot down accidently by the U.S. military based on documents circulating on the Web, it was clear that a lot of information found online simply could not be trusted. As a cautionary tale of the dangers of consumer-generated news, in the wake of 9/11, a raft of rumors began to circulate through the Web, including: NASA planned to photograph the site as a memorial; CNN used old pictures of Palestinians dancing to illustrate a story about their support of the attacks; and a person trapped on an upper floor of one of the buildings rode a piece of debris to safety. And, of course, there was no shortage of conspiracy theories about who was behind the attacks.[69]

Traditional journalists had long been skeptical of information on the Internet. How the public evaluated information from blogs was less certain. Nevertheless, blogs seemed to pose a threat to established news organizations. Commenting on the resignation of John Carroll, the editor of the *Los Angeles Times* in 2005, as a protest to cost cutting at the newspaper, Bill Keller, executive editor of the *New York Times,* said, "We've only got two things that distinguish us from blogs. One is we have reporting staffs who actually go out and see stuff and are trained professionals. And we have standards which are enforced by editors—you double-check things, make sure it's right—and all that costs money. If you aren't giving people the basics—good reliable news, smart analysis and in-depth investigations—then all they're going to see is the same stuff they can get on cable TV."[70] Bloggers often violated those standards. In 1994, for example, Ana Marie Cox published on her blog wonkette.com every unsubstantiated detail of a rumor floating around Washington, D.C., that Senator John Kerry, then a candidate for president of the United States, had had an affair. The story had originated on Matt Drudge's Web site but none of the Washington, D.C., gossip columnists reported it. Cox seemed unfazed when the story proved to be false.[71] Matt Drudge's site was routinely pilloried for posting unsubstantiated rumors, which did not seem to bother him.

While it was difficult to judge the credibility of an individual blog, blogs were becoming increasingly popular as news sources, particularly from places in which news organizations could not support their own correspondents, including societies not open to the U.S. media. For example, blogs launched by Iranian women gave them a forum to speak freely on issues that they were generally forbidden to discuss, including love, relationships, and the suppression of women.[72] A blog in China in which a twenty-five-year-old sex columnist described her intimate life attracted ten million visitors a day.[73] Bloggers could provide the eyes, ears, and reports from places that the traditional media simply could not or would not reach. In 2005, Michael Yon, a former member of the U.S. Army Special Forces, went to Iraq with the intention of staying for a month and then writing about his experiences. Instead, he stayed for three years, writing provocative and graphic accounts of the war on his own blog, michaelyon-online.com. Ultimately, Yon spent more time embedded with U.S. troops in Iraq than any other journalist.[74]

Yon himself admitted that he did not know the "rules of journalism" but slowly came to identify himself as a journalist. But what does it mean to be a journalist and could, or should, all bloggers who considered themselves to be journalists actually be considered journalists? The need to answer these questions surfaced in two ways. First, as with radio and television and then Web sites in the mid-1990s, the question was how to issue credentials to venues where news was regularly made, such as Congress, the White House, organizers of sporting events, and so on. The second question was whether legal protections that journalists claimed came from the First Amendment, if any, should be provided to bloggers?

The issue regarding press credentials came into sharp focus with the approach of the Democratic and Republican presidential nominating conventions in 2004. The Internet had been credited with playing a large role in the campaign of Howard Dean, the governor of Vermont, and although Dean did not win the nomination, online efforts were expected to play a role in the upcoming general election. How open would each party be to bloggers, who were seen as a potentially effective channel of communication to online communities, particularly young people who traditionally participated less in politics? Although each party expected to issue around 15,000 press credentials in total, according to a survey by the Pew Charitable Trusts, this would not begin to cover the five percent of 128 million American adults who used the Internet at that time and who said they had created a blog. Seventeen percent described themselves as blog readers.[75] While in the aggregate blogs had become a mass medium, it would clearly be impossible to accommodate all the bloggers who might want to attend the conventions.

More than two hundred bloggers applied for press credentials to the Democratic National Convention and in the end around thirty-five received them. Among those who received credentials were Jeralyn Merritt, who worked for a criminal defense attorney in Denver, Colorado, and ran the blog talkleft.com, where she commented on political and criminal justice issues, and Jay Rosen, a professor at New York University, who wrote the blog Pressthink.com. "Whomever they decide to let through the gate is now the press," Rosen said at the time. "What the credential means to me is that someone just expanded the idea of the press a little bit."[76]

While some bloggers slowly won recognition as journalists in the world of politics and elsewhere, the situation in the courts was murkier. In 1994, about a dozen reporters were criminally charged or were threatened with jail sentences for refusing to disclose their confidential sources for stories they had written about events that eventually led to criminal trials or other investigations. Worried that the threat of incarceration would inhibit whistle-blowing to the press, in 2005, Senator Richard Lugar and Representative Mike Pence introduced the Free Flow of Information Act, which would set national standards for subpoenas issued to reporters by the federal government. The goal was to strike a reasonable balance between the public's right to know and the fair administration of justice.[77] When asked, Lugar told the Inter American Press Agency that bloggers would probably not be covered.[78] In fact, the protections in the act were to be extended only to people who "regularly" engaged in the listed journalistic activities—such as gathering and publishing news and information for dissemination to the public—and who do so "for a substantial portion of the person's livelihood or for substantial financial gain." The definition of journalist was tied in large part to traditional media operations, both print and electronic.[79] In 2007, however, the bill was amended to encompass a more expansive definition of a journalist. In the amended version, journalism was defined as "gathering, preparing, collecting, photographing, recording, writing, editing, reporting or publishing of news or information that concerns local, national or international events or other matters of public interest for dissemination to the public." The measure did not require that people do journalism as an occupation or even on a regular basis. How the definition would ultimately be interpreted, the bill's sponsor said, would be up to the courts.[80]

The question of protection for bloggers came into full view in 2006. Josh Wolf, one of the first video bloggers, was jailed for eight months for refusing to testify to a grand jury or turn over to investigators video he shot of a crowd of anarchists as they protested the G8 summit, a meeting of the leaders of the top industrial countries in the world. Wolf had recorded demonstrators as they marched through San Francisco's Mission District, committing sporadic acts of vandalism, and had posted some of the video on his blog. Moreover, television news stations ran some of the material, for which Wolf was paid. Government authorities wanted the rest of his footage.

Wolf might have been protected by California's shield law,

which protects journalists from divulging their sources, but the case was being prosecuted as a federal offense. The government argued that Wolf was not a real journalist, but only an amateur using the claim of press freedom to protect his friends.[81] Wolf was finally released after answering two questions in writing from prosecutors. He then posted the rest of the video to his blog.[82]

Efforts to force bloggers to reveal their confidential sources continued to surface. Also in 2006, Apple Computer Corporation sued the blogger Powerpage.org to force it to release the names of individuals who leaked details about a new product, describing the leaks as a "very serious theft."[83] In 2007 in Hawaii, as a part of a lawsuit about the failure of the Ka Loko Dam, a lawyer sued to compel Malia Zimmerman, who wrote the Hawaii reporter.com blog, to turn over her confidential sources, claiming that as a blogger she was not entitled to withhold her sources of information.[84]

THE BLOGOSPHERE FLEXES ITS MUSCLES

The urgency to define the role of blogging within journalism was driven in part by the obvious impact that bloggers were beginning to have, particularly on politics. In December 2002, a party celebrating the one-hundredth birthday of Senator Strom Thurmond of South Carolina was held in the Dirksen Senate Office building in Washington, D.C. Thurmond had started his career as an ardent segregationist, bolting from the Democratic Party in 1948 to protest the civil rights plank in its party platform.[85] That year, Thurmond conducted a third-party campaign for the presidency based on the primacy of states' rights, code words for segregation of the races. During the great civil rights battles of the

1960s, Thurmond had joined the Republican Party. He eventually endorsed federal civil rights laws and ultimately came to be seen primarily as the oldest man to hold a seat in the Senate.

His birthday party was a convivial affair filled with well-wishers that was broadcast on C-SPAN and merited a front-page article in the next day's *Washington Post.* What was not mentioned in the *Post* article was that, in a toast to Thurmond during the party, Senator Trent Lott of Mississippi, then the majority leader of the Senate, said fondly that many in the room had voted for Thurmond when he ran for president, they were proud of that vote, and that if the country had followed their lead, it would not have faced many of the problems that came after. The remarks seemed to be an endorsement of segregation and a criticism of the Civil Rights movement. Although some of the press reports in newspapers and news broadcasts that followed noted the remarks, the focus of their reports was on the pleasant atmosphere at the party. They generally highlighted the Marilyn Monroe impersonator who kissed the centenarian senator; Thurmond was well known for his fondness for women. Only ABC News included criticism by the Leadership Conference on Civil Rights of Lott's remarks.

In years past, the moment may have passed relatively unnoticed. But at the time, there were close to a million registered blogs (although it was hard to estimate how many were active). As important, a community of high-profile blogs covering politics had begun to take shape, including InstaPundit, Talking Points Memo (started by Josh Micah Marshall, a journalist who had formerly worked for the liberal journal of ideas, *The American Prospect*), the anonymous Atrios, and others. Although Reynolds on Instapundit had as many as 50,000 visitors a week and Talking Points Memo had perhaps 20,000, the real audience for many of the political bloggers was the traditional media. Often, the traditional media was the megaphone through which a blogger could be heard nationally.

Eventually, word of the Lott toast reached Tom Edsall of the *Washington Post,* who in an earlier story had detailed Lott's connection to segregationist groups, connections Lott had denied. Edsall ultimately wrote a relatively short piece for the *Post* about the comments at the birthday party that included background on Thurmond's Dixiecrat party as well as critical reaction to the remarks from leading Democrats and Republicans. To drive home his point, Edsall closed with a complimentary comment from the head of the segregationist group with which Edsall had earlier linked Lott.

Edsall's story appeared on page 6 of the December 7 edition of the *Post,* a Saturday newspaper. The day before, both Josh Micah Marshall and Atrios had independently seen Lott's comments and began to blog about them. Both fleshed out the meaning of the remarks—that Lott was basically denigrating the voting and civil rights acts of the 1960s. For the next several days, both continued to blog on the story and criticize other reporters for not covering the story or not focusing on the remarks enough. InstaPundit eventually provided links to Atrios and Talking Point Memo and joined the barrage of criticism. Over time, the roar became so deafening (at least inside the Washington Beltway) that the mainstream press picked up the story again, reporting that Lott was in hot water over the remarks. Criticism of the remarks ultimately became so heated that Lott was forced to step down as majority leader. Although the bloggers had not broken the story, they kept it alive and stoked a conversation that ultimately had significant political consequences.

The Trent Lott affair was one of the first in which a conversation in the blogosphere had a clear impact on political events. It was not that a single blogger could exercise a powerful voice, but the conversation in which bloggers engaged with each other and with the nonblogging, megaphone press came to influence the course of coverage and the course of events. In 2002, Markos Moulitsas Zúniga started blogging at Daily Kos. An Army veteran, a former Republican, and the son of a Salvadoran mother and a Greek father, Moulitsas said that he started blogging because he was angry with what he perceived as the efforts of the administration of President George W. Bush to make all dissent seem unpatriotic.[86] In April 2004, Moulitsas posted a comment saying that he felt nothing about the deaths of four American contractors who had just been murdered in a most gruesome fashion in Iraq. Conservative bloggers demanded that advertisers and others dissociate themselves from Daily Kos. The opposite happened. By 2005, Daily Kos was attracting 400,000 visitors a week. Moreover, Moulitsas became a significant influence within the Democratic Party. He had been an early supporter of Howard Dean's campaign for the presidency of the United States, which attracted much more attention than had originally been expected. He was active in the opposition to Senator Joseph Lieberman of Connecticut in 2006. Lieberman lost the Democratic nomination for the Senate that year but was reelected anyway as an independent.[87]

Moulitsas did not just launch his own blog, he created a community of bloggers. By 2006, Daily Kos was drawing 600,000 visitors, and Moulitsas had organized an annual conference that similarly minded bloggers attended. Originally called Yearly Kos and then renamed Netroots Nation, the conference attracted many high-profile journalists from more established media outlets as well as most of the leading Democratic politicians, including most of the leading candidates for the Democratic nomination for the presidency.[88]

Daily Kos is only one cluster of liberal bloggers. In August 2005, Arianna Huffington launched The Huffington Post. Huffington had first come to public notice as the wife of Michael Huffington, heir to a Texas oil fortune and a member of the U.S. Congress from California, who, in 1994, spent $28 million of his own money in an attempt to unseat Senator Dianne Feinstein. At the time, it was the most expensive senatorial campaign in history. The couple divorced in 1997, and in 1998, Huffington revealed that he was bisexual and that his wife had married him knowing of his sexual interest in men.[89] Arianna Huffington revealed that she had become disillusioned with conservative policies and had become more liberal politically, befriending the poverty activist Jim Wallis and the comedian Al Franken.[90]

Somewhat improbably, after moving to Los Angeles, Arianna Huffington successfully remade herself as a liberal pundit. In 2003, she ran an independent campaign for governor of California, garnering almost no votes. In 2005, Kenny Lerer, a former America Online executive, and Jonah Peretti, a graduate of the MIT Media Laboratory and considered to be an expert in creating viral media—content that spreads from user to user on the Internet—teamed up to create The Huffington Post. The idea was to create a platform for bloggers with Huffington using her connections to recruit high-profile bloggers and Peretti using his techniques to spread the word otherwise. The concept worked. Over time, The Huffington Post gathered together 1,600 bloggers. Celebrities like John Cusack, Deepak Chopra, Nora Ephron, and Bill Moyers posted their thoughts on HuffPo, as it came to be affectionately called. By 2007, The Huffington Post was attracting 3.6 million visitors, and its users were generating 250,000 comments a month. The Huffington Post became a place for other journalists to visit regularly to get a pulse on the issues of the day.[91] Unlike most bloggers, who blogged primarily to express themselves and not for pay, The Huffington Post was intended to be an ongoing business. Through 2007, it raised $11 million in venture capital and then at the end of 2008 announced that it had raised another $25 million from Oak Investment Partners. The investment put a valuation on The Huffington Post at $100 million.[92]

The ability of the blogosphere to influence the course of political coverage continued to grow. In September 2004, with the presidential campaign in full gear, Dan Rather, on the television news magazine *60 Minutes II,* reported the explosive story of President George W. Bush receiving special treatment while serving in the Texas National Guard during the war in Vietnam. The charges had increased salience because President Bush was running against Senator John Kerry, who had won three Purple Hearts for being wounded during his service in Vietnam; Kerry's service was being attacked by other Vietnam veterans, and Kerry opposed the current war in Iraq, which Bush supported. CBS had based the story on four memos that were purported to be from the National Guard, which the news organization posted to its Web site. Nineteen minutes into the broadcast, bloggers began to question the story on a well-known conservative blog called Free Republic. Other posts followed and then a blog called Rathergate.com was established by Richard Viguerie, a major conservative fund-raiser, to serve as a clearinghouse for those questioning the story. The eruption in the blogosphere put CBS on the defensive. Ultimately the documents were judged to be forgeries, and Dan Rather was forced into retirement.[93]

The full potential for blogging in journalism reached beyond the ability to get people chattering about a specific subject and pushing it onto the public agenda. The idea was that with bloggers virtually everywhere, they could identify national stories that no single news organization could identify. Blogging could apply the approach of open source software development to journalism. A community could provide better reporting than a traditional organization.

Evidence of the potential came in 2008 when Talking Points Memo (TPM) won the George Polk Award for legal reporting. Through its correspondents, TPM had broken the story that the Bush administration had fired eight U.S. attorneys for what seemed to be political reasons. In pursuing the story, TPM combined original reporting with links to local articles about prosecutors being forced from office. In doing so, TPM was able to draw a national picture for its readers. Josh Micah Marshall had founded TPM in 2000, when he was serving as the Washington editor for *The American Prospect* and also a candidate for a Ph.D. in history at Brown University. Earlier in his career he had designed Web sites and published an online newsletter about Internet law. The idea behind TPM was to develop an outlet for his ideas as well as to track the recount in the presidential election in Florida in the year 2000. The blogger Mickey Kaus, who Marshall knew, added TPM to Kausfiles's blogroll, a list of blogs to which Kausfiles linked directly.[94]

Marshall followed the traditional Internet start-up route by starting small and building an audience first. In 2003, he began soliciting revenue and hired TPM's first full-time reporter. The objective was to report news, aggregate news from other news sources, and to allow TPM readers to contribute news and opinions. At times, Marshall openly solicited input on issues from readers. By 2005, TPM was generating advertising revenue from several sources, and from time to time, Marshall would directly solicit financial support from his readership. By 2008, TPM was attracting 750,000 unique visitors a month.[95]

As the blogosphere emerged as a channel of communication, many pundits suggested that it represented the liberal counterpart to talk radio, which traditionally was dominated by conservative voices. More important, it represented a flashpoint between traditional news media—online, electronic, and in print—and start-up news efforts shaped by the possibilities offered by the Internet. The Internet supported a different mix of reporting, aggregation, and personal commentary from journalists, experts, celebrities, commentators, and their audiences.

---◇---

SEVEN

THE ACCELERATION OF CHANGE

In 2002, Dave Winer, the creator of RSS (really simple syndication) and EditThisPagePHP blogging technology, made a bet with Martin Nisenholtz, then head of digital operations at the *New York Times.* Winer contended that by 2007 more people would get their news from blogs than from the *New York Times.*[1] Winer clearly did not win the bet, but in early 2009 it was not clear that he had lost either. By 2008, leading politicians routinely attended the annual conference organized by Markos Moulitsas, the founder of Daily Kos, and paid homage to the blogging community in the same way that they might visit the *New York Times* editorial board. Moreover, like the *New York Times,* blogs have demonstrated that they can push stories onto the national agenda.

Blogging has carved out a role in journalism. In January 2008, The Huffington Post was in the top 500 most visited sites on the Web and within the top 120 sites in the United States. However, those numbers pale in comparison to audiences the Web sites of what has come to be called the mainstream media attract. According to Alexa, a Web site that monitors Web traffic, in 2009 the Web site of the *New York Times* was the ninetieth most visited site, with nearly eighty times more traffic than Daily Kos and four times more traffic than The Huffington Post. The most visited news Web site, CNN.com, was the forty-ninth most visited Web site, with nearly twice the traffic of the *New York Times.* In 2008, CNN averaged approximately 485 million visitors a month.[2] Coupled with CNN's broadcast reach and the subscribers to the *New York Times* newspaper, clearly both are more powerful sources of news than bloggers.

But blogging is only one part of the equation for online news. Fifteen years after the *San Jose Mercury News* launched the Mercury Center and the *Raleigh News and Observer* started NandO .Net, the Web is a routine and growing platform to deliver the news. When Barack Obama was sworn in as the forty-fourth president of the United States, it was assumed that tens of millions of people around the world would watch the ceremony via the Web. By 2009, the idea that breaking news drives huge traffic to news Web sites is as unexceptional as cutting between images of the Brooklyn Bridge and the Golden Gate Bridge on television. On election day in 2008, CNN.com recorded 282 million page views, which represents more than 80 million visitors, nearly three times the amount that visited the site on election day in 2004. Officials in Washington, D.C. anticipated that tens of thousands of people would be blogging and sending their own pictures and video from the inaugural events in 2009. Extra cellular telephone network capacity was installed to handle the event, and warnings were issued that there could be delays if too much video was transmitted.[3]

As more people got Internet access and as using the Internet became a more routine part of people's daily activities, accessing news online became increasingly commonplace. The movement online posed a clear threat to newspapers. In 2004, the Carnegie Corporation commissioned a study that found among

18-to-34-year-old adults, while television was the most popular source of news for women and people with lower incomes, the Internet was emerging as the most popular source of news for men and people with higher incomes. Newspapers had no clear pockets of strength among any audiences. Moreover, nearly half of this demographic group reported using portals that also had daily news, such as Yahoo! and MSN.com. More than 40 percent of the respondents indicated that the Internet offered news when they wanted it, which was a very important consideration for them.[4]

Studies conducted by the Pew Charitable Trusts produced similar results. In the summer of 2006, Pew reported that 13 percent of all Americans were accessing online news about the midterm congressional elections, two and a half times more than the number who accessed political news online in the summer before the 2002 midterm elections.[5] At the end of 2008, the Pew Charitable Trusts reported the Internet had surpassed newspapers as a source of news. In a survey conducted by the Pew Research Center for the People and the Press in December 2008, 40 percent of the respondents reported that they get most of their news about national and international issues from the Internet, up from 24 percent in September 2007. Newspapers were a primary source of news for 35 percent of the respondents, while television continued to be the most popular news medium. Seventy percent of the respondents said that television was a main source of national and international news.

For younger people, the results were even more startling. Among people under the age of thirty, 59 percent reported that they got most of their national and international news online, figures that matched those of television. Only 28 percent of the respondents under the age of thirty reported that newspapers were a main source of news. The poll results marked a sharp change from

September 2007. By late 2008, the number of young people re-porting television as a main source of news had plunged eleven percentage points compared to 2007, while the number of people identifying the Internet as a main source of news had jumped an impressive twenty-five percentage points. In September 2007, twice as many young people said they relied mostly on televi-sion for news than mentioned the Internet. To fully understand the growth of the Internet as a primary source of news, in 2002, only 14 percent of the respondents to the Pew survey said that the Internet was a main source of national and international news while 82 percent said television was a main source of news. Forty-two percent relied on newspapers for national and international news.

The pronounced shift toward the Internet as a primary source of news is intertwined with at least three major relatively inde-pendent long-term trends. Each of these trends raises serious questions about the future structure and practice of journalism in the United States. The most obvious and immediate trend is that online journalism has placed urban daily newspapers under tremendous pressure, and the days of city newspapers supporting news rooms staffed with hundreds seem to be over. But the need to report local news remains. What kind of structures, if any, will replace city newspapers? Second, the established news media can no longer serve as gatekeepers for the news. News can get onto the Internet from anybody, anywhere, and at anytime. On the one hand, the diminishing role of big media calls into question who is a journalist and what is journalism. On the other hand, mainstream media currently serve as megaphones for online jour-nalism. Although unique stories may break on the Internet, their impact is magnified by the mainstream media. What happens if there is no megaphone? The third major trend is that the rate of technological change is accelerating. While the Web and blogging have already carved out roles within journalism, new technologies are emerging, including Wikis, handheld devices, and other communication technologies like Twitter, which may or may not play a role in journalism over time. The question remains as to which technologies will be suitable for a journalism that supports a rich social, cultural, and political life and which technologies may not? Taken together, the answers to these questions will have an enormous impact on American life.

IS THE BIG CITY NEWSPAPER DEAD?

The long-term, steady deterioration of newspaper readership had been well documented. According to the Newspaper Association of America, from 1972 to 1998, the percentage of people age thirty to thirty-nine who read a paper every day dropped from 73 percent to 30 percent. As the Web geared up, the situation got worse. Between 1997 and 2000, the percentage of people age eighteen to twenty-four who say they read yesterday's newspaper dropped by 14 percent. While newspapers created Web sites, many industry observers argued that newspapers never made a full commitment to Web and new product development. Their Web efforts were always seen as supplemental to the print newspaper.[6] For example, it was only in 2007 that the *Atlanta Journal-Constitution* made the commitment to put its digital operation on an equal footing with its print operation. Even then, the fear that the Web effort could hasten the demise of the print product was still evident.

News companies tried to pull off a balancing act between the Web and print. As a part of its reorganization, the *Journal-Constitution* consciously cut back the area in which the newspaper was distributed and reduced home-delivery discounts. The editorial staff was trimmed by 15 percent and coverage was focused more on local events. On the other hand, with the new attention to the Web site, by August 2007, page views climbed 22 percent compared to the prior year.[7]

Even with the nearly generation-long slide in newspaper readership and the clear understanding that online journalism posed a significant challenge to print, most people envisioned a long, and perhaps benign, transition along the lines the *Atlanta Journal-Constitution* was trying to engineer. Traditional newspaper companies may have been slow to fully grapple with both the risks and the rewards of the Web but most news organizations assumed that ultimately many of them would manage the transformation.[8] Moreover, the attrition that newspapers had experienced in the face of competition from television had occurred over two decades or more. Many anticipated a similarly long transition period.

A severe economic recession that started in 2008 dramatically altered the equation. Along with the slide of readership, the advertising base of newspapers had long been eroding. In the 1990s, there had been a sustained consolidation in department store chains and supermarkets, two stalwart advertisers. Classified advertising, particularly help wanted ads, had migrated largely to Web sites like Craigslist, which would post ads for free. The recession of 2008 hit two of the remaining advertising pillars for newspapers the hardest—automobiles and real estate. As the economy contracted, the impact on newspapers was swift and dramatic. In October 2008, the *Christian Science Monitor* announced that it would suspend its print edition and publish only online.[9] In December 2008, the Tribune Company, owner of the *Chicago Tribune,* the *Los Angeles Times,* and ten other newspapers, filed for bankruptcy, weighted down by the debt acquired during a leveraged buyout a year earlier. When the company filed for bankruptcy, it noted that advertising revenues were down 19 percent, the sharpest drop since the recession of 1981.[10] That same month, the *Detroit News* and the *Detroit Free Press* announced that they would stop home delivery of their newspaper four days a week, offering only a slimmer version of the newspaper for newsstand sales and online access. "My theory behind this continues to be, I'm going to invest less in paper, fuel, ink and distribution. It allows me to maintain my journalism," Dave Hunke, chief executive of the partnership and publisher of the *Free Press,* said at the time. The move also entailed laying off nine percent of the newspaper's work force.[11] In January 2009, the *Minneapolis Star Tribune* filed for bankruptcy.[12]

Even the *New York Times* was not immune to the problems. On the day that the Tribune Company filed for bankruptcy, the *New York Times* announced that it received $225 million through a sale and lease back arrangement of its new headquarters on Times Square. In January 2009, the company revealed that Mexican billionaire Carlos Slim had agreed to lend the company $250 million. The net result of the complicated deal would leave Slim owning 17 percent of the *Times.* In comparison, the Sulzberger family, the longtime owners of the *Times,* would hold only 19 percent of the company.[13]

As the winter turned into spring in 2009, the news got worse. In February, the *Rocky Mountain News* was closed after its parent company, E.W. Scripps, failed to find a buyer. Founded in 1859, the newspaper had lost $16 million over the past three years.[14] The same week, the Hearst Company threatened to sell or close the *San Francisco Chronicle* if it could not wring economic concessions from its unions.[15] In March 2009, the *Seattle Post-Intelligencer* stopped printing a newspaper and went to an all-Web delivery of the news. Although with the move the *Post-Intelligencer* became the largest daily to go to an all-Web format, as part of the process it cut its news staff from 165 people to 20. The future of the *Post-Intelligencer*'s competitor, the *Seattle Times,* with whom it had a joint operating agreement, was also in doubt.[16]

The economic difficulties faced by urban newspapers were not completely attributable to the competition from online journalism. From 2005 to 2007, many major newspapers had experienced ownership changes, fueled by the availability of easy credit. When the economic downturn hit and credit dried up, those companies were not in the position to manage their debt load. Nonetheless, with the demise of many urban newspapers apparently imminent, could online journalism fill the void they would leave as the dominant reporters of news in their geographic areas? The economic model of online journalism did not seem likely to be able to support the same kind of news gathering operations that urban newspapers supported. An analysis of the popular Web site of the *New York Times,* for example, suggested that it could only support about 20 percent of the current news staff.[17]

With the future of the city daily newspaper in doubt, many interesting online and hybrid news experiments have been launched. One approach is to create not-for-profit reporting teams whose work can then be used across a wide variety of media. In 2007, former managing editor of the *Wall Street Journal* Paul Steiger and Stephen Engelberg, a former managing editor of the *Oregonian* in Portland, helped to found ProPublica, an independent, nonprofit newsroom that produces investigative journalism in the public interest. Funded primarily by the Sandler Foundation, ProPublica was created to address what its founders felt was the contraction of original reporting. Although the Internet created a proliferation of publishing platforms, many of those sites aggregated material from elsewhere. ProPublica's goal was to be the largest, best-led, and best-funded investigative journalism operation in the United States.[18] In a twist on the same approach, Spot.us solicits contributions from readers to fund projects that can be published anywhere. Some of the stories that received funding addressed the rise of car and tent encampments in San Francisco and why the San Francisco transit authority doesn't run more express buses.[19]

In the spring of 2009, The Huffington Post launched a hybrid initiative to fund investigative journalism. It teamed with American News Project, an independent video journalism project, to create the Huffington Post Investigative Fund. The fund's initial $1.75 million budget was provided by both The Huffington Post and The Atlantic Philanthropies, whose mission is to bring lasting change to disadvantaged people. According to the announcement when the fund was launched, the fund will support long-form investigations as well as short, breaking news stories presented in a variety of media—including text, audio, and video. The stories will be available free for any media outlet to publish simultaneously.[20]

Politico represents yet another innovative approach for journalism. Founded in 2007 by John Harris and Jim VandeHei, two former *Washington Post* reporters, and owned by Allbritton Communications, a mainstream communications company that owns local District of Columbia television stations WJLA-TV and NewsChannel 8, Politico launched a Web site to give extensive coverage to the federal government. While Congress is in session, it also publishes a print edition, but the focus of its efforts is on the Web site. The idea was to cover the federal government extensively.[21] During the 2008 presidential election, this kind of focused coverage proved that it could attract an audience. For example, when Politico sponsored one of the Republican debates in May of that year, some 648,000 people visited its Web site, up 162 percent from April. Even more narrowly targeted Web sites such as

FiveThirtyEight, Pollster.com, and RealClearPolitics, which provided comprehensive coverage of all the polling taking place during the elections, also saw spikes in traffic.[22]

Finally, there has been a proliferation of independent citizen-based media efforts. The idea of citizen media was pioneered by the Korean Web site OhmyNews. Launched in the year 2000, by 2003 the site had forty editors posting two hundred stories a day and attracting two million visitors daily. The stories were being generated by 26,000 citizen-journalists. The site was given credit for helping to elect South Korea's progressive president, Roh Moo-hyun, in the early 2000s.[23] In 2007, the Knight Foundation, in conjunction with the Institute for Interactive Journalism, then housed at the University of Maryland, unveiled a Web portal to help citizens and journalists create community news sites.[24] Supporting what was called the Knight Citizen News Network, there were over 800 innovative community-based news efforts around the country.[25]

EVERYBODY IS A REPORTER

With the proliferation of citizen media, virtually anybody can post news. Even CNN encourages what it calls Ireporters to submit photos and videos of the events they attend. Within a short period of time, Ireports was receiving 10,000 submissions a month. So, on the one hand, news gathering is proliferating broadly. On the other hand, the distinction between professional news gathering and amateur news gathering is becoming blurred. For example, in 2008, Mayhill Fowler, a blogger for The Huffington Post, attended a closed-door fundraiser on behalf of presidential candidate Barack Obama in San Francisco. While there, using her cell phone, she videotaped Obama commenting that some small-town residents in Pennsylvania were bitter at being passed by in economic terms and therefore clung to religion and guns. She posted the videotape to The Huffington Post. When it was seized on and criticized by Hillary Clinton, Obama's chief rival for the Democratic nomination, it became the subject of heated debate and was seen as a major gaffe on the part of the Obama campaign. At one point, some pundits felt the remark could change the direction of the race. Ironically, Fowler was at the fundraiser because she was an Obama supporter but felt she had to post the video to fulfill her obligations as a journalist. Her responsibilities as a journalist, she said, outweighed her responsibilities as a supporter.[26]

Fowler's contribution to the 2008 presidential campaign would have been impossible prior to the spread of the Internet. Could what she did even be considered journalism? Fowler was part of a project launched by The Huffington Post called OffTheBus, in which it recruited 7,500 citizen journalists to be its eyes and ears during the presidential campaign. The idea was for the OffTheBus correspondents to sweep up information in hope of uncovering overlooked news of importance, establishing trends that might not otherwise be obvious, or simply establishing a strong database of information that could be used to bolster future reporting.[27]

The effectiveness of citizen journalists was an open question. Obviously, no news organization could actually support 7,500 correspondents. But the quality of the materials from 7,500 correspondents would be very uneven. Citizen journalists could perhaps capture and report on a demonstration in Bagdad or terrorist violence in Mumbai that would be beyond the reach of professional news organizations. But could citizen journalists provide accurate coverage of ongoing events consistently enough to keep people accurately informed about what they need to know?[28]

For citizen journalists, credibility and accuracy are major issues. In the OffTheBus project, correspondents had to acknowledge their political affiliations. But the possibility that an individual's personal perspective would color his or her coverage of a specific event is high. While a community developing a software application can be self-correcting, this is not necessarily the case in journalism. Social networks make mistakes.[29]

Since the very beginnings of Usenet, the Internet has been a medium for rumors, urban legends, hoaxes, and falsehoods. Although professional journalism organizations are not immune to making mistakes, there are safeguards in place. In the age of citizen journalism, those safeguards have weakened. For example, an incorrect citizen report on CNN's IReport site that Apple CEO Steve Jobs, whose health had been an open question, was rushed to the emergency room sent Apple stock plunging five percent in one day. In a similar example, false information about United Airlines led to a stock sell-off. When Matt Drudge reported that Oprah Winfrey refused to have Republican vice presidential candidate Sarah Palin on her show, it spread through the Internet and ultimately onto the NBC Nightly News, even though Winfrey denied it. New tools like Digg, a Web site designed to discover and share content on the Web, helped accelerate the rate at which mistakes spread through the Internet.[30]

But the widespread availability of news from all sources works in the other direction as well. In January 2008, MSNBC began to allow Web sites to embed video from the NBC Nightly News, making it easier for other Web sites to use MSNBC content on their sites.[31] This process has set up an echo chamber between the Web and other forms of media. For example, when the comedienne Tina Fey lampooned vice presidential candidate Sarah Palin on the television show *Saturday Night Live,* many more people watched the segment on YouTube than on the original broadcast. As Fey continued offering send-ups of the candidate, *Saturday Night Live*'s ratings soared, with the show ultimately airing a special edition on a Thursday night.[32]

ACCELERATING CHANGES

Online journalism is changing the way that content becomes available for public discussion. Anybody can upload words, images, or video that potentially can be read by the public, however the word *public* is defined. At the same time, professional news organizations are making at least part of their content available for anybody to embed into their own Web sites. These changes are enabled by the development of new technology, which continues to develop rapidly.

It took about two hundred years for all the technology that allowed for the development of the modern newspaper to emerge. By the early 1900s, however, newspapers began to look very much like they looked a hundred years later. It took about fifty years for the technology that enabled the modern television news broadcast to develop. But by the late 1980s, newscasts looked pretty much the same as they did twenty years later. For online journalism, the technology continues to develop at an accelerated clip, and there is no evidence to indicate when the rate of development may slow. It is not yet clear which technologies will shape the ultimate contours of online journalism.

In late 2008, the Israeli army invaded the Gaza Strip, a sliver of land ruled by its bitter enemy, the Palestinian organization Hamas. The invasion sparked protests around the world. To defend its position, the Israeli Consulate in New York conducted a news conference that could be attended by anybody. It used Twitter, a social medium that allows people to send messages of 140 characters or less. "Since the definition of war has changed, the definition of public diplomacy has to change as well," an Israeli diplomat who helped organize the news conference said at the time.[33] Twitter represented the next step in the development of an always-on communication culture that bypasses the traditional media. Celebrities, sports stars, politicians, and even business executives have taken to sending out regular updates regarding their thoughts, views, and whereabouts.[34]

Twitter, in turn, has been enabled by the proliferation of mobile and handheld devices. The release of the Apple iPhone in 2007 led to an explosion in the use of smart phones. Over the next two years, Apple's competitors, such as Research in Motion and Palm, also released devices that provided access to the Internet and a wide array of features found on personal computers. Even before the iPhone was released, text messaging had exploded as a channel of communication for younger people. When Barack Obama, who assiduously courted the youth vote, announced that Senator Joe Biden of Delaware was his choice to run for vice president, he sent a text message directly to supporters rather than holding a press conference. To go from text messaging and e-mail to downloading Web pages and receiving tweets, the name for Twitter messages, is a short leap. Since the release of the Apple iPod, many communities of people have become very used to downloading music and information onto a handheld device. Amazon.com joined the fray with the release of its Kindle reader, on which readers can not only download books but magazines and newspapers as well. Like in the early days of the online services, publishers are making content created for other media available to download on Kindle. These handheld devices have the potential to serve as delivery platforms for original online journalism.

Wiki technology also pushes the envelope of collaboration. Wikis are Web applications that allow multiple authors to add, remove, and edit content in a collaborative process. Wikipedia, the collaborative online encyclopedia, is the primary example of a large-scale wiki project. In 2004, Wikipedia launched Wikinews. The idea was that several authors could collaborate in writing a single article. The only requirements were that all sources of information must be cited and that articles should take a neutral point of view. Several other publications have tried developing articles using wiki technology. In 2005, *Esquire* used Wikipedia itself to develop an article about Wikipedia. It received 224 edits in twenty-four hours and ultimately received 500 edits before the article was closed to be printed. In 2006, *Wired* magazine experimented with an article about wikis. It received 348 edits. With that kind of interaction, some observers have argued the wikis are the next step in participatory journalism.[35]

The potential application of wiki technology to journalism slipped into sight in the aftermath of the sudden death of Tim Russert, the host of NBC's long-running Sunday political talk show *Meet the Press* and a pillar of the Washington, D.C., political media establishment. On June 13, 2008, Russert collapsed in NBC's Washington newsroom. He was rushed to the hospital and pronounced dead at 2:23 P.M. Customarily, television news organizations allow the network with which a journalist is affiliated to announce news of a death first. But about twenty minutes before Tom Brokaw of NBC News informed the world of Russert's death, Russert's page on Wikipedia had been updated with the news. A junior staffer at the Internet Broadcasting Services of St. Paul, Minnesota, which provides Web services to the local NBC affiliate, had seen the news and updated the page.[36]

WHAT WE KNOW

By 2009, online journalism had fully emerged as a significant platform for news, but it was not yet fully formed. Like newspapers in the 1830s, and television in the 1960s, online journalism already has had significant social impact and serves as an important platform for people to learn about the world around them. But because it is intertwined with computer technology, the technical underpinnings for online journalism are still under development. As with all media, the technological development shapes and conditions both the production and consumption of online journalism.

Media products can be judged on a spectrum ranging from intensive to extensive. Intensive products are fewer in number but those that are produced are used over and over again. The quintessential intensive product is the Bible. People who acquire a Bible tend to read it over and over again. Extensive products are generally shorter and used for a shorter duration of time. The daily newspaper is an extensive product. It is widely circulated but by the next day it is considered fit only to line birdcages. The Internet has generally been used to develop extensive news products. Blog posts are shorter and have a shorter shelf life than newspaper articles. Tweets are shorter and have a shorter shelf life than blog posts. The old joke about the newspaper *USA Today* is that it would never win a Pulitzer Prize because Pulitzer Prizes were not awarded for the best paragraph of the year. A paragraph is a standard length for a blog post and beyond the parameters of a tweet. Some critics claim that television helped to destroy the attention of its viewers through its cut-quick production. But a thirty-minute video is a long-form production on the Web.

On the other hand, with online journalism a lot more people have the opportunity to put what they have seen and what they think in front of the public. One of the fundamental pillars of the philosophy of free speech is that the truth is more likely to emerge from a multitude of tongues; online journalism could put that faith to the test.

But that test of faith has not come yet. Although major stories have been broken online, and online journalism already has the potential to have an impact on the public agenda, to date, generally speaking, the impact of news broken online has been felt through the megaphone of the mainstream media. Only after stories have been picked up by the national media have they become national issues. What will happen to the stories that break online if the megaphone media—large urban newspapers like the *Chicago Tribune,* the *Boston Globe,* or the *Los Angeles Times,* which make up a critical element of the national media—fail is hard to anticipate.

The established media do more than disseminate information. They put items on the agenda for discussion and perhaps entertain their readers and viewers. Both newspapers and national news broadcasts help to define specific communities.[37] By creating a shared sense of the news, national television broadcasts in part help define who is an American. Newspapers play an even greater role in shaping local identities. The urban newspaper has long been the primary engine for local reporting. Reading the *Baltimore Sun,* for example, defined who was a Baltimorean as opposed to people who read the *Washington Post* as their hometown newspaper.

Writing about the online service The WELL in the 1980s, Howard Rheingold, in what is generally considered to be a prescient book, wrote that online computer users have the ability to form communities among themselves.[38] It is true that people can form communities online, feeling a common bond and perhaps a sense of shared identity with people to whom have they no other connection except their online interactions. But can online journalism focused on local issues build the same sense of community for those who live geographically near each other, people who actually have a relationship to each other beyond their online interactions? Over time, perhaps it can, 140 characters at a time.

NOTES

◈

CHAPTER ONE

1. Nicholas G. Carr, "IT Doesn't Matter," http://www.nicholasgcarr .com/articles/matter.html (accessed March 21, 2009).

2. Neil Postman, *Amusing Ourselves to Death* (New York: Penguin Books, 1985), 8.

3. Ibid., 62.

4. Ibid., 100.

5. Mitchell Stephens, *A History of News* (New York: Viking Penguin, 1988), 14.

6. Sian Lewis, *News and Society in the Greek Polis* (Chapel Hill, N.C.: University of North Carolina Press, 1996), 127–42.

7. Elliot King, "The Impact of the Internet on Journalism," *Electronic Journal of Communication* 7, no. 2–4 (1997).

8. Pablo J. Boczkowski, *Digitizing the News: Innovation in Online Newspapers* (Cambridge, Mass.: MIT Press, 2005).

9. Stuart Allan, *Online News: Journalism and the Internet* (New York: Open University Press, 2006).

10. Michael Brian Salwen, Bruce Garrison, and Paul D. Driscoll, eds., *Online News and the Public* (Mahwah, N.J.: Lawrence Erlbaum Associates, 2004).

11. Barrie Gunter, *News and the Net* (Mahwah, N.J.: Lawrence Erlbaum Associates, 2003).

12. Randy Reddick and Elliot King, *The Online Journalist* (Dallas: Harcourt Brace College Publishers, 1995).

13. Michael Schudson, *Discovering the News* (New York: Basic Books, 1981), 5.

CHAPTER TWO

1. Bjorn Sorenssen, "A New Audiovisual Format Emerges: See It Now in Korea," http://www.hf.ntnu.no/ikm/bjornso/Bjornweb/Artikler/murrow.htm (accessed March 21, 2009).

2. Ron Simon, "See It Now," The Museum of Broadcast Communication, http://www.museum.tv/archives/etv/S/htmlS/seeitnow/seeitnow.htm (accessed March 21, 2009).

3. Eric Barnouw, *The Golden Web: A History of Broadcasting in the United States* (New York: Oxford University Press, 1966), 171.

4. "Top of the News," *Newsweek,* December 3, 1951, 38.

5. "Douglas Edwards Chronology," The Douglas Edwards Archives at St. Bonaventure University, http://web.sbu.edu/friedsam/archives/Edwards/chronology.htm (accessed March 28, 2009).

6. Reuven Frank, "1948: Live ... From Philadelphia ... It's the National Conventions," *The New York Times* Magazine, April 17, 1988.

7. Edward Bliss Jr., *Now the News: The Story of Broadcast Journalism* (New York: Columbia University Press, 1991), 224–25.

8. Simon, "See It Now."

9. Roger Wallis and Stanley J. Baran, *The Known World of Broadcast News: International News and the Electronic Media* (New York: Routledge, 1991), 9.

10. Adnan Almaney, "International and Foreign Affairs on Network Television News," *Journal of Broadcasting* 14, no. 4 (1970): 499.

11. Everette M. Rogers, *Diffusions of Innovation,* 4th ed. (New York: Simon and Schuster, 1994), 30–31.

12. Paul Arblaster, "Posts, Newsletters, Newspapers: England in a European System of Communications," *Media History* 11, nos. 1–2 (April-August 2005): 21.

13. Sandra Sider, *Handbook to Life in Renaissance Europe* (New York: Oxford University Press, 2007), 232.

14. Arblaster, "Posts, Newsletters, Newspapers," *Media History* 11, nos. 1–2 (Apr-Aug 2005): 26.

15. Mitchell Stephens, *A History of News* (New York: Viking Penguin, 1988), 155.

16. Paul Arblaster, "Policy and Publishing in Hapsburg Netherland 1585–1690," in *The Politics of Information in Early Modern Europe,* Brendan

Maurice Dooley and Sabrina Alcorn Baron, eds. (New York: Routledge, 2001), 180, 181.

17. Stephens, *A History of News,* 155.

18. Ibid., 153.

19. Joad Raymond, *Pamphlets and Pamphleteering in Early Modern Britain* (New York: Cambridge University Press, 2006), 1.

20. Charles John Sommerville, *The News Revolution in England: Cultural Dynamics of Daily Information* (New York: Oxford University Press, 1996), 192.

21. Jim Bernhard, *Porcupine, Picayune, and Post: How Newspapers Get Their Names* (Columbia: University of Missouri Press, 2007), 13.

22. "Breaking News: Renaissance Journalism and the Birth of the Newspaper," Exhibition at the Folger Shakespeare Library, September 25, 2008, to January 31, 2009.

23. Raymond, *Pamphlets and Pamphleteering in Early Modern Britain,* 23.

24. Joseph George Muddiman, *A History of English Journalism to the Foundation of the Gazette* (London: Longman, Green, 1908), 14.

25. "Breaking News: Renaissance Journalism and the Birth of the Newspaper," Exhibition at the Folger Shakespeare Library.

26. Sommerville, *The News Revolution in England,* 26–27.

27. Thomas Schroder, "The Origins of the German Press," in *The Politics of Information in Early Modern Europe,* Brendan Maurice Dooley and Sabrina Alcorn Baron, eds. (New York: Routledge, 2001), 123.

28. Ibid., 125–28.

29. Richard Cust, "News and Politics in Seventeenth-century England," *Past and Present* 112 (1986): 73, 87.

30. Arblaster, "Policy and Publishing in Hapsburg Netherland 1585–1690," 180, 181.

31. Joseph Frank, *The Beginnings of the English Newspaper 1620–1660* (Cambridge, Mass.: Harvard University Press, 1961), 6.

32. Michael Mendle, "News and the Pamphlet Culture in 17th Century England," in *The Politics of Information in Early Modern Europe,* Brendan Maurice Dooley and Sabrina Alcorn Baron, eds. (New York: Routledge, 2001), 58.

33. Raymond, *Pamphlets and Pamphleteering in Early Modern Britain,* 206.

34. Stephens, *A History of News,* 166–67.

35. Frank, *The Beginnings of the English Newspaper 1620–1660*, 267–69.

36. Sommerville, *The News Revolution in England*, 58, 77.

37. Jan De Vries, *The Industrious Revolution: Consumer Behavior and the Household Economy, 1650 to the Present* (Cambridge, England: Cambridge University Press, 2008), 156.

38. Robert Clark, "The Licensing Act (1662), The Literary Encyclopedia, http://www.litencyc.com/php/stopics.php?rec=true&UID=1407 (accessed March 21, 2009).

39. Michael Harris, *London Newspapers in the Age of Walpole: A Study of the Origins of the Modern English Press* (Madison, N.J.: Fairleigh Dickinson University Press, 1987), 19.

40. Kirstin Olsen, *Daily Life in 18th-century England* (Westport, Conn.: Greenwood Publishing Group, 1999), 184.

41. Stanley Morison, *The English Newspaper: Some Account of the Physical Development of Journals Printed in London Between 1622 and the Present Day* (Ann Arbor, Mich.: The University Press, 1932), 123–51.

42. David Paul Nord, "Teleology and News: The Religious Roots of American Journalism 1630–1730," *The Journal of American History* 77, no. 1 (June 1990): 16.

43. Richard Kielbowicz, *News in the Mail* (Westport, Conn.: Greenwood Press, 1989), 31.

44. Stephen Botein, "Printers and the American Revolution," in *The Press and the American Revolution,* Bernard Bailyn and John B. Hench, eds. (Worcester, Mass.: American Antiquarian Society, 1980), 11.

45. Kielbowicz, *News in the Mail,* 31.

46. Frank Luther Mott, *American Journalism: A History* (New York: Macmillan, 1962), 203.

47. Michael Emery, Edwin Emery, and Nancy Roberts, *The Press in America: An Interpretive History of the Mass Media,* 9th ed. (Boston: Allyn and Bacon, 2000), 95.

48. Mott, *American Journalism,* 204.

49. Emery, Emery, and Roberts, *The Press in America,* 95.

50. Chauncey Mitchell Depew, *1795–1895 One Hundred Years of American Commerce: A History of American Commerce by One Hundred Americans, with a Chronological Table of the Important Events of American Commerce and Invention Within the Past One Hundred Years* (New York: O. Haynes, 1895), 303–5.

51. Willard G. Bleyer, *Main Currents in the History of American Journalism* (New York: Houghton Mifflin Co., 1927), 187.

52. Ibid., 175.

53. Tom Standage, *The Victorian Internet* (New York: Berkley Books, 1999), 45–54.

54. Menahem Blondheim, *News Over the Wires: The Telegraph and the Flow of Public Information in America, 1844–1897* (Cambridge, Mass.: Harvard University Press, 1994), 33.

55. Standage, *The Victorian Internet,* 50.

56. Blondheim, *News Over the Wires,* 41.

57. Richard A. Schwarzlose, "The Nation's First Wire Service: Evidence Supporting a Footnote," *Journalism Quarterly* 57, no. 4 (Winter 1980): 558.

58. Ibid., 559.

59. Emery, Emery, and Roberts, *The Press in America,* 114–15.

60. Standage, *The Victorian Internet,* 156–57.

61. James Carey, "Technology and Ideology: The Case of the Telegraph," in James Carey, ed., *Communication as Culture,* 2nd ed. (London: Taylor and Francis, 2008), 155–77.

62. Donald L. Shaw, "News Bias and the Telegraph: A Study of Historical Change," *Journalism Quarterly* 44 (Spring 1967): 5–11.

63. David T. Z. Mindich, "Edwin M. Stanton, the Inverted Pyramid, and Information Control," *Journalism Monographs,* no. 140 (August 1993): 2.

64. Roger Fidler, *Mediamorphosis: Understanding New Media* (Thousand Oaks, Calif.: Pine Forge Press, 1997), 69.

65. Gerald J. Baldasty, *E. W. Scripps and the Business of Newspapers* (Champaign: University of Illinois Press, 1999), 2.

66. Bonnie Brennen and Hanno Hardt, *Picturing the Past: Media, History, and Photography* (Champaign: University of Illinois Press, 1999), 3.

67. George H. Douglas, *The Early Days of Broadcasting* (Jefferson, N.C.: McFarland and Company, 1987), 1.

68. Susan J. Douglas, *Inventing American Broadcasting, 1899–1922* (Baltimore, Md.: The Johns Hopkins University Press, 1987), 9–10.

69. G. H. Douglas, *The Early Days of Broadcasting,* 8–9.

70. Ibid., 11.

71. S. J. Douglas, *Inventing American Broadcasting,* 102.

72. Ibid., 240.

73. "The Radio Act of 1927," *Columbia Law Review* 27, no. 6 (June 1927): 726–33.

74. Lisa Gitelman, *Always Already New* (Cambridge, Mass.: The MIT Press, 2006), 59.

75. William C. Ackerman, "The Dimensions of American Broadcasting," *The Public Opinion Quarterly* 9, no. 1 (Spring 1945): 1–18.

76. Alfred N. Goldsmith and Austin C. Lescaroura, *This Thing Called Broadcasting* (New York: Henry Holt and Co., 1930), 186.

77. Ibid., 197.

78. Ibid., 198–203.

79. Emery, Emery, and Roberts, *The Press in America,* 276.

80. Ibid.

81. Christopher H. Sterling and John Michael Kittross, *Stay Tuned: A History of American Broadcasting* (Mahwah, N.J.: Lawrence Erlbaum Associates, 2002), 87.

82. Giraud Chester, "The Press-Radio War: 1933–1935," *The Public Opinion Quarterly* 13, no. 2 (Summer 1949): 255–56.

83. Ibid.

84. Lewis J. Paper, *Empire: William S. Paley and the Making of CBS* (New York: St. Martin's Press, 1987), 63.

85. Sterling and Kittross, *Stay Tuned,* 862.

86. Franklin Delano Roosevelt, Russell D. Buhite, and David W. Levy, *FDR's Fireside Chats* (Norman.: The University of Oklahoma Press, 1992), xiii.

87. Stuart Ewen, *PR! A Social History of Spin* (New York: Basic Books, 1998), 53.

88. Emery, Emery, and Roberts, *The Press in America,* 345.

89. J. Fred McDonald, *Don't Touch That Dial: Radio Programming in American Life 1920–1960* (Chicago: Nelson Hall, 1979), 18.

90. Paper, *Empire,* 63.

91. Ithiel de Sola Pool, *Technologies of Freedom* (Cambridge, Mass.: Harvard University Press, 1983), 108.

92. Ibid., 123.

93. Barnouw, *The Golden Web,* 72.

94. Gitelman, *Always Already New,* 25.

95. David Halberstam, *The Powers That Be* (Champaign: The University of Illinois Press, 2000), 226–27.

96. Barbie Zelizer, *Covering the Body: The Kennedy Assassination, the Media, and the Shaping of Collective Memory* (Chicago: University of Chicago Press, 1992), 62.

97. Reuven Frank, *Out of Thin Air: The Brief and Wonderful Life of Network News* (New York: Simon and Schuster, 1991), 181.

98. Stan Opotowsky, *TV: The Big Picture* (New York: E. P. Dutton and Co., 1961), 177.

99. Ford Rowan, *Broadcast Fairness: Doctrine, Practice, Prospects* (New York: Longman, 1984).

100. Margaret A. Blanchard, *Revolutionary Sparks: Freedom of Expression in Modern America* (New York: Oxford University Press, 1992), 405.

101. David Blum, *Tick . . . Tick . . . Tick: The Long Life and Turbulent Times of 60 Minutes* (New York: HarperCollins, 2004), 117–19.

102. Burns W. Roper, *Trends in Public Attitudes Toward Television and Other Mass Media 1959–1974* (New York: Roper Organization, 1975), 2.

103. David Carr, "'South Park,' a Vision and a Payoff," *New York Times,* March 1, 2009 (accessed online April 4, 2009).

104. Irving Fang, "Videotape," The Museum of Broadcast Communication, http://www.museum.tv/archives/etv/V/htmlV/videotape/videotape.htm (accessed March 21, 2009).

105. Gene Roberts and Hank Klibanoff, *The Race Beat* (New York: Alfred Knopf, 2006), 93, 346.

106. Ibid., 347.

107. Gareth Marples, "The History of Satellite TV—A Vision for the Future" TheHistoryOf.net, http://www.thehistoryof.net/history-of-satellite-tv.html (accessed March 21, 2009).

108. David J. Whalen, "Communications Satellites: Making the Global Village Possible," NASA History Division, http://www.hq.nasa.gov/office/pao/History/satcomhistory.html (accessed March 22, 2009).

109. Patrick R. Parsons and Robert N. Frieden, *The Cable and Satellite Television Industries* (Boston: Allyn and Bacon, 1998), 8.

110. Sterling and Kittross, *Stay Tuned,* 355–56.

111. Parsons and Frieden, *The Cable and Satellite Television Industries,* 1–2.

112. Mark Robichaux, *Cable Cowboy: John Malone and the Rise of the Modern Cable Business* (Hoboken, N.J.: John Wiley and Sons, 2002), 53.

113. Robert W. Crandall and Harold Furchtgott-Roth, *Cable TV: Regulation or Competition* (Washington, D.C.: The Brookings Institution, 1996), 6.

114. Robert Goldberg and Gerald Jay Goldberg, *Citizen Turner: The Wild Rise of an American Tycoon* (New York: Harcourt, Brace and Co., 1995), 135–37.

115. Ibid.

116. "Cable Network Begins Continuous News Program," *New York Times,* June 2, 1980, Metropolitan Report, Final Edition, B8.

117. Tony Schwartz, "The Expanding Role of TV News on Cable," *New York Times,* August 13, 1981 (accessed online April 4, 2009).

118. Andrew Rosenthal, "The News Media: Watching Cable News Network Grow," *New York Times,* December 16, 1987, Washington Talk (accessed online April 4, 2009).

119. James Clarity, "From TV Reporters in Iraq, News an Attack Has Begun," *New York Times* January 17, 1991 (accessed online April 4, 2009).

120. Blanchard, *Revolutionary Sparks,* 406.

121. Stephen R. Knowlton and Karen L. Freeman, *Fair and Balanced: A History of Journalistic Objectivity* (Northport, Ala.: Vision Press, 2005), 7.

122. Michale Pfau, "The Mass Media and American Politics: A Review Essay," *Political Research Quarterly* 42, no. 1 (1989): 173.

123. David R. Davies, *The Postwar Decline of American Newspapers* (Westport, Conn.: Praeger Publishers, 2006), 133.

124. James McCartney, "USA Today Grows Up," *American Journalism Review* 19, no. 7 (September 1997): 18.

125. Ibid., 19.

CHAPTER THREE

1. A. M. Turing, "On Computable Numbers, with an Application to the Entscheidungsproblem," *Proceedings of the London Mathematical Society,* series 2, no. 42 (1936–37): 230–65, in *The Essential Turing,* B. J. Copeland, ed. (New York: Oxford University Press, 2004), 58–91.

2. A. M. Turing, "Lecture on the Automatic Computing Engine," in *The Essential Turing*, B. J. Copeland, ed. (New York: Oxford University Press, 2004), 362–95.

3. "Charles Babbage," http://www.charlesbabbage.net/ (accessed March 22, 2009).

4. "IBM's ASCC Introduction," IBM Archives, http://www-03.ibm .com/ibm/history/exhibits/markI/markI_intro.html (accessed March 22, 2009).

5. "Inventors of the Modern Computer: The Harvard MARK I Computer—Howard Aiken and Grace Hopper," About.com: Inventors, http://inventors.about.com/library/weekly/aa052198.htm (accessed March 22, 2009).

6. "Inventors of the Modern Computer: The Atanasoff-Berry Computer, the First Electronic Computer—John Atanasoff and Clifford Berry," About.com: Inventors, http://inventors.about.com/library/weekly/ aa050898.htm (accessed March 22, 2009).

7. Dilys Winegrad and Atsushi Akera, "A Short History of the Second American Revolution," http://www.upenn.edu/almanac/v42/ n18/eniac.html (accessed March 22, 2009).

8. Alexander Randall, "Q&A: A Lost Interview with ENIAC Co-inventor J. Presper Eckert," *Computerworld*, February 14, 2006, http://www .computerworld.com/printthis/2006/0,4814,108568,00.html (accessed March 22, 2009).

9. Robert Reinholi, "Dr. Vannevar Bush Is Dead at 84," *New York Times,* June 30, 1974.

10. "Vannevar Bush," Internet Pioneers, http://www.ibiblio.org/ pioneers/bush.html (accessed March 22, 2009).

11. Vannevar Bush, "As We May Think," *Atlantic Monthly,* July 1945, (accessed online March 22, 2009).

12. Karl Kempf, "Electronic Computers Within the Ordinance Corp: Chapter III—EDVAC," http://ftp.arl.mil/~mike/comphist/61ordnance/ chap3.html (accessed March 22, 2009).

13. "Inventors of the Modern Computer: The History of the UNIVAC Computer—J. Presper Eckert and John Mauchly," About.com: Inventors, http://inventors.about.com/library/weekly/aa062398.htm (accessed March 22, 2009).

14. Kardex, http://www.kardexeng.com/images/History_Kardex.PDF (accessed September 3, 2009).

15. K. Ryan Weston, "Univac: The Paul Revere of Computer Revolution," http://ei.cs.vt.edu/~history/UNIVAC.Weston.html (accessed March 22, 2009).

16. "Inventors of the Modern Computer: The History of the UNIVAC Computer—J. Presper Eckert and John Mauchly," About.com: Inventors, http://inventors.about.com/library/weekly/aa062398.htm (accessed March 22, 2009).

17. "IBM 701: A Notable First," IBM Archives, http://www-03.ibm.com/ibm/history/exhibits/701/701_intro.html (accessed March 22, 2009).

18. "The Invention of the Transistor," Following the Path of Discovery, http://www.juliantrubin.com/bigten/transistorexperiments.html (accessed March 22, 2009).

19. Ira Flatow, "Transistorized! Introduction," PBS, http://www.pbs.org/transistor/album1/index.html (accessed March 22, 2009).

20. Flatow, "Transistorized! The Sandwich Transistor," PBS, http://www.pbs.org/transistor/science/events/sandtran.html (accessed March 22, 2009).

21. Flatow, "Transistorized! Integrated Circuits," PBS, http://www.pbs.org/transistor/background1/events/icinv.html (accessed March 22, 2009).

22. "The History of Computer Data Storage: The Timeline," USByte,http://www.usbyte.com/common/history_of_storage.htm (accessed March 22, 2009).

23. "The Fifties," IBM Archives, http://www-03.ibm.com/ibm/history/history/decade_1950.html (accessed March 22, 2009).

24. John McCarthy, "Reminiscences on the History of Time Sharing" (1983), http://www-formal.stanford.edu/jmc/history/timesharing/timesharing.html (accessed March 22, 2009).

25. "Guide to the Collection of Digital Equipment Corporation PDP-1 Computer Materials," Online Archive of California, http://content.cdlib.org/view?docId=kt0t1nc9fw&chunk.id=bioghist-1.3.6&brand=oac (accessed March 22, 2009).

26. "Inventors of the Modern Computer: Spacewar! The First Com-

puter Game Invented by Steve Russell," About.com: Inventors, http://inventors.about.com/library/weekly/aa090198.htm (accessed March 22, 2009).

27. J. C. R. Licklider, "Man-Computer Symbiosis," *IRE Transactions on Human Factors in Electronics,* Vol: HFE-1 (March 1960): 4.

28. "Ted Nelson Discovers Hypertext," Living Internet, http://www.livinginternet.com/w/wi_nelson.htm (accessed March 22, 2009).

29. EDS: About, http://www.eds.com/about/history/timeline.aspx (accessed March 22, 2009).

30. Roger Summit, "Reflections on the Beginnings of Dialog: The Birth of Online Information Access" (June 2002), Dialog,http://support.dialog.com/publications/chronolog/200206/1020628.shtml (accessed March 22, 2009).

31. Susanne Bjørner and Stephanie C. Ardito, "Online Before the Internet, Part 1: Early Pioneers Tell Their Stories," Information Today, http://www.infotoday.com/searcher/jun03/ardito_bjorner.shtml (accessed March 22, 2009).

32. Charles P. Bourne and Trudi Bellardo Hahn, *A History of Online Information Services, 1963–1976* (Cambridge, Mass.: MIT Press, 2003), 157.

33. Lucy Heckman, *NASDAQ: A Guide to Information Sources* (New York: Routledge, 2001), 8.

34. Michael A. Banks, *On the Way to the Web: The Secret History of the Internet and Its Founders* (Berkeley, Calif.: Apress, 2008), 10.

35. Bourne and Bellardo Hahn, *A History of Online Information Services,* 212.

36. Paul Martijn, "History of Tymnet," http://parmasoft.com/ (accessed March 22, 2009).

37. Norman Hardy, "The Origins of Tymnet," http://www.cap-lore.com/Tymnet/ETH.html (accessed March 22, 2009).

38. Cornelis Robat, ed., "The History of the Internet 1957–1976," The History of Computing Project, http://www.thocp.net/reference/internet/internet1.htm (accessed March 22, 2009).

39. Banks, *On the Way to the Web,* 12.

40. "MCI WorldCom, Inc.," Funding Universe, http://www.fundinguniverse.com/company-histories/MCI-WorldCom-Inc-Company-History.html (accessed May 11, 2009).

41. Robert Cannon, "The Legacy of the Federal Communications Commission's Computer Inquiries," *Federal Communication Law Journal* 55, no. 2 (March 2003), http://www.law.indiana.edu/fclj/pubs/v55/no2/cannon.pdf (accessed March 22, 2009).

42. Ibid.

43. De Sola Pool, *Technologies of Freedom,* 221.

44. Donald E. Kimberlin, "Telex and TWX History" (1986), http://www.baudot.net/docs/kimberlin—telex-twx-history.pdf (accessed March 22, 2009).

45. "Ceefax Marks 30 Years of Service," BBC News, September 22, 2004, http://news.bbc.co.uk/1/hi/entertainment/tv_and_radio/3681174.stm (accessed March 22, 2009).

46. Mark Cook and Mike Brown, "Teletext Timeline," MB21, http://teletext.mb21.co.uk/timeline/ (accessed March 22, 2009).

47. "Videotext," Nationmaster Encyclopedia, http://www.nationmaster.com/encyclopedia/Videotext (accessed March 22, 2009).

48. James Arnold, "France's Minitel: 20 Years Young," BBC News, May 14, 2003, http://news.bbc.co.uk/2/hi/business/3012769.stm (accessed March 22, 2009).

49. Maite Selignan, "France's Precursor to the Internet Lives On," *Washington Post,* September 25, 2003 (accessed online May 26, 2009).

50. Nadine Epstein, "Et Voila! Le Minitel," *New York Times,* March 9, 1986, magazine (accessed online April 4, 2009).

51. Eva Hoffman and Margot Slade, "Think Electronic, Publishers Urged," *New York Times,* May 2, 1982, Week in Review (accessed online April 4, 2009).

52. "Knight Ridder, Inc.," Funding Universe, http://www.fundinguniverse.com/company-histories/Knight-Ridder-Inc-Company-History.html (accessed March 22, 2009).

53. Roger Fidler, *Mediamorphosis: Understanding New Media* (Thousand Oaks, Calif.: Pine Forge Press, 1997), 144–46.

54. "Knight Ridder in Affiliated Tie," *New York Times,* April 23, 1982 (accessed online April 4, 2009).

55. Peter Kerr, "Are Viewers Looking to 'Videotex'?" *New York Times,* December 4, 1983 (accessed online April 7, 2009).

56. Andrew Pollack, "Citicorp, Penney, RCA Holding Videotex Talks," *New York Times,* November 6, 1984 (accessed online April 7, 2009).

57. Richard Stevenson, "Videotex Players Seek a Workable Formula," *New York Times*, March 25, 1986 (accessed online April 7, 2009).

58. "Knight Ridder Shuts Videotex," *New York Times,* March 18, 1986 (accessed online April 7, 2009).

59. Jonathan Friendly, "Study Finds No Mass Market for Newspapers on Home TV," *New York Times,* October 2, 1982 (accessed online April 7, 2009).

60. Stevenson, "Videotex Players Seek a Workable Formula."

61. John Markoff, "A Media Pioneer's Quest: Portable Electronic Newspapers," *New York Times,* June 28, 1992, Financial Desk (accessed online April 7, 2009).

62. "Inventors of the Modern Computer: Intel 4004—The World's First Single Chip Microprocessor," About.com: Inventors, http://inventors.about.com/od/mstartinventions/a/microprocessor.htm (accessed March 22, 2009).

63. Thayer Watkins, "Early History of the Personal Computer," http://www.sjsu.edu/faculty/watkins/pc.htm (accessed March 22, 2009).

64. Stephen Wozniak, "Homebrew and How the Apple Came to Be," Atariarchives.org., http://www.atariarchives.org/deli/homebrew_and_how_the_apple.php (accessed March 22, 2009).

65. Banks, *On the Way to the Web,* 20.

66. "Software Arts and Visicalc," Dan Bricklin's Web Site, http://www.bricklin.com/history/sai.htm (accessed March 22, 2009).

67. M. L. Clayton, "Atari History," http://www.heartbone.com/comphist/Atari.htm (accessed March 22, 2009).

68. Banks, *On the Way to the Web,* 24–27.

69. Ray Tomlinson, "The First Network Email," http://openmap.bbn.com/~tomlinso/ray/firstemailframe.html (accessed May 27, 2009).

70. Janet F. Asteroff, "Electronic Bulletin Boards, A Case Study," The Columbia University Center for Computing Activities, http://www.columbia.edu/acis/history/bboard.html (accessed March 22, 2009).

71. Banks, *On the Way to the Web,* 58.

72. Sara Fitzgerald, "Electronic Publishing Project Includes *Post*," *Washington Post,* March 2, 1981, Washington Business, Final Edition.

73. Banks, *On the Way to the Web,* 33–35.

74. Ibid., 80, 87, 210.

75. Christos J. P. Moschovitis, Hilary Poole, Tami Schuyler, and Theresa M. Senft, *History of the Internet: A Chronology, 1843 to the Present* (Santa Barbara, Calif.: ABC-CLIO, 1999), http://www.historyoftheinternet.com/chap5.html (accessed May 27, 2009).

76. Cheryl C. Sullivan, "Can Computers Take the Paper Out of 'Newspaper'?" *Christian Science Monitor,* February 9, 1982, Midwestern Edition.

77. "CompuServe Extends Its Reach," *Business Week,* December 7, 1981, 88.

78. Banks, *On the Way to the Web,* 106.

79. Katie Hafner, "The Epic Saga of The Well: The World's Most Influential Online Community (And It's Not AOL)," Wired, http://www.wired.com/wired/archive/5.05/ff_well_pr.html (accessed March 22, 2009).

80. David Killick and Sonya Sandham, "Policing the Techno-Nasties," *Sydney (Australia) Morning Herald*, December 18, 1993, Late Edition.

81. Joseph P. Treaster, "Hundreds of Youths Trading Data on Computer Break-ins," *New York Times,* September 5, 1983, Late City Final Edition, National Desk, 1.

82. Martin Lansden, "Of Bytes and Bulletin Boards," *New York Times,* August 4, 1985, Late City Final Edition.

83. Andrew Pollack, "Free Speech Issues Surround Computer Bulletin Board Use," *New York Times,* November 12, 1984, A1.

84. Michael Schrage, "Disastrous to Computer Growth, Sources Claim; Charge-By-Minute Investigated," *Washington Post,* December 31, 1983, Final Edition.

85. Margie G. Quimpo, "Prodigy Venture Plans More Computer Services; Joint IBM-Sears Effort Seeks to Widen Appeal," *Washington Post,* September 6, 1990, Final Edition.

86. "Knight-Ridder to Buy Lockheed's Dialog Unit," *New York Times,* July 12, 1988, Late City Final Edition.

87. Lawrence M. Fisher, "News Corp. Buys On-Line Network," *New York Times,* September 2, 1993, Late City Final Edition.

CHAPTER FOUR

1. Kristie Moore, "The Sputnik Effect: Space Age at 50 Marks a Milestone," *Washington Times,* October 4, 2007.

2. James Gillies and Robert Cailliau, *How the Web Was Born: The Story of the World Wide Web* (New York: Oxford University Press, 2000), 12.

3. Defence Advanced Research Projects Agency, http://www.darpa.mil/history.html (accessed March 22, 2009).

4. Gillies and Cailliau, *How the Web Was Born,* 13.

5. Katie Hafner and Matthew Lyon, *Where Wizards Stay Up Late: The Origins of the Internet* (New York: Simon and Schuster, 2006), 37–39.

6. Leonard Kleinrock, *Information Flows in Large Communication Nets,* Ph.D. proposal, http://www.cs.ucla.edu/~lk/LK/Bib/REPORT/PhD/part1.pdf (accessed March 22, 2009).

7. Janet Abbate, *Inventing the Internet* (Cambridge, Mass.: MIT Press, 2000), 14–23.

8. Ronda Hauben, "The Birth and Development of the ARPANET," http://www.columbia.edu/~rh120/ch106.x08 (accessed March 22, 2009).

9. Michael Hauben, "Part I: The History of ARPA Leading Up to the ARPANET," http://www.dei.isep.ipp.pt/~acc/docs/arpa—1.html (accessed March 22, 2009).

10. Ronda Hauben, "The Birth and Development of the ARPANET."

11. Barry M. Leiner, Vinton G. Cerf, et. al, *A Brief History of the Internet,* http://www.isoc.org/internet/history/brief.shtml#Origins (accessed March 22, 2009).

12. "The Launch of NSFNET," National Science Foundation, http://www.nsf.gov/about/history/nsf0050/internet/launch.htm (accessed March 22, 2009).

13. "NSFNET—National Science Foundation Network" Living Internet, http://www.livinginternet.com/i/ii_nsfnet.htm (accessed March 22, 2009).

14. "New Mexico Network Links Agencies, Academia and Private Sector to Cray-Class Supercomputers," *Aviation Week and Space Technology,* July 25, 1988, 43.

15. "NSFNET: Bringing the World of Ideas Together," Living Internet, http://www.livinginternet.com/doc/merit.edu/nsfnet.overview .txt (accessed March 22, 2009).

16. Abbate, *Inventing the Internet,* 196.

17. "NSFNET—National Science Foundation Network."

18. Lawrence G. Roberts, "The ARPANET and Computer Networks" (May 1995), http://www.packet.cc/files/arpanet-computernet .html (accessed March 22, 2009).

19. Hafner and Lyon, *Where Wizards Stay Up Late,* 189–94.

20. Ronda Hauben, "ARPANET Mailing List and Usenet Newsgroups: Creating an Open and Scientific Process for Technology Development and Diffusion," http://www.ais.org/~jrh/acn/text/acn9-1 .articles/acn9-1.15.txt (accessed March 22, 2009).

21. "Mailing List History," Living Internet, http://www.livinginternet .com/l/li.htm (accessed May 27, 2009).

22. Elizabeth A. Muenger, "Ames During NASA's Golden Years, 1958–1969," in *Searching the Horizon: A History of Ames Research Center, 1940–1976* (Washington, D.C.: NASA, 1985), http://history.nasa .gov/SP-4304/ch6.htm (accessed March 22, 2009).

23. "The Maze War 30-Year Retrospective," DigiBarn Computer Museum, http://www.digibarn.com/collections/games/xerox-maze -war/index.html#palmer (accessed March 22, 2009).

24. "Alto by Xerox PARC," Lexicon's History of Computing, http://www.computermuseum.li/Testpage/Xerox-PARC-Alto-1973. htm (accessed March 22, 2009).

25. Greg Thompson, "The Amazing History of Maze," http://www .docstoc.com/docs/1046782/The-aMazing-History-of-Maze (accessed March 22, 2009).

26. "Here's Where It All Began," The Colossal Cave Adventure Page, http://www.rickadams.org/adventure/a_history.html (accessed March 22, 2009).

27. David Cuciz, "The History of MUDs: Part II," Gamespy.com, http://archive.gamespy.com/articles/january01/muds1/index5.shtm (accessed March 22, 2009).

28. Richard Bartle, "Interactive Multi-User Computer Games" (De-

cember 1990), ftp://ftp.lambda.moo.mud.org/pub/MOO/papers/mud report.txt (accessed March 22, 2009).

29. Sherry Turkle, *Life on the Screen: Identity in the Age of the Internet* (New York: Simon and Schuster, 1995), 50.

30. Charles Severance, "A Brief History of Unix," http://www.hsrl .rutgers.edu/ug/unix_history.html (accessed March 22, 2009).

31. "Usenix Timeline," Usenix, http://www.usenix.org/about/ history/firsts.html (accessed March 22, 2009).

32. "1981: B News & Rapid Expansion," Giganews, http://www .giganews.com/usenet-history/bnews.html (accessed March 22, 2009).

33. "Early Usenet Hierarchies History," Living Internet, http://www .livinginternet.com/u/ui_early.htm (accessed March 22, 2009).

34. "20-Year Usenet Timeline," Google Group, http://www.google .com/googlegroups/archive_announce_20.html (accessed March 22, 2009).

35. Paul McFedries, "A Usenet Primer: Netiquette Niceties for Usenet," http://www.mcfedries.com/Ramblings/usenet-netiquette.asp (accessed March 22, 2009).

36. "1987: The Great Renaming," Giganews, http://www.giganews .com/usenet-history/renaming-1.html (accessed March 22, 2009).

37. Dave Hayes, "Alternative Viewpoints: Case Histories and Stories," *An Alternative Primer on Net Abuse, Free Speech, and Usenet* (1996), http:// www.faqs.org/faqs/usenet/freedom-knights/free-speech-faq/section -7.html (accessed March 22, 2009).

38. Richard Sexton, "The Origins of Alt.sex," Living Internet, http://www.livinginternet.com/u/ui_alt_sex.htm (accessed March 22, 2009).

39. "A Brief History of Bit.net," http://www.bit.net/ (accessed March 22, 2009).

40. "CREN History and Future," Corporation for Research and Educational Networking, http://www.cren.net/cren/cren-hist-fut.html (accessed March 22, 2009).

41. "History of LISTSERV," L-Soft, http://www.lsoft.com/products/ listserv-history.asp (accessed March 22, 2009).

42. Charlene O'Hanlon, "Robert Metcalfe," Channel Web, De-

cember 12, 2003, http://www.crn.com/it-channel/18825021 (accessed March 22, 2009).

43. PARC, About, http://www.parc.com/about/history/ (accessed March 22, 2009).

44. "Alto by Xerox PARC."

45. "Robert Metcalfe," The Centre for Computing History, http://www .computinghistory.org.uk/cgi-bin/sitewise.pl?act=det&p=2929 (accessed March 22, 2009).

46. Hadriel Kaplan and Robert Noseworthy, "The Ethernet Evolution: From 10 Meg to 10 Gig, How It All Works!" http://www.iol.unh .edu/services/testing/ethernet/training/The%20Ethernets%20new%20 handout.pdf (accessed March 22, 2009).

47. "Short case history—Standards—Speech by 3Com Corp. VP Robert M. Metcalfe on Ethernet 1990," BNET, http://findarticles .com/p/articles/mi_m0REL/is_nDIRECT_v90/ai_8547188/pg_2 (accessed March 22, 2009),

48. Andrew Pollack, "Next, a Computer on Every Desk," *New York Times,* August 23, 1981 (accessed online April 7, 2009).

49. Brad A. Myers, "Interesting and Useful Numbers about Computers," Computer Almanac, http://www.cs.cmu.edu/afs/cs/user/bam/ www/numbers.html (accessed March 22, 2009).

50. Douglas Engelbart, "Augmenting Human Intellect: A Conceptual Framework," Stanford Research Institute (October 1962), http://www .invisiblerevolution.net/engelbart/full_62_paper_augm_hum_int.html (accessed March 22, 2009).

51. Jeremy Riemer, "A History of the GUI," Ars Technica, http:// arstechnica.com/articles/paedia/gui.ars (accessed March 22, 2009).

52. Mike Tuck, "The Real History of the GUI," August 13, 2001, http://www.sitepoint.com/article/real-history-gui/5/ (accessed March 22, 2009).

53. "NYSERNet History—Organizational Overview," NYSER-Net, http://www.nysernet.org/about/history.php (accessed March 22, 2009).

54. "Richard L. Adams," Free Encyclopedia of Ecommerce, http:// ecommerce.hostip.info/pages/2/Adams-Richard-L.html (accessed March 22, 2009).

55. "Internet Service Provider (ISP) History and Development," Free Encyclopedia of Ecommerce, http://ecommerce.hostip.info/pages/623/Internet-Service-Provider-ISP-HISTORY-DEVELOPMENT.html (accessed March 22, 2009).

56. "A Brief History of the Internet," Walt Howe's Internet Learning Center, http://www.walthowe.com/navnet/history.html (accessed March 22, 2009).

57. Thomas Palmer, "Newspapers Expand Services: More Information Seen a Key to Survival," *Boston Globe,* April 15, 1991, Economics Section, City Edition.

58. Jim Rosenberg, "Prototype for a National Info Superhighway?" *Editor & Publisher,* October 9, 1993, 26–32.

59. Chip Brown, "Fear.com," *American Journalism Review* (June 1999): 50.

60. William Glaberson, "Newspapers Redefining Themselves," *New York Times,* April 26, 1993, Financial Desk, Late Edition Final.

61. "A Less Brief History of ClariNet," ClariNet, http://www.clari.net/history.html (accessed March 22, 2009).

62. Rosenberg, "Prototype for a National Info Superhighway?"

63. Chick Whiteside, Mary Ann. "Computers - just another reporting tool," *Editor & Publisher,* November 2, 1991, 1–3.

64. Tim Berners-Lee, *Weaving the Web: The Original Design and Ultimate Destiny of the World Wide Web by Its Inventor* (San Francisco: HarperCollins, 1999), 4.

65. Gillies and Cailliau, *How the Web Was Born,* 178.

66. Berners-Lee, *Weaving the Web,* 15, 16.

67. Ibid., 19, 20.

68. Ibid., 23.

69. Ibid., 30.

70. Ibid., 37–39.

71. Ibid., 45–47.

72. "Web Browser History," Living Internet, http://www.livinginternet.com/w/wi_browse.htm (accessed March 22, 2009).

73. Berners-Lee, *Weaving the Web,* 69.

74. Global Network Navigator, http://oreilly.com/gnn/ (accessed March 22, 2009).

75. Brown, "Fear.com."

76. William Glaberson, "In San Jose, Knight-Ridder Tests a Newspaper Frontier," *New York Times,* February 7, 1994 (accessed online March 22, 2009).

77. M. L. Stein, "First Step to a Multimedia Future," *Editor & Publisher,* April 10, 1993, 18.

78. Glaberson, "In San Jose, Knight-Ridder Tests a Newspaper Frontier."

79. Stein, "First Step to a Multimedia Future."

80. Brown, "Fear.com."

CHAPTER FIVE

1. David Davies, *The Postwar Decline of American Newspapers, 1945–1965* (Westport, Conn.: Praeger Publishers, 2006), 114–22.

2. William David Sloan and Lisa Mullikin Parcell, *American Journalism: History, Principles, Practices* (Jefferson, N.C.: McFarland, 2002), 122.

3. John C. Busterna and Robert G. Picard, *Joint Operating Agreements: The Newspaper Preservation Act and Its Application* (Westport, Conn.: Greenwood Publishing Group, 1993), 3.

4. "A Brief Company History," Gannett.com, http://www.gannett.com/about/history.htm (accessed March 29, 2009).

5. Charles Kaiser, "The Big Mac of Newspapers," *Newsweek,* January 17, 1983, 48.

6. Roger Wallis and Stanley J. Baran, *The Known World of Broadcast News: International News and the Electronic Media* (London: Routledge, 1990), 8–9.

7. Philip S. Cook, Douglas Gomery, and Lawrence W. Lichty, *The Future of News: Television, Newspapers, Wire Services, Newsmagazines* (Washington, D.C.: Woodrow Wilson Center Press, 1992), 10–11.

8. Constance L. Hayes, "Turmoil in China," *New York Times,* June 10, 1989 (accessed online March 29, 2009).

9. Leon Sigal, "Editorial Notebook," *New York Times,* June 13, 1990 (accessed online March 29, 2009).

10. "Times Will Fax Short Version of Itself to the Far East," *Deseret News,* November 14, 1989 (accessed online March 29, 2009).

11. William Glaberson, "Newspapers Redefining Themselves," *New York Times,* April 26, 1993, Financial, Section D1, Final.

12. M. L. Stein, "Audiotex Success at Newspapers," *Editor & Publisher,* February 20, 1993, 11.

13. M. L. Stein, "Where Are All the Editors?" *Editor & Publisher,* March 27, 1993, 22.

14. Robert Cannon, "The Legacy of the Federal Communications Commission's Computer Inquiry," *Federal Communications Law Journal* 55, no. 2, http://www.law.indiana.edu/fclj/pubs/v55/no2/cannon.pdf (accessed March 29, 2009).

15. Debra Gersh, "Neuharth Pulls No Punches," *Editor & Publisher,* March 28, 1992, 7.

16. John F. Kelsey, "A Future in Electronic Services," *Editor & Publisher,* March 6, 1993, 16.

17. "The Press" Cartoon Section, *Editor & Publisher,* October 23, 1982, 5.

18. George Mannes, "Delivering the Fax," American Heritage.com, http://www.americanheritage.com/articles/magazine/it/1999/4/1999_4_40.shtml (accessed March 29, 2009).

19. Nina Munk, *Fools Rush In: Steve Case, Jerry Levin, and the Unmaking of AOL Time Warner* (New York: HarperCollins, 2005), 75–78.

20. David Noack, "Interactive Newspapers: A Look at Services Provided by the *Chicago Tribune* and Gannett's *Florida Today,*" *Editor & Publisher,* May 15, 1993, 57.

21. William Glaberson, "The Media Business: The Building Blocks of Newspaper Networks," *New York Times,* August 16, 1993 (accessed online March 29, 2009).

22. "Compuserve and CNN Team Up to Bring Live Online Participation to CNN Programs," *Internet Librarian,* October 1994, 49.

23. "The National Information Infrastructure: Agenda for Action, Executive Summary," http://www.ibiblio.org/nii/NII-Executive-Summary.html (accessed March 29, 2009).

24. John Markoff, "The Executive Computer: A Web of Networks, an Abundance of Services," *New York Times,* December 28, 1993 (accessed online March 29, 2009).

25. "Information Superhighway: The Digital Future Can Mean Great

News for Newspapers, Journalists and News Consumers," *American Journalism Review* 16, no. 4 (May 1994): 4.

26. The Research Group of the Freedom Forum Media Studies Center, "Special Report: Separating Fact from Fiction on the Information Superhighway" (New York: Freedom Forum Media Studies Center, April 1994), 5–7.

27. "Information Superhighway."

28. Al Gore, Remarks Delivered to the Superhighway Summit, January 11, 1994, http://clinton1.nara.gov/White_House/EOP/OVP/other/superhig.html (accessed March 29, 2009).

29. Paul M. Eng, "On Ramps to the Info Highway," *Business Week,* February 7, 1994, 108.

30. Jim Rosenberg, "*Washington Post* to Go On Line with Ziff-Davis," *Editor & Publisher,* April 9, 1994, 40.

31. George Garneau, "Billion-dollar Electronic Investment," *Editor & Publisher,* December 17, 1994, 11.

32. William Webb, "New Influx of Cash for Raleigh Online Service," *Editor & Publisher,* June 10, 1995, 26.

33. Christopher Harper, "Online Newspapers: Going Somewhere or Going Nowhere?" *Newspaper Research Journal* 17, nos. 3–4 (Summer-Fall 1996): 2.

34. John Consoli, "Newspapers and the Superhighway," *Editor & Publisher,* July 2, 1994, 28.

35. Harper, "Online Newspapers."

36. Columbia University Graduate School of Journalism First Amendment Leaders' Breakfast, transcript, May 25, 1994.

37. Michael Crichton, "Mediasaurus," *Wired* (September/October 1993), http://www.wired.com/wired/archive/1.04/mediasaurus.html (accessed March 29, 2009).

38. W. Bender, et. al, "Enriching Communities: Harbingers of News in the Future," *IBM Systems Journal* 35, nos. 3–4 (1996), 369–80.

39. Columbia University Graduate School of Journalism First Amendment Leaders' Breakfast, transcript, May 25, 1994.

40. M. Conniff, "A Tangled Web for Newspapers," *Editor & Publisher,* February 4, 1995, 4.

41. Scott B. Anderson, "Technology: The Story That May Affect Us

Most," *The American Editor,* June 9, 1999, http://www.asne.org/index.cfm?ID=2131 (accessed January 3, 2009).

42. David Mindich, *Tuned Out: Why Americans Under 40 Don't Follow the News* (New York: Oxford University Press, 2005), 2.

43. Robert Hof, "From the Man Who Brought You Silicon Graphics," *Business Week,* October 24, 1994, 90.

44. Amy Cortese, "Cyberspace," *Business Week,* February 27, 1995, 78.

45. Amy Dunkin and Edward Baig, "Pounding the Virtual Pavement," *Business Week,* September 30, 1996, 52.

46. Saul Hansell, "Hackers Bazaar: Online Auction," *New York Times,* April 2, 1998 (accessed online March 31, 2009).

47. "Company News: First Official Stock Sale in Four Weeks Raises $63 Million," *New York Times,* September 24, 1998 (accessed online March 31, 2009).

48. Jon Leibowitz, "Five Years and Counting," The Article Bin, http://art-bin.com/art/alabovitz.html (accessed March 31, 2009).

49. Nicholas Stein, "Slate vs. Salon," *Columbia Journalism Review,* January/February 1999, 56–59.

50. "Salon Press Information Killer Lineup: James Carville and Anne Rice," July 29, 1996, http://www.salon.com/press/releases/1996/7-29.html (accessed March 31, 2009).

51. "Time Magazine Names Salon 'Best Web Site of 1996,'" December 16, 1996, http://www.salon.com/press/releases/1996/12-16.html (accessed March 31, 2009).

52. Nicholas Stein, "Slate vs. Salon," *Columbia Journalism Review,* January/February 1999, 56–59.

53. "Salon.com Reports First Fiscal Quarter Results," August 9, 1999, http://www.salon.com/press/releases/1999/08/09/q1fy00/ (accessed March 31, 2009).

54. "The Street.com," Free Encyclopedia of Ecommerce, http://ecommerce.hostip.info/pages/985/Thestreet-Com-Inc.html (accessed March 31, 2009).

55. Gary Wolf, *Wired: A Romance* (New York: Random House, 2003), 204.

56. Beth Lipton Krigel, "News Corp., The Street.com in IPO Deal," CNET News, May 7, 1999, http://news.cnet.com/News-Corporation

,-TheStreet.com-in-IPO-deal/2100-1023_3-225571.html (accessed March 31, 2009).

57. Elizabeth Corcoran, "Justice Dept. Again Scrutinizing Microsoft; Probe to Focus on Upcoming On-Line Network," *Washington Post,* June 9, 1995, Financial, Final Edition.

58. Louise Kehoe, "The Battle for Cyberspace: Online Service Providers Brace for Entry of Powerful New Competitor Next Week with Launch of Microsoft Network," *The (Toronto) Financial Post,* August 17, 1995, News, Daily Edition, 24.

59. Stephen D. Isaacs, "The Bill Gates Factor," *Columbia Journalism Review,* July/August 1995, 53.

60. "Justice Department Files Antitrust Suit Against Microsoft for Unlawfully Monopolizing Computer Software Markets," May 18, 1998, http://www.usdoj.gov/atr/public/press_releases/1998/1764.htm (accessed March 31, 2009).

61. Alica Shepard, "Webward Ho," *American Journalism Review,* March 1997, Vol 19 No. 2, 32–38.

62. Steve Lohr, "Kinsley Hired for New Microsoft Magazine," *New York Times,* November 7, 1995 (accessed online March 31, 2009).

63. Dierdre Carmody, "Conde Nast Jumps into Cyberspace," *New York Times,* May 1, 1995, Business, Late Edition Final, D10.

64. Lohr, "Kinsley Hired for New Microsoft Magazine."

65. Hugo Cornwell, "Pornography: Do We Protest Too Much?" *The (London) Guardian,* June 23, 1994, 8.

66. Al Gore, Remarks Delivered to the Superhighway Summit.

67. Lyle Denniston, "A SLOW sign on the Information Highway," *American Journalism Review* 16, no. 2 (March 1994): 54.

68. Daniel A. Tysver, *Cubby, Inc. v. Compuserve, Inc.,* http://www.bitlaw.com/source/cases/copyright/cubby.html (accessed March 31, 2009).

69. Pamela Coyne, "TechnoTrial," *ABA Journal,* October, 1994, 66.

70. Dale Herbeck, "Bad Words and Good Samaritans: Defamatory Speech in Cyberspace," paper delivered to the International Communications Association, San Diego, California, May 23, 2003.

71. Eric Easton, "Journalism Ethics and the Internet: Ethical Implications of a Canadian Publication Ban," Communication Institute for

Online Scholarship, http://www.cios.org/EJCPUBLIC/007/4/007415 .HTML (accessed March 31, 2009).

72. "Link to Internet by China May Be Forum for Dissent," *Wall Street Journal,* January 27, 1995, A6.

73. "Censorship in Cyberspace," *The Economist,* April 8, 1995, 16.

74. "An Analysis of S. 314," Center for Democracy and Technology, http://www.cdt.org/speech/cda/950309s314analysis.html#text (accessed March 31, 2009).

75. Federal Communications Commission, Telecommunication Act of 1996, www.fcc.gov/telecom.html (accessed March 31, 2009).

76. Solveig Bernstein, "Policy Analysis: Beyond the Communications Decency Act, Constitutional Lessons of the Internet," The Cato Institute, November 4, 1996, http://www.cato.org/pubs/pas/pa-262.html (accessed March 31, 2009).

77. Federal Communications Commission, Telecommunication Act of 1996.

78. "U.S. Policy: The Telecommunications Act of 1996," The Museum of Broadcasting, http://www.museum.tv/archives/etv/U/htmlU/uspolicyt/uspolicyt.htm (accessed March 31, 2009).

79. Jon Hart, *Web Publishing Law* (Washington, D.C.: Dow Lohnes & Albertson, 2002), 3.

80. Ibid., 104.

81. "Zeran v. AOL Opinion," AOL Legal Department, Decisions and Litigation, http://legal.web.aol.com/decisions/dldefam/zeranopi.html (accessed March 31, 2009).

82. Todd Oppenheimer, "Virtual Reality Check," *Columbia Journalism Review,* March/April 1996, 27.

83. Everette E. Dennis, "The Race for Content on the Information Superhighway: Self-Interest vs. the Public Interest" (New York: The Freedom Forum Media Studies Center, June 19, 1994).

84. "Web Covers Oklahoma City," Newsbytes, April 21, 1995 (accessed March 31, 2009).

85. Jeff Sallot, "Internet Overloaded After Bombing," *The Globe and Mail,* August 27, 1995 (accessed March 31, 2009).

86. Stephen C. Miller, "Terror in Oklahoma: The Internet," *New York Times,* April 25, 1995, National, Late Edition Final, A21.

87. Wade Rowland, "The New News: Digital, Online, Multimedia Technology Is Changing the Nature of News," *The Toronto Star,* April 30, 1995, Context, Final Edition, F1.

88. Jeff Sallot, "Internet Overloaded After Bombing."

89. T. E. Ruggiero and S. P. Winch, "The Media Downing of Pierre Salinger: Journalistic Mistrust of the Internet as a News Source," *Journal of Computer-Mediated Communication* 10, no. 2, (2004), http://jcmc.indiana .edu/vol10/issue2/ruggiero.html (accessed March 31, 2009).

90. Jocelyn Noveck, "Pierre Salinger Claims Navy Missile Shot Down TWA Flight 800," Associated Press, November 8, 1996, http://www .welfarestate.com/twa800/pierre.htm (accessed March 31, 2009).

91. Matthew Wald, "Cyber Mouse That Roared, Implausibly," *New York Times,* October 10, 1996, Week in Review, Late Edition Final.

92. Ruggiero and Winch, "The Media Downing of Pierre Salinger."

93. John Consoli, "Online Usage: 'More Than a Fad,'" *Editor & Publisher,* August 9, 1997, 26.

94. Hoag Levins, "Growing U.S. Audience Reads News on Net," *Editor & Publisher,* February 21, 1998, 14.

95. David Noack, "Bias Against Online News Reporters: The Second Class Citizens of Journalism," *Editor & Publisher,* January 31, 1998, S13.

96. Rebecca Quick, "Web Journalists Are Finding Themselves Out of the Loop" *Wall Street Journal,* August 14, 1997, B5.

97. Jon Katz, "Online or Not, Newspapers Suck," Wired (September 1994), http://www.wired.com/wired/archive/2.09/news.suck.html ?topic=&topic_set= (accessed March 31, 2009).

98. David Noack, "Paid Web Site Falters: St. Paul (Minn.) Pioneer Press Eliminates Readers' Fees for Access to Its Online Service," *Editor & Publisher,* May 24, 1997, 27.

99. David Noack, "Express-News Caves on Web Site Fees," *Editor & Publisher,* April 4, 1998, 22.

100. David Rapp, "How Matt Drudge Changed the World of News," American heritage.com, http://www.americanheritage.com/articles/web/ 20070118-drudge-report-blogs-blogging-clinton-lewinsky-starr-impeachment -website.shtml (accessed March 31, 2009).

101. Richard Pachter, "By Linking News Sites, Matt Drudge Created

an Internet Success," Words on Words.com, http://www.wordsonwords .com/reviews/Drudge903.html (accessed March 31, 2009).

102. Reese Cleghorn,. "The News: It May Never Be the Same," *American Journalism Review* 20, no. 2 (March 1998): 4.

103. Michelle Rafter, "Internet Creates Multitude of Momentous Moments from Monica to Mergers," *The Globe and Mail,* December 31, 1998, Business, C2.

104. David Noack, "Readers Flock to Watch Clinton Squirm," *Editor & Publisher,* September 26, 1998, 10.

CHAPTER SIX

1. Orla Healy, "Victoria Bares All," *New York Daily News,* August 2, 1995, News, 8.

2. Rebecca Quick, "Victoria's Secret Causes a Stir with Web Blitz," *Wall Street Journal,* February 4, 1999, B6.

3. Lisa Napoli, "Was the Victoria's Secret Show a Web Failure?" *New York Times,* February 8, 1999, Business, Late Edition Final, C10.

4. Elizabeth Gleick, "It Was the Marker We Were Waiting For," http://www.time.com/time/reports/cult/heavensgate/heavensgate1 .html (accessed March 31, 2009).

5. David Noack, "The Wave from Heaven's Gate," *Editor & Publisher,* April 26, 1997, 88.

6. Stuart Allan, *Online News: Journalism and the Internet* (New York: Open University Press, 2006), 25–26.

7. Frank Houston, "What I Saw in the Digital Sea," *Columbia Journalism Review,* July/August 1999, 36.

8. Dylan McClain, "Web Sites Set to Transmit Images from Mars After a Craft's Landing Today," *New York Times,* July 4, 1997, National, Late Edition Final.

9. Rajiv Chandrasekaran, "Web Is Red Hot with Landings on Mars Sites," *Washington Post,* July 9, 1997, National, Final Edition, A10.

10. Howard Kurz, "Bureau Chief Ousted Over Hyde Affair Story, Disagreement Rankles Salon Editor," *Washington Post,* September 29, 1998, Style, Final Edition, D1.

11. John Bresnahan, "Harry Hyde Dies," The Politico, http://www .politico.com/blogs/thecrypt/1107/Henry_Hyde_dies.html (accessed March 31, 2009).

12. Wendy Dibean and Bruce Garrison, "Online Newspaper Market Size and the Use of World Wide Web Technologies," in *Online News and the Public,* Michael B. Salwen, Bruce Garrison, and Paul D. Driscoll, eds. (Mahwah, N.J.: Lawrence Erlbaum Associates, 2004), 257.

13. "PC Growth to Drop in '97, Web Users to Double—IDC," Newsbytes, January 7, 1997 (accessed March 31, 2009).

14. Leslie Kaufman and Saul Hansell, "Estimates for On-Line Shopping Exceed the Most Bullish Forecasts," *New York Times,* December 29, 1998, Business, Late Edition Final, A1.

15. "Apache Becomes Favorite Web Server," Newsbytes, April 4, 1996 (accessed March 31, 2009).

16. "On the Number of Web Sites in the World," Pandia, http://www .pandia.com/searchworld/2000-39-oclc-size.html (accessed March 31, 2009).

17. Neil Hickey, "Revolution in Cyberia," *Columbia Journalism Review,* July/August 1995, 42.

18. Nicholas Economides, "Economics of Networks: The Telecommunications Act of 1996 and its Impact" (September 1998), http:// archive.nyu.edu/bitstream/2451/26249/2/98-08.pdf (accessed September 4, 2009).

19. "Lessons from the 1996 Telecommunications Act: Deregulation Before Meaningful Competition Spells Consumer Disaster," Consumers Union (February 2001), http://www.consumersunion.org/telecom/ lessondc201.htm (accessed March 31, 2009).

20. "The Fallout from the Telecommunications Act of 1996: Unintended Consequences and Lessons Learned," Common Cause Educational Fund (May 9, 2005), http://www.commoncause.org/atf/cf/%7B8A2D1D15 -C65A-46D4-8CBB-2073440751B5%7D/FALLOUT_FROM_THE _TELECOMM_ACT_5-9-05.PDF (accessed March 31, 2009).

21. Lawrence Lessig and Robert W. McChesney, "No Tolls on the Internet," *Washington Post,* June 8, 2006, A23 (accessed online March 31, 2009).

22. "U.S. v. Microsoft: Timeline," Wired, http://www.wired.com/techbiz/it/news/2002/11/35212 (accessed March 31, 2009).

23. Nicholas Economides, "The Microsoft Antitrust Case: A Case Study for MBA Students," http://www.stern.nyu.edu/networks/exmba/microsoftcase.pdf (accessed March 31, 2009).

24. Peter Lewis, "Cruising the Web with a Browser," *New York Times,* Febraury 7, 1995, Science, Late Edition Final, C8.

25. David Flynn, "Microsoft Steps Up Pressure," *Sydney (Australia) Morning Herald,* October 10, 1995, Late Edition, 5.

26. Eric S. Raymond, "An Open Letter to AOL," Open Source, http://www.opensource.org/pressreleases/aol-letter.php (accessed March 31, 2009).

27. Rajiv Chandrasekaran, "At Justice, a Sense of Urgency About Web Domination," *Washington Post,* October 22, 1997, Financial, Final Edition, C9.

28. Peter H. Salus, "A History of Free and Open Source—The Daemon, the GNU, and the Penguin," http://www.groklaw.net/article.php?story=20050407114834583 (accessed March 31, 2009).

29. "Brief History of Open Source," Open Options, http://www.netc.org/openoptions/background/history.html (accessed March 31, 2009).

30. Eric S. Raymond, "The Cathedral and the Bazaar," http://fringe.davesource.com/Fringe/Computers/Philosophy/Cathedral_Bazaar/ (accessed March 31, 2009).

31. Tom Spooner, "Olympics Online: The Old Media Beat the New Media," Pew Internet & American Life Project (October 4, 2000), http://www.pewinternet.org/~/media//Files/Reports/2000/PIP_Olympics_Report.pdf.pdf (accessed March 31, 2009).

32. Lawrence K.Grossman, "Will Success Spoil Network News?" *Columbia Journalism Review,* May/June 1999, 58.

33. Howard Finberg, "Digital Media Credibility Study," Online News Association (2002), www.mjbear.com/presentations/AUSTIN.ppt (accessed March 31, 2009).

34. Denise Caruso, "Show Me the Money," *Columbia Journalism Review,* July/August 1997, 32–33.

35. Saul Hansell and Amy Harmon, "Caveat Emptor on the Web: Ad

and Editorial Lines Blur," *New York Times,* February 26, 1999 (accessed online March 31, 2009).

36. Caruso, "Show Me the Money."

37. "Brock Meeks's CyberWire Dispatch, R.I.P.," December 31, 2003, http://www.mail-archive.com/politech@politechbot.com/msg02484 .html (accessed March 31, 2009).

38. Andy Wang, "Cutting Through the Online Clutter," *New York Times,* August 2, 1999, C10 (accessed online March 31, 2009).

39. Adnan Quaium, "Ten Blogging Tips from the Ultimate Blogger," http://maqtanim.wordpress.com/2007/12/18/ten-blogging-tips-from -the-ultimate-blogger/ (accessed March 31, 2009).

40. Rebecca Blood, "Weblogs: A History and Perspective," Rebec- ca's Pocket (September 7, 2000), http://www.rebeccablood.net/essays/ weblog_history.html (accessed March 31, 2009).

41. Cameron Barrett, "Anatomy of a Weblog," Camworld (January 26, 1999), http://www.camworld.com/journal/rants/99/01/26.html (ac- cessed March 31, 2009).

42. Reyhan Harmanci, "Time to Get a Life: Pioneer Blogger Justin Hall Bows Out at 31," *San Francisco Chronicle,* February 20, 2005 (accessed online March 31, 2009).

43. Jeffrey Rosen, "Your Blog or Mine," *New York Times,* December 19, 2004, Magazine (accessed online March 31, 2009).

44. "A Brief History of Blogs," *Columbia Journalism Review,* Septem- ber/October, 2003, 22.

45. Steve Levy, "Living in the Blog-osphere," *Newsweek,* August 26, 2002, 42.

46. Tim O'Reilly, "Blogging and the Wisdom of Crowds," http://tim .oreilly.com/pub/a/oreilly/tim/news/2005/09/30/what-is-web-20. html?page=3 (accessed March 31, 2009).

47. "State of the Blogosphere, October 2004," Sifry's Alerts, http://www .sifry.com/alerts/archives/000387.html (accessed March 31, 2009).

48. Rebecca Mead, "You've Got Blog," *The New Yorker,* Novem- ber 13, 2000, 102.

49. "Andrew Sullivan," Spiritus-Temporis.com, http://www.spiritus -temporis.com/andrew-sullivan/biography.html (accessed March 31, 2009).

50. Andrew Sullivan, "Why I Blog," *The Atlantic Magazine,* http://www

.theatlantic.com/doc/200811/andrew-sullivan-why-i-blog/2 (accessed March 31, 2009).

51. "Mickey Kaus," NationMaster.com, http://www.nationmaster .com/encyclopedia/Mickey-Kaus (accessed March 31, 2009).

52. Samela Harris, "Keeping Track of Disaster," *The Advertiser,* September 15, 2001, 68.

53. Robert Andrews, "9/11: Birth of a Blog," *Wired,* September 11, 2006, http://www.wired.com/techbiz/media/news/2006/09/71753 (accessed March 31, 2009).

54. Matt Welch, "Blogworld and Its Gravity," *Columbia Journalism Review,* September/October 2003, 24.

55. Steven Schneider, Kirsten Foot, et. al, "One Year Later: September 11 and the Internet," Pew Internet and American Life Project, September 5, 2002, http://www.pewinternet.org/~/media//Files/Reports/ 2002/PIP_9-11_Report.pdf. (accessed March 31, 2009).

56. Andrews, "9/11: Birth of a Blog."

57. Levy, "Living in the Blog-osphere."

58. "State of the Blogosphere, October 2004," Sifry's Alerts.

59. Peter Meyers, "Fact-Driven? Collegial? This Site Wants You," *New York Times,* September 20, 2001, Late Edition Final, G2.

60. Hawatha Bray, "One Great Source If You Can Trust It," *Boston Globe,* July 12, 2004, Business, Third Edition, C2.

61. Curtis Krueger, "There Is No End," *St. Petersburg Times,* November 8, 2004, Floridian, South Pinellas Edition, 1E.

62. "The History of YouTube," http://www.youtube.com/watch ?v=x2NQiVcdZRY (accessed March 31, 2009).

63. Dan Gillmor, "Google Buys Pyra: Blogging Goes Big time," eJournal (February 15, 2003), http://web.archive.org/web/ 20031008161432/http://weblog.siliconvalley.com/column/dangillmor/ archives/000802.shtml (accessed March 31, 2009).

64. "News Corp in $580m Internet Buy," BBC News (July 19, 2005), http://news.bbc.co.uk/2/hi/business/4695495.stm (accessed March 31, 2009).

65. "Google Buys YouTube for $1.65 Billion," MSNBC (October 10, 2006), http://www.msnbc.msn.com/id/15196982/ (accessed March 31, 2009).

66. Matt Welch, "Blogworld and Its Gravity," *Columbia Journalism Review,* September/October 2003, 24.

67. Eric Alterman, "The Seven-Year (Old) Snitch," *The Nation,* November 22, 1999, http://www.thenation.com/doc/19991122/alterman (accessed March 31, 2009).

68. Stephen Levy, "Will the Blogs Kill Old Media?" *Business Week,* May 20, 2002, 54.

69. Amy Harmon, "The Search for Intelligent Life on the Internet," *New York Times,* September 23, 2001 (accessed online March 31, 2001).

70. Peter Johnson, "Changing of the Guard in L.A.," *USA Today,* July 20, 2005 (accessed online March 31, 2009).

71. Julie Bosman, "First with the Scoop, If Not the Truth," *New York Times,* April 18, 2004 (accessed online May 27, 2009).

72. Nazila Fathi, "Taboo Surfing: Click Here for Iran," *New York Times,* August 4, 2002 (accessed online March 31, 2009).

73. Jim Yardley, "Internet Sex Column Thrills, and Inflames, China," *New York Times,* November 30, 2003 (accessed online March 31, 2009).

74. Richard Perez-Pena, "Frontline Blogger Covers War in Iraq With a Soldier's Eyes," *New York Times,* January 21, 2008 (accessed online May 27, 2009).

75. Joanna Weiss, "Blogs Colliding with Traditional Media," *Boston Globe,* May 10, 2004, Metro-Regional, Third Edition, B1.

76. Jennifer Lee, "Year of the Blog? Web Diarists Are Now Official Members of Convention Press Corps," *New York Times,* July 26, 2004, National Desk, Late Edition Final, P7.

77. Mike Pence and Richard G. Lugar, "Protecting the Press—And the Public," *Washington Post,* April 15, 2005 (accessed online March 31, 2009).

78. James Watkins, "Are Bloggers Journalists?" http://jameswatkins.agathongroup.com/bloggers.htm (accessed March 31, 2009).

79. "Definition of a Journalist," ASNE, http://www.asne.org/index.cfm?id=6775 (accessed March 31, 2009).

80. Anne Broache, "Bills Propose Reporter's Shield for Bloggers," CNET News (May 4, 2007), http://news.cnet.com/Bills-propose-reporters-shield-for-bloggers/2100-1028_3-6181531.html (accessed March 31, 2009).

81. Josh Harkinson, "Reporter Behind Bars," *Mother Jones,* February 20, 2007, http://www.motherjones.com/interview/2007/02/Josh_Wolf.html (accessed May 27, 2009).

82. Howard Kurtz, "Blogger Makes Deal, Is Released from Jail," *Washington Post,* April 4, 2007, C1.

83. "Apple Argues That Blogger Can't Protect Source," The Register, http://www.theregister.co.uk/2006/04/24/apple_blogger_appeal/ (accessed March 31, 2009).

84. "Internet Journalist's Sources Should Be Kept Confidential," *Honolulu Star Bulletin,* May 23, 2007, http://archives.starbulletin.com/2007/05/23/editorial/editorial01.html (accessed March 31, 2009).

85. E. Scott, "Big Media Meets the Bloggers," (Cambridge, MA: Kennedy School of Government Case Program C14-04-1731.0, March 2004).

86. "About Daily Kos," http://www.dailykos.com/special/about2#dk (accessed March 31, 2009).

87. Dean Barnett, "Taking Kos Seriously," *The Weekly Standard,* February 2, 2005, http://www.weeklystandard.com/Content/Public/Articles/000/000/005/207exwra.asp (accessed March 31, 2009).

88. Jonathan Darman, "The War's Left Front," *Newsweek,* July 3, 2006, 34.

89. John Cloud, "A Politician Comes Out," *Time*, December 21, 1998, 55.

90. Andrew Ferguson, "The Arianna Sideshow: The Activist and Socialite Has Plans for Two 'Shadow Conventions' She Hopes Will Roil the Establishment" *Time*, July 31, 2000, 22.

91. Richard Siklos, "Meet Ariana Huffington 2.0," *Fortune,* October 29, 2007, http://money.cnn.com/2007/10/26/magazines/fortune/huffington.fortune/?postversion=2007102911 (accessed March 31, 2009).

92. Robin Wauters, "The Huffington Post Raises $25 Million from Oak Investment Partners," Tech Crunch, http://www.techcrunch.com/2008/12/01/the-huffington-post-raises-25-million-from-oak-investment-partners/ (accessed March 31, 2009).

93. Howard Kurtz, "After Blogs Got Hit, CBS Got a Black Eye," *Washington Post,* September 20, 2004 (accessed online March 31, 2009).

94. Noam Cohen, "Blogger, Sans Pajamas, Rakes Muck and a Prize," *New York Times,* February 25, 2008 (accessed online March 31, 2009).

95. David Glenn, "The Marshall Plan," *Columbia Journalism Review,* September/October 2007, 22, 27.

CHAPTER SEVEN

1. Stephen Levy, "Will the Blogs Kill Old Media?" *Business Week,* May 20, 2002, 54.

2. Brian Stelter, "Can the Go-to Site Get You to Stay?" *New York Times,* January 17, 2009 (accessed online March 31, 2009).

3. Matt Richtel, "Inauguration Crowd Will Test Cell Phone Networks," *New York Times,* January 18, 2009 (accessed online March 31, 2009).

4. Merrill Brown, "Abandoning the News," *The Carnegie Reporter* 3, no. 2 (Spring 2005): 2–12.

5. "Internet Overtakes Newspapers as News Source," Pew Research Center Publications, December 23, 2008, http://pewresearch.org/pubs/1066/internet-overtakes-newspapers-as-news-source (accessed April 1, 2009).

6. Brown, "Abandoning the News," 5.

7. Julia M. Klein, "If You Build It . . . ," *Columbia Journalism Review,* November/December 2007, 40–45.

8. Michael Hirschorn, "End Times," *The Atlantic,* January/February 2009, http://www.theatlantic.com/doc/200901/new-york-times (accessed April 1, 2009).

9. Stephanie Clifford, "Christian Science Paper to End Daily Print Edition," *New York Times,* October 28, 2008 (accessed online April 1, 2009).

10. Richard Perez Pena, "Tribune Company Seeks Bankruptcy Protection," *New York Times,* December 8, 2008 (accessed online April 1, 2009).

11. Richard Perez Pena, "Fewer Papers Will Hit the Porch in Detroit," *New York Times,* December 15, 2008 (accessed online April 1, 2009).

12. Richard Perez Pena, "Bankruptcy Protection Filing at Minneapolis Star Tribune," *New York Times,* January 15, 2008 (accessed online April 1, 2009).

13. Eric Dash, "Mexican Billionaire Invests in Times Company," *New York Times,* January 19, 2009 (accessed online April 1, 2009).

14. Richard Perez-Pena, "Rocky Mountain News Fails to Find Buyer and Will Close," *New York Times,* February 26, 2009 (accessed online April 1, 2009).

15. Richard Perez-Pena, "Hearst Threatens to End San Francisco Paper," *New York Times,* February 24, 2009 (accessed online April 1, 2009).

16. William Yardley and Richard Perez-Pena, "Seattle Paper Shifts Entirely to the Web," *New York Times,* March 17, 2009 (accessed online April 1, 2009).

17. Hirschorn, "End Times."

18. "About Us," Pro Publica, http://www.propublica.org/about (accessed April 1, 2009).

19. "What Is Spot.Us About?" Spot.us, http://spot.us/pages/about (accessed April 1, 2009).

20. "The Huffington Post to Launch Non-Profit Investigative Journalism Venture," http://journalism.nyu.edu/pubzone/weblogs/pressthink/2009/03/26/flying_seminar.html#comment52571 (accessed September 4, 2009).

21. Howard Kurtz, "Politico: Niche Web Site Isn't Yet a Notch Above," *Washington Post,* January 29, 2007, Style, Final Edition, C1.

22. Tom Regan, "Political Websites: Clocks That Never Stop," *Christian Science Monitor,* November 25, 2008, Innovation, 25.

23. Leander Kahney, "Citizen Reporters Make the News," *Wired,* May, 17, 2003, http://www.wired.com/culture/lifestyle/news/2003/05/58856 (accessed April 1, 2009).

24. Institute for Interactive Journalism, http://www.j-lab.org/kcnn_launch_release.shtml (accessed April 1, 2009).

25. "Directory of Citizen Media Sites," Knight Citizen News Network, http://www.kcnn.org/citmedia_sites/ (accessed April 1, 2009).

26. Katharine Q. Seelye, "Blogger Is Surprised by Uproar Over Obama Story, But Not Bitter," *New York Times,* April 14, 2008 (accessed online April 1, 2009).

27. Katharine Q. Seelye, "Citizen Journalism Project Gains a Voice in the Campaign," *New York Times,* July 25, 2008 (accessed online April 1, 2009).

28. Jack Shafer, "Blog Overkill: The Danger of Hyping a Good Thing into the Ground," Slate, January 26, 2005, http://www.slate.com/default .aspx?search_input=Jack+Shafer&search_loc=on&qt=Jack+Shafer&id =3944&x=9&y=5 (accessed April 1, 2009).

29. "A Group Is Its Own Worst Enemy," Clay Shirky's Writing about the Internet, http://www.shirky.com/writings/group_enemy.html (accessed April 1, 2009).

30. Noam Cohen, "Spinning a Web of Lies at Digital Speed," *New York Times,* October 12, 2008 (accessed online April 1, 2009).

31. "Exclusive: NBC Nightly News and Other MSNBC Shows Will Be Sharable via Embed," Beet.TV, http://www.beet.tv/2008/01/exclusive -nbc-n.html (accessed April 1, 2009).

32. Bill Carter, "An Election to Laugh About," *New York Times,* October 8, 2008 (accessed online May 27, 2009).

33. Noam Cohen, "The Toughest Q's Answered in the Briefest Tweets," *New York Times,* January 4, 2009 (accessed online April 1, 2009).

34. Noam Cohen, "All a-Twitter About Stars Who Tweet," *New York Times,* January 5, 2008 (accessed online April 1, 2009).

35. Paul Bradshaw, "Wiki Journalism: Are Wikis the New Blogs?" Paper presented at the Future of the Newspaper Conference, September 2007, http://onlinejournalismblog.files.wordpress.com/2007/09/wiki _journalism.pdf (accessed April 1, 2009).

36. Noam Cohen, "Delaying the News in the Era of the Internet," *New York Times,* June 23, 2008 (accessed online April 1, 2009).

37. Benedict Anderson, *Imagined Communities: Reflections on the Origin and Spread of Nationalism,* 2nd ed. (London: Verso, 1991).

38. Howard Rheingold, *The Virtual Community: Finding Connection in a Computerized World,* rev. ed. (Cambridge, Mass.: MIT Press, 2000).

SELECTED BIBLIOGRAPHY

◈

BOOKS AND MONOGRAPHS

Abbate, Janet. *Inventing the Internet*. Cambridge, Mass.: MIT Press, 2000.

Allan, Stuart. *Online News: Journalism and the Internet*. New York: Open University Press, 2006.

Anderson, Benedict. *Imagined Communities: Reflections on the Origin and Spread of Nationalism,* 2nd ed. London: Verso, 1991.

Bailyn, Bernard, and John B. Hench. *The Press and the American Revolution*. Worcester, Mass.: American Antiquarian Society, 1980.

Baldasty, Gerald J. *E. W. Scripps and the Business of Newspapers*. Champaign: University of Illinois Press, 1999.

Banks, Michael A. *On the Way to the Web: The Secret History of the Internet and Its Founders*. Berkeley, Calif.: Apress, 2008.

Barnouw, Eric. *The Golden Web: A History of Broadcasting in the United States*. New York: Oxford University Press, 1966.

Berners-Lee, Tim. *Weaving the Web: The Original Design and Ultimate Destiny of the World Wide Web by Its Inventor.* San Francisco: HarperCollins, 1999.

Bernhard, Jim. *Porcupine, Picayune, & Post: How Newspapers Get Their Names*. Columbia: University of Missouri Press, 2007.

Bernstein, Solveig. *Policy Analysis: Beyond the Communications Decency Act: Constitutional Lessons of the Internet*. Cato Policy Analysis No. 262, Washington, D.C.: Cato Institute, November 4, 1996.

Blanchard, Margaret A. *Revolutionary Sparks: Freedom of Expression in Modern America*. New York: Oxford University Press, 1992.

Bleyer, Willard G. *Main Currents in the History of American Journalism*. New York: Houghton Mifflin Co., 1927.

Bliss, Edward, Jr. *Now the News: The Story of Broadcast Journalism*. New York: Columbia University Press, 1991.

Blondheim, Menahem. *News Over the Wires: The Telegraph and the Flow of Public Information in America, 1844–1897.* Cambridge, Mass.: Harvard University Press, 1994.

Blum, David. *Tick . . . Tick . . . Tick: The Long Life and Turbulent Times of 60 Minutes.* New York: HarperCollins, 2004.

Boczkowski, Pablo J. *Digitizing the News: Innovation in Online Newspapers.* Cambridge, Mass.: MIT Press, 2005.

Bourne, Charles P., and Trudi Bellardo Hahn. *A History of Online Information Services, 1963–1976.* Cambridge, Mass.: MIT Press, 2003.

Brennen, Bonnie, and Hanno Hardt. *Picturing the Past: Media, History, and Photography.* Champaign: University of Illinois Press, 1999.

Busterna, John C., and Robert G. Picard. *Joint Operating Agreements: The Newspaper Preservation Act and Its Application.* Westport, Conn.: Greenwood Publishing Group, 1993.

Carey, James. *Communication as Culture,* 2nd ed. London: Taylor & Francis, 2008.

Cook, Philip S., Douglas Gomery, and Lawrence W. Lichty. *The Future of News: Television, Newspapers, Wire Services, Newsmagazines.* Washington, D.C.: Woodrow Wilson Center Press, 1992.

Copeland, B. J., ed. *The Essential Turing.* New York: Oxford University Press, 2004.

Crandall, Robert W., and Harold Furchtgott-Roth. *Cable TV: Regulation or Competition.* Washington, D.C: The Brookings Institution, 1996.

Davies, David R. *The Postwar War Decline of American Newspapers.* Westport, Conn.: Praeger Publishers, 2006.

de Sola Pool, Ithiel. *Technologies of Freedom.* Cambridge, Mass.: Harvard University Press, 1983.

De Vries, Jan. *The Industrious Revolution: Consumer Behavior and the Household Economy, 1650 to the Present.* Cambridge, England: Cambridge University Press, 2008.

Dennis, Everette E. *The Race for Content on the Information Superhighway: Self-Interest vs. the Public Interest.* New York: The Freedom Forum Media Studies Center, 1994.

Depew, Chauncey Mitchell. *1795–1895 One Hundred Years of American Commerce: A History of American Commerce by One Hundred Americans, with a Chronological Table of the Important Events of American*

Commerce and Invention Within the Past One Hundred Years. New York: O. Haynes, 1895.

Dooley, Brendan Maurice, and Sabrina Alcorn Baron, eds. *The Politics of Information in Early Modern Europe.* New York: Routledge, 2001.

Douglas, George H. *The Early Days of Broadcasting.* Jefferson, N.C.: McFarland and Company, 1987.

Douglas, Susan J. *Inventing American Broadcasting, 1899–1922.* Baltimore, Md.: The Johns Hopkins University Press, 1987.

Emery, Michael, Edwin Emery, and Nancy Roberts. *The Press in America: An Interpretive History of the Mass Media,* 9th ed. Boston: Allyn and Bacon, 2000.

Ewen, Stuart. *PR! A Social History of Spin.* New York: Basic Books, 1998.

Fidler, Roger. *Mediamorphosis: Understanding New Media.* Thousand Oaks, Calif.: Pine Forge Press, 1997.

Frank, Joseph. *The Beginnings of the English Newspaper 1620–1660.* Cambridge, Mass.: Harvard University Press, 1961.

Frank, Reuven. *Out of Thin Air: The Brief and Wonderful Life of Network News.* New York: Simon and Schuster, 1991.

Gillies, James, and Rovert Cailliau. *How the Web Was Born: The Story of the World Wide Web.* New York: Oxford University Press, 2000.

Gitelman, Lisa. *Always Already New.* Cambridge, Mass.: MIT Press, 2006.

Goldberg, Robert, and Gerald Jay Goldberg. *Citizen Turner: The Wild Rise of an American Tycoon.* New York: Harcourt, Brace and Co., 1995.

Goldsmith, Alfred N., and Austin C. Lescaroura. *This Thing Called Broadcasting.* New York: Henry Holt and Co., 1930.

Gunter, Barrie. *News and the Net.* Mahwah, N.J.: Lawrence Erlbaum Associates, 2003.

Hafner, Katie, and Matthe Lyon. *Where Wizards Stay Up Late: The Origins of the Internet.* New York: Simon and Schuster, 2006.

Halberstam, David, *The Powers That Be.* Champaign: The University of Illinois Press, 2000.

Harris, Michael. *London Newspapers in the Age of Walpole: A Study of the Origins of the Modern English Press.* Madison, N.J.: Fairleigh Dickinson University Press, 1987.

Hart, Jon. *Web Publishing Law.* Washington, D.C.: Dow Lohnes & Albertson, 2002.

Heckman, Lucy. *NASDAQ: A Guide to Information Sources.* New York: Routledge, 2001.

Kielbowicz, Richard. *News in the Mail.* Westport, Conn.: Greenwood Press, 1989.

Knowlton, Stephen R., and Karen L. Freeman, eds. *Fair & Balanced: A History of Journalistic Objectivity.* Northport, Ala.: Vision Press, 2005.

Lewis, Sian. *News and Society in the Greek Polis.* Chapel Hill: University of North Carolina Press, 1996.

McDonald, J. Fred. *Don't Touch That Dial: Radio Programming in American Life 1920–1960.* Chicago: Nelson Hall, 1979.

Mindich, David. *Tuned Out: Why Americans Under 40 Don't Follow the News.* New York: Oxford University Press, 2005.

Morison, Stanley. *The English Newspaper: Some Account of the Physical Development of Journals Printed in London Between 1622 & the Present Day.* Ann Arbor, Mich.: The University Press, 1932.

Moschovitis, Christos J. P., Hilary Poole, Tami Schuyler, and Theresa M. Senft. *History of the Internet: A Chronology, 1843 to the Present.* Santa Barbara, Calif.: ABC-CLIO, 1999.

Mott, Frank Luther. *American Journalism: A History.* New York: Macmillan, 1962.

Muddiman, Joseph George. *A History of English Journalism to the Foundation of the Gazette.* London: Longman, Green, 1908.

Munk, Nina. *Fools Rush In: Steve Case, Jerry Levin, and the Unmaking of AOL Time Warner.* New York: HarperCollins, 2005.

Olsen, Kirstin. *Daily Life in 18th-century England.* Westport, Conn.: Greenwood Publishing Group, 1999.

Opotowsky, Stan. *TV: The Big Picture.* New York: E. P. Dutton and Co., 1961.

Paper, Lewis J. *Empire: William S. Paley and the Making of CBS.* New York: St. Martin's Press, 1987.

Parsons, Patrick R., and Robert N. Frieden. *The Cable and Satellite Television Industries.* Boston: Allyn and Bacon, 1998.

Postman, Neil. *Amusing Ourselves to Death.* New York: Penguin Books, 1985.

Raymond, Joad. *Pamphlets and Pamphleteering in Early Modern Britain.* New York: Cambridge University Press, 2006.

Reddick, Randy, and Elliot King. *The Online Journalist.* Dallas: Harcourt Brace College Publishers, 1995.

The Research Group of the Freedom Forum Media Studies Center. *Special Report: Separating Fact from Fiction on the Information Superhighway.* New York: Freedom Forum Media Studies Center, April 1994.

Rheingold, Howard. *The Virtual Community: Finding Connection in a Computerized World,* rev. ed. Cambridge, Mass.: MIT Press, 2000.

Roberts, Gene, and Hank Klibanoff. *The Race Beat.* New York: Alfred Knopf, 2006.

Robichaux, Mark. *Cable Cowboy: John Malone and the Rise of the Modern Cable Business.* Hoboken, N.J.: John Wiley and Sons, 2002.

Rogers, Everette M. *Diffusions of Innovation,* 4th ed. New York: Simon and Schuster, 1994.

Roosevelt, Franklin Delano, Russell D. Buhite, and David W. Levy. *FDR's Fireside Chats.* Norman: The University of Oklahoma Press, 1992.

Roper, Burns W. *Trends in Public Attitudes Toward Television and Other Mass Media 1959–1974.* New York: Roper Organization, 1975.

Rowan, Ford. *Broadcast Fairness: Doctrine, Practice, Prospects.* New York: Longman, 1984.

Salwen, Michael B., Bruce Garrison, and Paul D. Driscoll, eds. *Online News and the Public.* Mahwah, N.J.: Lawrence Erlbaum Associates, 2004.

Schudson, Michael. *Discovering the News.* New York: Basic Books, 1981.

Sider, Sandra. *Handbook to Life in Renaissance Europe.* New York: Oxford University Press, 2007.

Sloan, William David, and Lisa Mullikin Parcell, eds. *American Journalism: History, Principles, Practices.* Jefferson, N.C.: McFarland, 2002.

Sommerville, Charles John. *The News Revolution in England: Cultural Dynamics of Daily Information.* New York: Oxford University Press, 1996.

Standage, Tom. *The Victorian Internet.* New York: Berkley Books, 1999.

Stephens, Mitchell. *A History of News.* New York: Viking Penguin, 1988.

Sterling, Christopher H., and John Michael Kittross. *Stay Tuned: A History of American Broadcasting.* Mahwah, N.J.: Lawrence Erlbaum Associates, 2002.

Turkle, Sherry. *Life on the Screen: Identity in the Age of the Internet.* New York: Simon and Schuster, 1995.

Wallis, Roger, and Stanley J. Baran. *The Known World of Broadcast News: International News and the Electronic Media.* New York: Routledge, 1991.

Wolf, Gary. *Wired: A Romance.* New York: Random House, 2003.

Wolff, Michael. *Burn Rate.* New York: Simon and Schuster, 1999.

Zelizer, Barbie. *Covering the Body: The Kennedy Assassination, the Media, and the Shaping of Collective Memory.* Chicago: University of Chicago Press, 1992.

ARTICLES

Ackerman, William C. "The Dimensions of American Broadcasting." *The Public Opinion Quarterly* 9, no. 1 (Spring 1945): 1–18.

Almaney, Adnan. "International and Foreign Affairs on Network Television News." *Journal of Broadcasting* 14, no. 4 (1970): 499.

Alterman, Eric. "The Seven-Year (Old) Snitch." *The Nation,* November 22, 1999. http://www.thenation.com/doc/19991122/alterman (accessed April 9, 2009).

Arblaster, Paul. "Posts, Newsletters, Newspapers: England in a European System of Communications." *Media History* 11, nos. 1–2 (April-August 2005): 21–36.

Bender, W., et. al. "Enriching Communities: Harbingers of News in the Future." *IBM Systems Journal* 35, nos. 3–4 (1996): 369.

"A Brief History of Blogs." *Columbia Journalism Review* 42, no. 3 (September-October 2003): 20.

Brown, Chip. "Fear.com." *American Journalism Review* 20, no. 10 (June 1999): 50–77.

Brown, Merrill. "Abandoning the News." *The Carnegie Reporter* 3, no. 2 (Spring 2005). http://www.carnegie.org/reporter/10/news/ (accessed April 9, 2009).

Bush, Vannevar. "As We May Think." *Atlantic Monthly* (July 1945).

http://www.theatlantic.com/doc/194507/bush (accessed March 22, 2009).

Cannon, Robert. "The Legacy of the Federal Communications Commission's Computer Inquiries." *Federal Communication Law Journal* 55, no. 2 (March 2003): 167–206.

Carr, Nicholas G. "IT Doesn't Matter." http://www.nicholasgcarr .com/articles/matter.html (accessed March 21, 2009).

Caruso, Denise. "Show Me the Money." *Columbia Journalism Review* 36, no. 2 (July–August 1997): 32–36.

Chester, Giraud. "The Press-Radio War: 1933–1935." *The Public Opinion Quarterly* 13, no. 2 (Summer 1949): 252–64.

Cleghorn, Reese. "The News: It May Never Be the Same." *American Journalism Review* 20, no. 2 (March 1998): 4.

Cust, Richard. "News and Politics in Seventeenth Century England." *Past and Present* 112 (1986): 60–90.

Denniston, Lyle. "A SLOW sign on the Information Highway." *American Journalism Review* 16, no. 2 (March 1994): 54.

Easton, Eric. "Journalism Ethics and the Internet: Ethical Implications of a Canadian Publication Ban." *Electronic Journal of Communication* 7, no. 4 (1997). http://www.cios.org/EJCPUBLIC/007/4/007415 .HTML (accessed April 9, 2009).

Glenn, David. "The Marshall Plan." *Columbia Journalism Review* 46, no. 3 (September-October 2007): 22–28.

Grossman, Lawrence K. "Will Success Spoil Network News?" *Columbia Journalism Review* 38, no. 1 (May-June 1999): 58–60.

Harkinson, Josh. "Reporter Behind Bars." *Mother Jones,* February 20, 2007. http://www.motherjones.com/interview/2007/02/Josh_Wolf.html (accessed April 10, 2009).

Harper, Christopher. "Online Newspapers: Going Somewhere or Going Nowhere?" *Newspaper Research Journal* 17, nos. 3–4 (Summer-Fall 1996): 2–13.

Hickey, Neil. "Revolution in Cyberia." *Columbia Journalism Review* 34, no. 2 (July–August 1995): 40–48.

Hirschorn, Michael. "End Times." *The Atlantic,* January/February 2009. http://www.theatlantic.com/doc/200901/new-york-times (accessed April 9, 2009).

Houston, Frank. "What I Saw in the Digital Sea." *Columbia Journalism Review* 38, no. 2 (July–August 1999): 34–38.

"Information Superhighway: The Digital Future Can Mean Great News for Newspapers, Journalists and News Consumers." *American Journalism Review* 16, no. 4 (May 1994): 4–8.

Isaacs, Stephen D. "The Bill Gates Factor." *Columbia Journalism Review* 34, no. 2 (July–August 1995): 53–54.

King, Elliot. "The Impact of the Internet on Journalism." *Electronic Journal of Communication* 7, nos. 2–4 (1997). http://www.cios.org/www/ejcrec2.htm (accessed April 9, 2009).

Klein, Julia M. "If You Build It . . . ." *Columbia Journalism Review* 46, no. 4 (November–December 2007): 40–46.

Licklider, J. C. R. "Man-Computer Symbiosis." *IRE Transactions on Human Factors in Electronics* (March 1960): 4–11.

McCartney, James. "USA Today Grows Up." *American Journalism Review* 19, no. 7 (September 1997): 18–26.

Mead, Rebecca. "You've Got Blog." *The New Yorker,* November 13, 2000, 102.

Mindich, David T. Z. "Edwin M. Stanton, the Inverted Pyramid, and Information Control." *Journalism Monographs,* no. 140 (August 1993).

Nord, David Paul. "Teleology and News: The Religious Roots of American Journalism 1630–1730." *The Journal of American History* 77, no. 1 (June 1990): 9–38.

Oppenheimer, Todd. "Virtual Reality Check." *Columbia Journalism Review* 34, no. 6 (March–April 1996): 27–30.

Pfau, Michale. "The Mass Media and American Politics: A Review Essay." *Political Research Quarterly* 42, no. 1 (1989): 173–86.

"The Radio Act of 1927." *Columbia Law Review* 27, no. 6 (June 1927): 726–33.

Raymond, Eric S. "The Cathedral and the Bazaar." http://fringe.davesource.com/Fringe/Computers/Philosophy/Cathedral_Bazaar/.

Ruggiero, T. E., and S. P. Winch. "The Media Downing of Pierre Salinger: Journalistic Mistrust of the Internet as a News Source." *Journal of Computer-Mediated Communication* 10, no. 2 (2004). http://jcmc.indiana.edu/vol10/issue2/ruggiero.html (accessed April 9, 2009).

Schwarzlose, Richard A. "The Nation's First Wire Service: Evidence Supporting a Footnote." *Journalism Quarterly* 57, no. 4 (Winter 1980): 555–62.

Shaw, Donald L. "News Bias and the Telegraph: A Study of Historical Change." *Journalism Quarterly* 44 (Spring 1967): 3–12.

Shepard, Alicia, and Christopher Harper. "Webward Ho." *American Journalism Review* 19, no. 2 (March 1997): 32–38.

Stein, Nicholas. "Slate vs. Salon." *Columbia Journalism Review* 37, no. 5 (January-February 1999): 56–60.

Sullivan, Andrew. "Why I Blog." *The Atlantic Magazine.* http://www.theatlantic.com/doc/200811/andrew-sullivan-why-i-blog/2.

Welch, Matt. "Blogworld and Its Gravity." *Columbia Journalism Review* 42, no. 3 (September-October 2003): 20–28.

INDEX

◈